Professional Chef

Level 1 Diploma

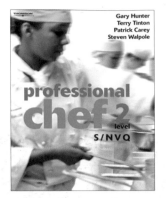

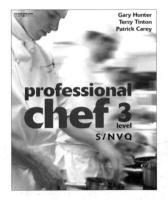

NEIL RIPPINGTON

Professional Chef

Level 1 Diploma

THOMSON

Australia • Canada • Mexico • Singapore • Spain • United Kingdom • United States

THOMSON

The Professional Chef: Level 1 Diploma
Neil Rippington

Publishing Director	**Publisher**	**Development Editor**
John Yates	Lib Wight	Lizzie Catford
Content Project Editor	**Manufacturing Manager**	**Marketing Manager**
Lucy Mills	Helen Mason	Leo Stanley
Typesetter	**Production Controller**	**Cover Design**
Book Now Ltd, London, UK	Maeve Healy	HarrisCookTurner
Text Design	**Printer**	
Design Deluxe Ltd, Bath, UK	Canale, Italy	

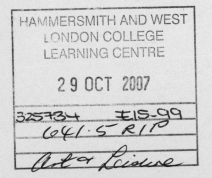

CONTENTS

325734

About the author

Neil Rippington grew up in Bournemouth and got a taste for the catering industry at an early age by working in hotels while at school and college. Following a chefs' programme at The Bournemouth and Poole College, Neil went on to work in a Michelin starred restaurant in France and in London's Capital Hotel in Knightsbridge. Neil then went to work in the USA for two years before returning to the UK as a head chef in a country house hotel in the New Forest.

In 1994, Neil was presented with the opportunity to return to education as a chef lecturer at South East Essex College. After five years, he moved on to Redbridge College as a Programme Manager for Hospitality and Catering, later taking up the post as Quality Manager for the College.

In 2003, Neil took the position of Head of Centre for Hospitality and Food Studies at Colchester Institute (CoVE). In November 2006, the Centre was awarded Grade 1 for outstanding provision, the first in the history of Colchester Institute.

Neil's purpose for writing the book was because he believes that learners entering Colleges or the industry need a foundation of skills and knowledge before they can progress to more technical work. With proficient knife skills and the ability to apply the fundamental cookery processes across a range of foods, learners will have the foundations to build a successful career in the industry.

Neil is married to Amanda and they have three children, Joseph, Luke and Freya. Neil is a keen sportsman and (still) plays football at club level.

Acknowledgements

Annie Kettle for the photography and Martin Fordham for the food preparation and cooking behind the photographic sequences of techniques and cookery processes.

Amanda, my wife, for helping out when I broke my wrist half way through writing the book as well as being so patient during a very busy time.

Gary Hunter co-author of the other two books in the series for his openness and willingness to share ideas and materials.

The chefs, Gary Rhodes, Mark Salter, Mark Dodson, Alan Bird, Herbert Berger and Stas Anastasiades for their valuable and inspiring input.

Steve Thorpe of City College, Norwich, Shyam Patiar of Coleg Llandrillo and Raj Mandal of Bedford College for their detailed reviews of the manuscript.

The Publisher and Author would also like to thank the following for the use of their artwork:

Chubb Fire Ltd

Cookware UK

Eureka

Lincat Catering Equipment

Nisbets

Russums

Shop-Equip Ltd

Foreword

Just over 30 years have passed since my first day of professional college training. It was more than a daunting experience, standing amongst my peers with a huge knife in one hand, wiping away the oniony tears with the other. We all stood silently waiting for instruction to begin.

To educate and teach in the culinary world it is essential to begin with the basics. In my experience it really is true that you can't 'run before you can walk'.

With that in mind, and as a chef with many restaurants to my name, this is why the *Professional Chef Level 1* really needs to be shared and shouted about! These pages tell the true professional story.

The purpose of this book is to provide a valuable resource for the development of initial skills and knowledge for aspiring chefs entering the world of professional cooking.

As a 'Fellow of the City & Guilds of London Institute' I welcomed this book with open arms, realising it follows the structure of the new City & Guilds curriculum for the Level 1 Diploma in Professional Cookery. It is written in a format that is useful for anyone wishing to enter the industry, or those studying towards a qualification at a similar level.

Throughout the book, learners are introduced to a broad range of skills and information and are prepared to meet the needs of the industry. *Professional Chef Level 1* covers all the primary cookery processes, stewing, braising, boiling, poaching, steaming, roasting, grilling and much more! It is finely seasoned, with clear explanations that will add a new depth to your personal kitchen, food and cookery knowledge. Throughout the book little secrets are shared in the chefs' tip boxes, which offer insider advice that adds extra bite to your general understanding of the method behind a finished dish.

Here you will find guidance for delivery of best practice.

The Result? To receive a final grade for each unit honoured at three levels – Pass, Merit and Distinction.

This textbook places every learner in the driving seat, creating a track for them to follow, and helping them to achieve their goal with determination and enthusiasm, so they have the best chance of making a success in the catering industry.

Quick reference guide to the Diploma units

The following 12 units make up the diploma in Introduction to Professional Cookery.

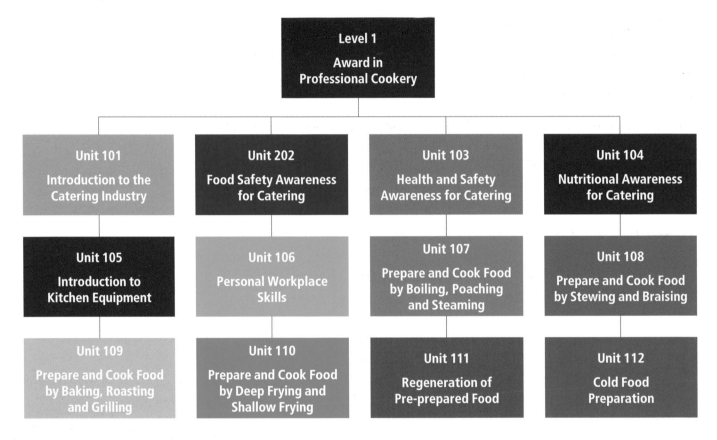

Level 1
Award in Professional Cookery

Unit 101
Introduction to the Catering Industry

Unit 202
Food Safety Awareness for Catering

Unit 103
Health and Safety Awareness for Catering

Unit 104
Nutritional Awareness for Catering

Unit 105
Introduction to Kitchen Equipment

Unit 106
Personal Workplace Skills

Unit 107
Prepare and Cook Food by Boiling, Poaching and Steaming

Unit 108
Prepare and Cook Food by Stewing and Braising

Unit 109
Prepare and Cook Food by Baking, Roasting and Grilling

Unit 110
Prepare and Cook Food by Deep Frying and Shallow Frying

Unit 111
Regeneration of Pre-prepared Food

Unit 112
Cold Food Preparation

The units are structured in a standard format and comprise of the following:

Unit reference number and title – e.g. Unit 108 Prepare and cook food by stewing and braising

Rationale – explaining the aims and purpose of the unit

Connections with other qualifications – e.g. NVQs and Key Skills

Assessment details – detailing the requirements for the assessment of practical skills and underpinning knowledge

Learning outcomes – specifying the practical skills and/or the underpinning knowledge to be covered

Range – providing detail as to the content of each learning outcome

Guidance – for delivery and best practice

About the book

Performance criteria

The philosophy behind the diploma is that a chef needs to have a sound foundation of high quality skills and to be able to apply these skills across a range of processes and commodities.

The qualification has been designed for delivery in a College environment or similar. It does not replace the S/NVQs but intends to provide learners with a broader range of skills and knowledge and to make them better prepared to meet the needs of industry. There is also more emphasis on teaching and learning in comparison to the assessment model presented by the S/NVQ.

All candidates enrolled on a Diploma in Professional Cookery will follow a specific programme, completing a range of theoretical and practical tasks and activities. Individuals will also receive a final grade for each unit to highlight areas of high achievement.

Features within chapters

Each chapter addresses a specific unit of the Diploma in Introduction to Professional Cookery qualification

Learning objectives at the start of each chapter explain the skills and knowledge you need to understand by the end of the chapter

7
Prepare and cook food by boiling, poaching and steaming

Unit 107 Prepare and cook food by boiling, poaching and steaming

LEARNING OBJECTIVES

On completion of this chapter, learners will be able to
- Describe the methods of boiling, poaching and steaming
- Identify foods that can be boiled, poached and steamed
- Identify the liquids that are used to boil, poach and steam
- Select suitable techniques associated with boiling, poaching and steaming

 CHEF'S TIP

It is very important that sauces to be reduced are not seasoned with salt and pepper until the reduction is complete. If seasoned in advance of reducing, the amount of seasoning will remain the same but in less liquid, making it too severe and potentially ruining the sauce.

Chef's Tip boxes share the author's experience of the catering industry

HEALTH & SAFETY

Physical/mental state – we are less likely to slip, trip or fall when we are fresh in our minds and concentrating on the tasks ahead.

Health and safety tip boxes draw your attention to important health and safety information

ACTIVITY

Think of several potential causes of fire in the kitchen. How could each of these be prevented?

Activity boxes provide additional tasks for you to try out

Quality points provide information to help you assess ingredients

QUALITY POINTS TO LOOK FOR IN STEWED ITEMS

- Main items are of even size (e.g. meat)

Step-by-step: **Roast chicken**

STEP 1 Roughly crush a few cloves of garlic

STEP 2 Peel the zest from a fresh lemon

STEP 3 Remove the wish-bone from the chicken and stuff the cavity of the chicken with the lemon and garlic

Step-by-step sequences illustrate each process and provide an easy-to-follow guide

STEP 4 Place a trivet of vegetables into a roasting tray. Place the prepared chicken on top of the trivet and baste with vegetable oil. Season the chicken with salt and freshly ground black pepper

STEP 5 Roast the chicken in a pre-heated oven at 200°C, basting on a regular basis and turning the chicken throughout to ensure that the legs of the chicken are sufficiently roasted.

STEP 6 Once cooked, place the chicken onto a rack to relax in a warm environment for at least 10–15 minutes before carving. The core temperature of the chicken will remain safe and this will allow the structure of the chicken time to relax and become less tense (taut), making carving much easier and efficient

Assessment of knowledge and understanding at the end of each chapter contains questions, so you can test your learning

Assessment of knowledge and understanding

You have now learned about the different sectors of the industry. The hospitality, leisure, travel and tourism sector is an important sector across the whole of the United Kingdom, in terms of employment and economic output. In most cases it is seen as a priority sector.

To test your level of knowledge and understanding, answer the following short questions.

Hospitality and catering

1 Describe the term 'hospitality'.

Gary Rhodes' beef and potatoes braised in Guinness

INGREDIENTS	4 PORTIONS
Olive oil for cooking	
Large onions, sliced	3
Pieces of chuck steak or braising beef	4 × 175g (6oz)–225g (8oz)
Flour for dusting	
Salt and pepper	
Guinness	440ml
Tablespoon muscavado sugar	1
Tin of beef consommé or stock	400ml
Large potatoes, peeled and halved	4

Recipes provide examples of the different cooking processes for you to try out

CHEF'S PROFILE

Name: ALAN BIRD

Position: Head Chef

Establishment: The Ivy Restaurant, I–5 West Street, London WC2H 9NQ

Training and experience:

1982–1986   West Lodge Park Hotel, Hertfordshire
Apprentice Chef for three years. Attended Southgate Technical College on part-time day release. Left as a Chef Tournant.

1986–1988   Goring Hotel, London
I joined the Goring as First Commis on the sauce section and was promoted to Chef Saucier in 1987. I gained 18 months experience in this position before leaving in 1988.

September 1988–August 1990   Simply Nicos, London SW1
I joined Simply Nicos as Chef De Partie on the fish section. I held this position until new premises were opened on May 1989, whereupon I was promoted to Sous

Chef profiles provide advice from leading industry figures

2 The food is placed into a deep poaching liquid. For example, an egg is poached in simmering water which is three or four times as deep as the shelled egg. A poached egg can be blanched, *refreshed* and reheated for service in a similar way to the way that vegetables are reheated for service. The sequence below demonstrates an egg being poached.

Step-by-step: **Poaching an egg**

VIDEO CLIP
Deep poaching salmon

Video presentations – if your college adopts the online Virtual Kitchen Level 1 you can view video demonstrations of the key processes being carried out

1

Introduction to the catering and hospitality industry

Unit 101 Introduction to the catering and hospitality industry

LEARNING OBJECTIVES

At the end of this chapter you will be able to:

- Understand the terms 'hospitality' and 'catering'
- Compare the sectors and different types of operations in the industry
- Describe the main features of establishments within the different sectors
- Identify staffing structures and job roles in different establishments
- Identify training opportunities, related qualifications and employment rights and responsibilities
- List some of the associations related to professional cookery

HOSPITALITY AND CATERING

The hospitality and catering, leisure, travel and tourism sector covers the following 14 industries:

1	Hotels	8	Events
2	Restaurants	9	Gambling
3	Pubs	10	Travel services
4	Bars and nightclubs	11	Tourist services
5	Contract food service providers	12	Visitor attractions
6	Hospitality services	13	Hostels
7	Membership clubs	14	Holiday centres and self catering accommodation.

Each operation is unique, but each has in common the provision of food and drink and/or accommodation. A large number of people are employed in core hospitality occupations such as chefs, kitchen assistants, reception staff, food service and bar staff. The main industries employing the majority of these people are as follows:

- Travel
- Retail
- Business
- Education
- Healthcare
- Corporate and executive dining
- Government and local authority provision
- Leisure venues and events (concerts, sporting events, parties)
- Restaurants
- Hotels.

The dining area of a cruise ship

The sectors and different types of operations within the industry

The scope for employment in this industry is huge with many career pathways available. As leisure time continues to increase so have the many venues people can visit to enjoy their free time. Theme parks, family friendly pubs, coffee shops, restaurants, major sporting events and hotels have been established to accommodate this growing trend.

The industry is broken down into two main sectors, described as the commercial sector and the catering services sector. Organizations can be categorized into the two sectors according to the main purpose and aim of the business.

The commercial sector – in this case, the provision of hospitality and catering is the main purpose of the organization which aims to make a profit in return for the supply of their products and services. Examples include restaurants and hotels.

The catering services sector – in this case, the provision of hospitality and catering is a secondary purpose of the organization, although the organization may still aim to make a profit in return for the supply of their products and services. Examples include the catering supplied to employees working in a large bank or factory. In these examples, banking and production are the main purposes of the organizations and catering is supplied as a secondary feature, a 'service' to the staff employed in either of these organizations.

For example, an employer has 20 staff. The caterers quote a price of £3.50 to supply lunch for each member of staff (Total – 20 × £3.50 = £70.00). As a perk (benefit) to the staff, the employer contributes £30.00 to the caterer, reducing the total cost to £40.00. Each member staff now has a reduced (subsidized) cost to purchase their lunch (£40.00 ÷ 20 = £2.00). Each time a lunch is sold, the employee spends £2.00, the employer has contributed £1.50 and the caterer receives the £3.50 originally quoted.

THE MAIN FEATURES OF ESTABLISHMENTS WITHIN THE DIFFERENT SECTORS

Contract food service

Contract food service providers support a number of wider industries from hotels and restaurants to schools and airlines. Traditionally the sector has provided food and drink service but it is increasingly developing into other areas such as retail opportunities, facilities management, fine dining restaurants, vending, healthcare, school meals provision and prison catering.

CHEF'S TIP

Some catering services may be subsidized by the company. A 'subsidy' is a payment by the company to keep the selling price at a low rate to individual employees

TASK

Identify the scope of the local industry by finding two organizations that would fall into the commercial sector and two that would fall into the catering service sector.

Commercial sector

1 _____

2 _____

Catering service sector

1 _____

2 _____

An overview of the sectors within the hospitality and catering industry

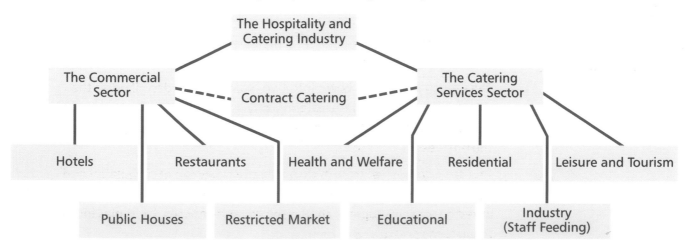

CHEF'S TIP

Hospital catering is sometimes classified as 'welfare catering'. The object is to assist the medical staff to get a patient back to health as soon as possible.

Healthcare and hospitals

Healthcare homes provide accommodation, meals and personal care, but also have professional registered nurses and experienced care assistants in constant attendance. The focus is to provide a balanced nutritious diet using fresh, quality ingredients and to maintain high standards of food production and presentation. The dishes prepared can be designed to include the requests of residents. The residents may also choose to eat a meal in the home's dining room or, if they prefer, in the comfort of their own room.

In many hospitals the patients are provided with a daily menu choice of breakfast, lunch and supper. This is usually ordered a day in advance. Dieticians are employed to liaise with the head chef or catering manager to help plan each menu, to design specialized diets for individual patients and to help introduce diet conscious recipes and advice to patients.

Dining area at the Ritz hotel

HOTELS

It is estimated that there are over 12,000 individual hotels in the UK. With the addition of smaller hotels and guest houses the total is probably nearer 30,000. The structure of hotels is defined into the following categories:

- Budget hotels
- Bed and breakfast accommodation (guest houses)
- One star
- Two star
- Three star
- Four star
- Five star (luxury).

Large hotel chains generally have the market share of business and comprise the majority of hotels found across the world today. Aside from food and drink service where chefs, kitchen assistants and service staff are required, hotels will also employ staff in other specialized areas to cater for the accommodation and leisure facilities. For instance in areas such as:

- Reception
- Housekeeping
- Front office management
- Porter service
- Leisure management
- Events and banquet management.

BUSINESS SERVICES

Because hotels are residential they will provide breakfast, lunch, tea, dinner and snacks (sometimes for 24 hours a day). Banquets and functions will also play an important role in the business.

RESTAURANTS

The restaurant sector is the largest area in the hospitality and catering industry. This has had a steady increase of turnover and it is estimated that there are over 65,000 restaurants in the UK.

Restaurants can be classified by their origin of cuisine; European, North American, Asian, Oriental, Central and South American. The restaurant industry is broken down into four different segments:

- Fast food establishments
- Cafes and coffee shops
- Mainstream restaurants
- Fine dining restaurants

PUBLIC HOUSES, BARS AND CLUBS

A high proportion of the industry's workforce is employed on a part-time basis. In this sector custom tends to be concentrated into a short number of hours (evenings and weekends) so the amount of staff needed in peak hours is considerably higher than at quieter times. A relatively high proportion of this workforce describe their employment as casual, many of whom may be working in the industry while studying.

Public houses and bars provide alcoholic and non-alcoholic beverages. They are increasingly also providing snacks or food through a restaurant service. There are many similarities between a bar and a public house, but the most obvious factor is the style and ambience. One way to segment the sector has been to look at ownership:

- **Managed houses** – include those which are owned by a brewery and employ salaried staff who manage and work in the outlet.
- **Tenanted or leased pubs** – are owned by a brewery but are occupied by licensees who pay rent to the brewery and agree to take their supply of beer and alcohol from them.
- **Freehouses** – are owned and managed by the licensee and deal with a number of different suppliers and brewers.

Nightclubs are establishments where the primary offer is that of dancing to music and where drink and food are offered as a secondary service (or where there is a legal requirement to do so).

Bars can obviously be found in other sectors, such as hotels and restaurants and other areas, such as sports grounds.

Food signs at a theme park

VISITOR ATTRACTIONS

The visitor attraction industry is small in terms of establishments, employment and turnover. However, popular visitor attractions that attract high numbers of visitors are vital to local economies.

- Theme parks and gardens
- Sporting locations (e.g. football stadium)
- Museums
- Other attractions – including theatres.

Usually there will be some form of food and drink provision from vending facilities to restaurants, some of which may be sub-contracted out to the catering services industry.

QUALIFICATIONS, TRAINING AND EXPERIENCE WITHIN THE INDUSTRY

Staffing structures and job roles

Organizations, regardless of their size will have a staffing structure, with members of staff performing different job roles that contribute to the overall aims of the organization.

Organizations range from individuals working by themselves to very large companies with thousands of employees.

Staffing structures can be divided into three main categories. These are as follows:

Operational staff – Operational staff are the employees who perform the everyday practical operations. They are the staff who cook the food and serve the customers, clean the bedrooms and public areas and generally provide the services that customers expect from the organization.

Supervisory staff – Supervisory staff are generally more experienced than operational staff. They will oversee the work and performance of operational staff and deal with any day-to-day issues as they arise. Supervisory staff should also provide a first point of call for operational staff if they have a problem that they need help with.

Management staff – Managers have responsibility for ensuring that the organization is performing well, that suitably trained staff are employed and customers receive the products and services they expect. Managers have many other responsibilities including planning for the future, managing finance and ensuring health and safety policies and employment laws are followed.

CHEF'S TIP

In the case of the smaller organizations, it is likely that individuals will have to perform a wide variety of roles as all operational (and management) requirements have to be completed by a few people. In larger organizations, job roles are likely to be more specific as many people are working towards the aims of the organization and the breakdown of roles can be more detailed.

CHEF'S TIP

Depending on the size of the organization, managers often perform supervisory and operational roles. As organizations become larger that managers perform these tasks on a less frequent basis, or perhaps never at all.

Examples of staff in a medium to large kitchen operation would be:

Manager – Head Chef (In larger organizations, sometimes referred to as the executive head chef).

Supervisor/s – Sous chef (second chef); Chef de partie (Section chefs).

Operational – Commis chefs; Apprentices.

TASK

Other than the examples provided above, think of two additional roles that operational, supervisory and management staff perform as part of their job role.

Operational	Supervisory	Management
1	1	1
2	2	2

Staffing structures of a large city centre hotel

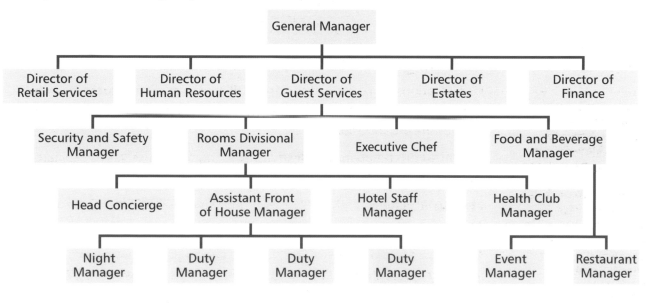

Training opportunities, related qualifications and employment rights and responsibilities

Working in the hospitality industry and particularly as a chef is a never ending learning opportunity. There is always more to learn with constant innovation from very talented chefs from around the world. The innovative ways in which to work with new commodities and applying different approaches and techniques can make working in the industry an interesting and personally rewarding experience.

As someone entering the industry without any, or very much, experience, the training opportunities are vast and varied. The following describes some of the ways in which training is provided:

On the job – this refers to bite size, regular chunks, of training that is provided while at work. Occasionally, short courses (e.g. one or two days) may be provided to learn about specific aspects of the job – health and safety and food hygiene, for example.

College based – most colleges in the UK offer courses and qualifications in hospitality and catering. This provides the opportunity for students to learn about the industry and develop skills in an educational environment. There are also opportunities to learn other subjects and improve other skills such as the use of language, number and IT.

Training providers – work in conjunction with employers and perform the assessment of skills for apprentices in the workplace.

E-learning – although it may be considered more difficult to learn skills through IT based resources, modern materials are being produced with a very interactive and personalized approach. The streaming of video-based material also makes it possible for learners to review material at their own pace.

Work placement – a placement provides a controlled period of time when there is a great opportunity to observe the way in which an organization operates and performs tasks.

QUALIFICATIONS

There are many qualifications designed for people working or aspiring to work in the catering and hospitality industry. For trainee chefs, there are vocational (career based) qualifications that are designed to meet the current needs of the industry. The two main routes, although there are others, are the NVQ (National Vocational Qualification) and the Diploma qualification.

NVQs are designed as an assessment based qualification in which candidates prove their competence (capability and knowledge) against a range of tasks. For example, it will take a period of time before a developing chef will be able to fillet a fish correctly and accurately. However, after a period of practising, his or her skills and confidence will improve to a point where an assessment of the skill can take place. Successful assessments build up until sufficient skills and knowledge have been gained for the student to be awarded the overall qualification.

Diplomas have been designed as a college-based qualification. There is much more emphasis on teaching and learning in comparison to the assessment based NVQ. All candidates enrolled on a Diploma in Professional Cookery will follow the same programme, completing the same theoretical and practical tasks. Individuals will also receive a final grade for each unit to highlight areas of high achievement.

Attached to college-based qualifications and the apprenticeship framework are key skills. Key skills are seen as an important addition to vocational qualifications as they are intended to improve the functional skills of individuals. The main key skills are in the areas of communication (written, spoken, body language, etc.), the application of number (use of number in vocational contexts) and IT. These additional skills are seen as vital additional attributes to individuals at work, making them more employable and increasing potential promotion opportunities in the future.

As well as main qualification aims, as described above, there are many short courses that people working in the industry may take to increase their knowledge in specific areas. Examples include short courses in health and safety, food safety, communication and the certificate for personal licence holders.

Qualifications are also written at different levels to enable individuals to build on their existing skills and knowledge.

NVQs and VRQs in Food Preparation and Cooking/Professional Cookery are written at levels 1, 2 and 3. This intends to develop skills and knowledge from a broad and sound base to a refinement of skills as candidates move from one level to the next.

There are also academic (more scholarly/less practical) qualifications written for the hospitality and catering industry. Such qualifications usually take a broader view of the industry from a more business oriented perspective. Qualifications and courses along this route range from level 1 through to Foundation, Bachelors and Masters Degrees.

EMPLOYMENT RIGHTS AND RESPONSIBILITIES

Employers and employees have certain rights and responsibilities.

Employers must supply a job description and contract of employment, detailing the following:

- Contracted working hours, and
- Holiday entitlement.

They must also provide a healthy and safe working environment.

Employees must:

- Work to the conditions as described in their job description and contract of employment, and
- Follow organizational policies.

They must also follow health and safety working practices, including food safety.

Some of the associations related to professional cookery

- The Academy of Culinary Arts
- The Association Culinaire Française
- The Craft Guild of Chefs
- Euro Toques
- Craft Guild of Chefs and Master Craftsmen of Great Britain
- PACE (Professional Association of Catering Education)
- HCIMA (Hotel, Catering, International Management Association).

Assessment of knowledge and understanding

You have now learned about the different sectors of the industry. The hospitality, leisure, travel and tourism sector is an important sector across the whole of the United Kingdom, in terms of employment and economic output. In most cases it is seen as a priority sector.

To test your level of knowledge and understanding, answer the following short questions.

Hospitality and catering

1 Describe the term 'hospitality'.
2 Describe the term 'catering'.
3 Explain the difference between 'commercial' and 'service' sectors.

Hospitality and catering establishments

Explain the difference in menus between the following catering/hospitality operations:

- Healthcare home
- Guest house
- Restaurant
- Large city bank.

Research task

Explain the types of qualifications that may be required for the following job roles:

- Head chef
- Commis chef
- Waiter
- Bar manager.

2

Food safety in catering

LEARNING OBJECTIVES

At the end of this chapter you will be able to:

- Be aware of your responsibility for personal cleanliness during food preparation and cooking in the workplace and unsafe behaviour
- Maintain clean and hygienic work surfaces and equipment
- Check food into the premises and identify specific labels
- Understand the correct use of storage control, the stock rotation system and keeping records
- Know how to safely defrost and thoroughly wash food
- Know the regulations for the safe cooking, the safe holding and the safe re-heating of food
- Chill and freeze cooked food not for immediate consumption
- Identify food bacteria and other organisms and food hazards in the workplace

INTRODUCTION

Food hygiene implies more than just the sanitation of work areas. It includes all practices, precautions and legal responsibilities involved in the following:

1 Protecting food from risk of contamination.
2 Prevention of organisms from multiplying to an extent which would pose a health risk to customers and employees.
3 Destroying any harmful bacteria in food by thorough heat treatment or other techniques.

WHAT IS FOOD POISONING?

Food poisoning is a group of medical conditions that result from eating food that is contaminated with harmful bacteria or toxic poisons from bacteria. Bacteria are a part of all living things and are found on all raw agricultural products. Harmful bacteria can be transferred from food to people, from people to food, or from one food to another.

WHAT IS FOOD HYGIENE?

Food hygiene is defined as all conditions and measures necessary to ensure the safety and suitability of food to be consumed.

PERSONAL HYGIENE

Good hygiene systems are required to be followed by all food handlers.

Regular hand washing is a requirement of the chef. The following procedures should apply:

1 An approved hand washing detergent should be provided by the employer, preferably in liquid form and from a dispenser.
2 Hot water and an approved drying system should be in place.
3 The application of an alcohol-based hand disinfectant allows for maximum disinfection.

Hand washing must be undertaken:

- Before commencing work (to wash away general bacteria)
- After using the toilet or being in contact with faeces
- After breaks
- Between touching raw food and cooked food
- Before handling raw food
- After disposing of waste
- After cleaning the work space
- After any first aid or dressing changes
- After touching face, nose, mouth or blowing your nose

Cuts, boils and septic wounds

Food handlers should always cover cuts, grazes, boils and septic wounds with the appropriate dressing or with brightly coloured (blue) waterproof plasters. Cuts on fingers may need extra protection with waterproof fingerstalls or latex disposable gloves.

Smoking

This is prohibited where food is being prepared due to the following issues:

■ The danger of contaminating food by Staphylococci from the fingers which may touch the lips and from saliva from the cigarette end.

■ Smoking encourages coughing.

Jewellery and cosmetics

Food handlers and chefs should not wear earrings, watches, rings or other piercings because they can harbour dirt and bacteria. Plain wedding bands are permitted, but these can still harbour significant levels of bacteria. Strong smelling perfume may cause food to be tainted and make-up should be used minimally.

Reporting procedures

It is essential that incidents and other problems are reported as soon as possible to avoid any further developments. Examples of situations that require reporting include:

■ Accidents
■ Sickness
■ Problems with pests
■ Complaints
■ Equipment failure.

A CLEAN AND HYGIENIC WORK AREA

The use of premises which are clean and can be correctly maintained is essential for the preparation, cooking and service of food. Cross-contamination risks should be minimized by the provision of separate preparation areas for the various raw and cooked foods. The chart below describes the various fittings and fixtures that need to be considered in a kitchen before the main equipment is thought of.

An example of an unclean, cluttered kitchen

EQUIPMENT

Work surfaces and equipment for the preparation, cooking and service of food should be impervious (resistant) and easy to clean. Equipment should be constructed from materials which are non-toxic, corrosion resistant, smooth and free from cracks. An apparatus such as a Bain-Marie should be able to store hot food for up to two hours at an ambient temperature of

FIXTURES AND FITTINGS	RECOMMENDATIONS
Ceilings	White in colour to reflect the light. Smooth textured, without cracks or peeled paint/plaster. Usually panelled to hide the ventilation system.
Floors	Should have a durable, non-slip and non-permeable material.
Lighting	Good lighting is essential to avoid eye strain.
Ventilation	The requirements for a modern kitchen is for a high performance kitchen ventilation system.
	The extracted air should be free from grease and odours.
	A canopy system should be built around the existing structure of the kitchen to cover at least all cookery areas.
Walls	In the past, ceramic wall tiles have been considered the best surface for areas where liquids splash a wall surface, potentially overcoming a damp or hygiene problem.
	Modern alternatives to ceramic wall tiles include PVC wall cladding systems, resin wall coatings and screed mortars. They offer a hygienic finish capable of withstanding heavy impact.

CHEF'S TIP

If you have a dishwasher, this is a very effective way to clean plastic chopping boards. Dishwashers can wash at a very high temperature, which kills bacteria. Otherwise, wash chopping boards thoroughly with hot water and washing-up liquid.

63 °C and regular temperature checks should be taken. The surfaces should be easy to clean even when hot and should allow the food to be presented in an attractive manner.

Worktops and chopping boards

It is very important to keep all worktops and chopping boards clean because they touch the food your customers are going to eat. If they are not properly clean, bacteria could spread to food and make your customers ill.

- Always wash worktops before you start preparing food.
- Wipe up any spilt food straight away.
- Always wash worktops thoroughly after they have been touched by raw meat, including poultry, or raw eggs.
- Never put ready-to-eat food, such as tomatoes or fruit, on a worktop or chopping board that has been touched by raw meat, unless you have washed it thoroughly first.

Cleaning products

Different cleaning products are designed to perform different tasks. The following describes the purpose of the main categories of cleaning products.

Detergent – a detergent is defined as a compound, or a combination of compounds, that is put to use for cleaning purposes. Detergents are created in a way that water is an essential requirement in the cleaning process.

Sanitizer – A sanitizer is an anti-microbial product. Before sanitizer is used, the area concerned must be thoroughly cleaned. Sanitizer is a chemical that reduces the number of micro-organisms, such as bacteria and viruses, to safe levels.

Disinfectant – A substance that destroys micro-organisms with the potential of spreading bacteria.

Sterilizer – A product that is used after cleaning to make a surface sterile (germ-free).

Bactericide – A chemical or element that kills, destroys or controls bacteria.

Ideally, it is standard practice to have separate chopping boards for raw meat and for other foods. A standardized system of coloured boards and knife handles that help to minimize cross contamination are widely available. They should be as follows:

- ■ Red   Raw meat and poultry
- ■ Yellow   Cooked meat and poultry
- ■ Blue   Raw fish (in this book, white and wooden backgrounds may be used for photographic purposes)
- ■ Brown   Vegetables
- ■ Green   Fruit and salads
- ■ White   Dairy and pastry items

These boards must be cleaned between use, ideally with sanitizer. Storage of such boards must be in racks and not touching each other. If boards become damaged they should be discarded because bacteria can multiply in cracks and blemishes, and be the cause of contamination.

Kitchen cloths

Dirty, damp cloths are the perfect breeding ground for bacteria. So it is very important to wash all cleaning cloths and sponges regularly.

Ideally, try to keep different cloths for different jobs. For example, use one cloth to wipe worktops and another to wash dishes. This helps to stop bacteria spreading.

The safest option is the use of disposable kitchen towels to wipe worktops and chopping boards. This is because you throw the kitchen towel away after using it once, so it is less likely to spread bacteria than cloths you use again.

Tea towels can spread bacteria, so it's important to wash them regularly and be careful how you use them.

Knives, spoons and other utensils

It is important to keep knives, wooden spoons, spatulas, tongs and other utensils clean to help stop bacteria spreading to food. It is especially important to wash them thoroughly after using them with raw meat, because otherwise they could spread bacteria to other food.

Chart to show colour-codes for chopping boards

 **HEALTH & SAFETY**

Remember, if you wipe your hands on a tea towel after you have touched raw meat, this will spread bacteria to the towel. Then, if you use the tea towel to dry a plate, the bacteria will spread to the plate.

HEALTH & SAFETY

HACCP

HACCP stands for 'Hazard Analysis Critical Control Point'. It is an internationally recognized and recommended system of food safety management. It focuses on identifying the 'critical points' in a process where food safety problems (or 'hazards') could arise and putting steps in place to prevent things going wrong. This is sometimes referred to as 'controlling hazards'. Keeping records is also an important part of HACCP systems.

HACCP involves the following seven steps:

1 identify what could go wrong (the hazards)
2 identify the most important points where things can go wrong (the critical control points – CCPs)
3 set critical limits at each CCP (e.g. cooking temperature/time)
4 set up checks at CCPs to prevent problems occurring (monitoring)
5 decide what to do if something goes wrong (corrective action)
6 prove that your HACCP Plan is working (verification)
7 keep records of all of the above (documentation)

Your HACCP plan must be kept up to date. You will need to review it from time to time, especially whenever something in your food operation changes. You may also wish to ask your local Environmental Health Officer for advice.

Remember that, even with a HACCP plan in place, you must comply with all requirements of current food safety legislation.

HEALTH & SAFETY

The Food Hygiene (England) Regulations 2006 provide the framework for the EU legislation to be enforced in England. The main new requirement is to have 'food safety management procedures' and keep up-to-date records of these.

Disposal of waste is another HACCP matter, as bacteria and pathogens can multiply at an alarming rate in waste disposal areas. Waste bins in the kitchen should be emptied at regular and short intervals and be kept clean. Food waste can be safely disposed of in a waste disposal unit. Oil can only be disposed of by a specialist oil disposal company and must not be placed in a sink or waste disposal unit.

REPORTING MAINTENANCE ISSUES

Food for cookery must be prepared on surfaces that are hygienic and suitable for use. Work surfaces, walls and floors can become damaged, and they too can be a source of contamination and danger to customers and staff alike. This should be reported to your line manager. A maintenance reporting system can easily be designed to suit each establishment and each section in that kitchen. Areas for attention are:

- Cracks in walls
- Damage to tables and work benches
- Cooking equipment such as pots, pans and utensils
- Windows, sanitary systems and lights
- Flooring and any other structural issues
- Electrical equipment relating to that particular operation.

SAFE FOOD STORAGE

The HACCP food management system will also examine the point of food storage. It should cover the receiving of goods where the core temperatures and condition of the delivery is thoroughly checked. Fresh meat that has been delivered should have a core temperature of a maximum of 8°C. All fresh produce should be delivered in unbroken, clean packaging and in clean delivery vehicles that are refrigerated. If you suspect a delivery has not met the requirements of your HACCP it should not be accepted and returned immediately to the supplier.

A well laid out storeroom

Maintenance Report Sheet

Date _____
Name _____
Production area _____

Nature of Problem

Action taken

Reported to

Follow-up action taken

Weekly maintenance checklist ✓		
	Date	Comments
Sinks		
Freezers		
Refrigerators		
Tables		
Food processors		
Mincers		
Ovens		
Stoves		
Windows		
Evidence of pests		
Other equipment		

Signature _____

Example of a Maintenance Report Sheet

<table>
<tr><td colspan="8">Chef's name _____

Production area _____</td></tr>
</table>

Date	Time	Supplier	Order correct	Delivery note/ Invoice number	Fault (Identify product)	Action	Temperature reading

Goods Received Checklist

Example of a Goods Received Checklist

SATURDAY

MM Sabado - Samedi

Item: _____

Prep Date: _____ Time: _____ ☐ AM ☐ PM

Shelf Life: _____ ☐ Shifts ☐ Fresh Daily

Use By: _____ ☐ 4 PM ☐ Close Emp: _____

A food label to record details of when food was made and when it should be used by.

After the commodity has been received it needs to be correctly stored. Raw meat and fish should be stored, covered, in separate refrigerators at 1°C to 4°C. However if there is not enough capacity for two separate refrigeration systems, **cooked products must be stored above fresh meat**. Fish should be stored as low in the refrigerator as possible. This is the coldest part of the refrigerator and a layer of crushed ice will help to keep the temperature down. This method eliminates cross contamination from storage and optimizes quality. All foods should be labelled with the date of delivery or production, a description of the contents and the recommended use by date.

BACTERIA AND FOOD POISONING

Salmonella

 CHEF'S TIP

There are approximately over 2000 types of salmonella.

The commonest variety is *salmonella enteriditis* and *salmonella typhimurium.* These organisms survive in the intestine and can cause food poisoning by releasing a toxin on the death of the cell. The primary source of salmonella is the intestinal tract of animals and poultry and will therefore be found in:

a) Human and animal excreta
b) Excreta from rats, mice, flies and cockroaches
c) Raw meat and poultry
d) Some animal feed.

Staphylococcus aureus

CHEF'S TIP

About 40–50 per cent of adults carry this organism in their nose, mouth, throat, ears and hands.

If present in food, *Staphylococcus aureus* will produce a toxin which may survive boiling for 30 minutes or more. The majority of outbreaks are caused by poor hygiene practices which result in direct contamination of the food by people from sneezing or uncovered septic cuts and abrasions. Frequently, the cooked food has been handled while still slightly warm and this has encouraged the organism to produce its toxin.

Clostridium perfringens

This is commonly found in human and animal faeces and is present in raw meat and poultry. This organism forms spores which may survive boiling temperatures for several hours. Outbreaks can involve stews and large joints of meat which have been allowed to cool down slowly in a warm kitchen and either eaten cold or inadequately reheated the following day.

Bacillus cereus

This is a spore forming organism. The spores survive normal cooking and rapid growth will occur if the food has not been cooled quickly and refrigerated. This bacteria will induce nausea and vomiting within five hours of ingestion.

THE DEVELOPMENT OF BACTERIA

Timeline

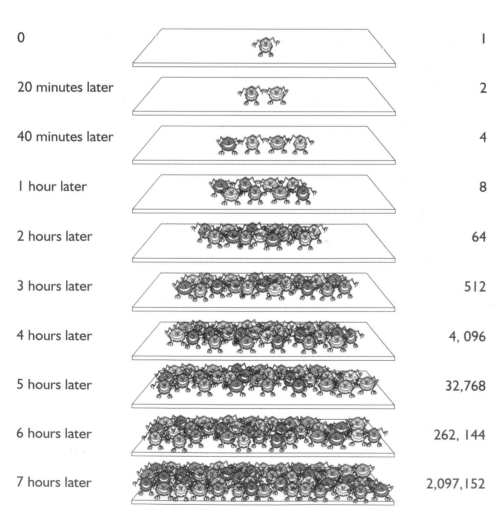

0	1
20 minutes later	2
40 minutes later	4
1 hour later	8
2 hours later	64
3 hours later	512
4 hours later	4, 096
5 hours later	32,768
6 hours later	262, 144
7 hours later	2,097,152

FOOD STORAGE AND TEMPERATURES

■ Raw meat, poultry and game
4 °C or below — *Store away from cooked meat and cooked meat products to avoid any risk of cross-contamination.*

■ Cooked meat
4 °C or below — *Keep away from raw meat and meat products.*

■ Uncooked fish
2 °C or below — *Keep in separate compartments or in plastic fish trays with lids if possible and away from other foods which may become tainted.*

■ Frozen food
−18 °C or below — *Thaw only immediately prior to using the commodity.*

■ Fish (smoked or cured)
5 °C — *Keep in chilled storage away from other foods, which may become tainted.*

■ Fruit (fresh and dried) — *Store in cool, dry, well-ventilated area. Away from other food, at least 15 cm from the ground. Discard at the first sign of mould growth. Do not overstock.*

■ Pasta, rice and cereals — *Store in self-closing tightly lidded containers in dry cool storeroom or cupboard.*

■ Eggs
Refrigerate at 8 °C or below — *Use strictly in rotation and ensure the shells are clean.*

■ Fats, butter, dairy and non dairy spreads
5 °C or below — *Keep covered and away from highly flavoured food, which may taint.*

■ Milk and cream
5 °C or below — *In a separate dairy refrigerator that is used for no other purpose and in strict rotation.*

■ Prepared desserts
4 °C or below — *Should be prepared only on day of use.*

■ Sauces and soups
5 °C or below — *Should be prepared only on day of use and stored in plastic containers with a tight fitting lid.*

■ Salads and fresh herbs
5 °C or below — *Always wash before use.*

■ Canned and bottled goods — *Cool, dry, well-ventilated storage area. Blown, rusty or split tins must not be used.*

■ Root vegetables — *Store in sacks or nets as delivered in cool, well ventilated area*

■ Leaf and green vegetables
5 °C — *Use on day of delivery.*

Freezers, whether upright or chest freezers, should be maintained at a maximum temperature of −18 °C. All food should be covered to prevent freezer burn and labelled with the date of production and a use by date.

Ambient stores should be clean and well ventilated, with mesh over windows and doors to help with pest control. All foodstuffs must be stored away from the floor and be rotated on a first in and first out basis.

PREPARING, COOKING AND STORING FOOD SAFELY

Frozen food should be defrosted in a refrigerator and treated as fresh food with the same use by date. All root vegetables must be washed prior to peeling and then rewashed after peeling. Leaf vegetables such as cabbage and spinach should be washed in several changes of cold water to allow soil and grit to go to the bottom of the sink. A separate preparation area should be facilitated ideally to help prevent cross contamination.

In large scale catering operations such as hospitals and schools, during cooking a core temperature of 70°C will be maintained for two minutes as a core temperature of 75°C will kill pathogens; however, a consequence of this is that all foods will be well done. In restaurants and hotels the core temperature is dependent on the requirements of the customer.

Chilling food not for immediate use should ideally be achieved in blast chillers where the core temperature is brought down from 70°C to 4°C in 90 minutes or less. With these temperature ranges both pathogenic and bacterial growth is inhibited although not completely stopped.

If food that has been cooked is not for immediate consumption, or is to be frozen, it should be well covered with cling film or ideally vacuum packed to create an airtight barrier and prevent freezer burn. Storage should be within manufacturer's guidelines and the foods must be clearly labelled as previously mentioned.

HAZARD ANALYSIS

Critical points to note in the preparation and cooking of food come in the following forms:

- Bacterial and other organisms
- Chemical

Chemicals such as degreasers, polishes, detergents and sanitizers, must be stored in a designated area away from food production.

HAZARD CONTROLS

- Regular servicing of equipment
- Use a temperature probe to check on food storage
- Use a temperature probe to check on food storage equipment
- Investigate all complaints of suspected food-borne illnesses
- Regular inspections by a health and safety officer
- Frequent self inspections
- Comprehensive cleaning programmes in place
- Adequate staff training in food handling and hygiene practices.

(Please see page 200 for a table of where hazards might occur.)

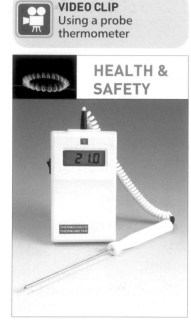

VIDEO CLIP
Using a probe thermometer

HEALTH & SAFETY

A probe is an hygienic way to test the core temperature of food.

IMAGE COURTESY OF RUSSUMS

CHEF'S TIP

For information regarding allergies, refer to pages 45–6 in chapter 4 (unit 104) – Introduction to Healthier Foods and Special Diets

Food safety temperature guide

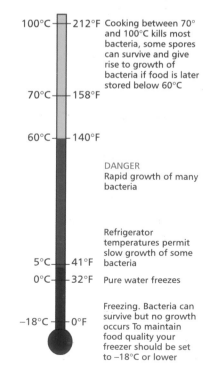

100°C — 212°F Cooking between 70° and 100°C kills most bacteria, some spores can survive and give rise to growth of bacteria if food is later stored below 60°C

70°C — 158°F

60°C — 140°F

DANGER
Rapid growth of many bacteria

Refrigerator temperatures permit slow growth of some bacteria

5°C — 41°F

0°C — 32°F Pure water freezes

Freezing. Bacteria can survive but no growth occurs To maintain food quality your freezer should be set to −18°C or lower

−18°C — 0°F

Assessment of knowledge and understanding

1 Explain what food poisoning is.

_____

_____

2 Give 3 examples of times when you should wash your hands.

i) _____

ii) _____

iii) _____

3 Explain why different coloured chopping boards should be used.

_____

_____

4 By drawing a line, match up the colour chopping board with the food items it should be used to prepare.

red   vegetables

yellow   dairy and pastry items

blue   raw meat and poultry

brown   fruits and salads

green   raw fish

white   cooked meat and poultry

5 What does HACCP stand for?

_____

_____

6 Give the correct food storage temperature for the food items listed below.

Raw meat   _____ °C or below

Cooked meat   _____ °C or below

Uncooked fish   _____ °C or below

Milk   _____ °C or below

7 Give 3 ways in which you can help to control hazards in the workplace.

i) _____

ii) _____

iii) _____

3

Health and safety awareness for catering and hospitality

Unit 103 Health and safety awareness for catering and hospitality

LEARNING OBJECTIVES

At the end of this chapter you will be able to:

- Understand the need for health and safety practices in the workplace
- Identify hazards in the workplace
- Understand the importance of following health and safety procedures
- Describe the types and use of safety signs and the types of hazards and incidents that require reporting.

HEALTH AND SAFETY PRACTICES IN CATERING AND HOSPITALITY

What is health and safety?

Health is described as an individual's physical and mental wellbeing. If a person is in good health, they will feel well, stable in their mind and not be suffering from any illness or disease.

Safety refers to the absence of risks that could potentially damage someone's health. Whatever function you have in the hospitality industry, everyone is required to behave safely and professionally. Reasonable care must be taken for the health and safety of yourself and others who may be affected by what you do.

What are the factors that affect health and safety in the workplace?

There are a number of factors that affect health and safety in the workplace. These can be broken down into the following three areas.

Occupational factors

'Occupational' refers to issues that are specific to the type of work being undertaken. For example:

- *The type of equipment being used* – Kitchens have many pieces of equipment that could cause harm if used incorrectly, e.g. gravity food slicers, electric mixer, blenders, etc.
- *The chemicals used for cleaning* – It is essential that the manufacturer's instructions are followed carefully and that personal protective equipment is used as required to prevent injury through direct contact or inhalation.
- *The processes being used to produce food* – Food preparation and cookery processes have risks attached. For example, when smoking foods there is the risk of inhalation of smoke.
- *The food itself* – Certain foods can present a risk without any of the above. For example, the tiny particles in flour can cause respiratory problems if someone is exposed to working in this type of environment for a long period of time. It is recommended that a flour mask is worn in such cases to reduce inhalation.

Environmental factors

The 'environment' refers to the surroundings in which a person works and the conditions to which they may be exposed. For example:

- *High levels of noise* – High levels of noise can cause damage to a person's ears, especially if the exposure is over a long period of time.
- *Poor lighting* – Poor lighting reduces vision and increases the possibility of an accident.

■ *Temperature* – For example, if we get overheated, this can make us feel dizzy, faint and even nauseous (sick).

■ *Facilities* – Facilities should be clean, safe and fit for purpose. A variety of welfare facilities should also be provided for employees:

■ Toilets	■ Washing facilities
■ Changing areas	■ PPE storage facilities
■ Drinking water	■ Rest facilities

Human factors

The way in which we behave at work has a massive impact on the health and safety of ourselves, those working near us and any customers we serve. For example:

■ *Carelessness* – A lack of concentration or a carefree approach could result in something going wrong with the task in hand.

■ *Inexperience or a lack of training* – A lack of experience and/or training may expose the person performing the task to danger and a risk to their personal health and safety as well as the health and safety of others. It is essential that inexperienced staff are properly supervised and provided with the required training to perform tasks safely.

■ *Physical and/or mental state* – The physical and mental state of a person can be critical in the way that they perform at work. The way in which a task is approached can change due to stress and anxiety. It can be difficult to focus and concentrate when suffering from stress.

Someone that is under the influence of alcohol or drugs is obviously a danger to themselves and others and should be prevented from working immediately.

The benefits of following good health and safety practices?

■ Reduce accidents and illness

Health and safety practices are intended to protect people from any form of harm, injury or illness. If such practices are well planned and monitored with regular training and updating for all staff concerned, the likelihood of accidents and illness is reduced significantly.

■ Preserves and promotes a good reputation

The benefits of reducing accidents and potential ill-health include the prospect of a contented and motivated workforce. Such a workforce is much more likely to achieve increased productivity, an enhanced reputation and eventually improved profitability.

On the contrary, a damaged reputation to a business can lead to eventual closure due to insufficient trade.

HEALTH & SAFETY

If good practices are developed and there is regular training and monitoring of health and safety, it is much less likely that anyone will become subject to harm.

HEALTH & SAFETY

The personal costs can be equally damaging. An accident can be particularly painful and may affect the rest of a person's life. Someone's life is the ultimate cost. In the most serious cases, people can die from poor health and safety practices.

■ Prevents legal action and associated costs

People have the right to seek legal action if their health and safety have been put at risk or harmed as a result of another's actions. An employer has a responsibility to protect staff, visitors and customers from any form of risk to their health and safety.

■ Helps to control costs

Any accident or illness related directly or indirectly to the workplace could have a cost implication. This could be from increased sick leave, poor performance and staff turnover. There is also the possibility that a case could lead to prosecution, fines, high legal costs and compensation claims.

Responsibilities for health and safety and the consequences of non-compliance

Everyone has a responsibility for health and safety

Employers have a duty to provide and maintain a working environment which is safe and healthy. This includes regular checking and servicing of equipment and also ensuring that chemical substances are handled safely and with due care and attention. An employer has a responsibility to train all employees in health and safety on a regular basis and ensure that the work environment is in good repair with sufficient lighting, ventilation, temperature control and that safety equipment and clothing are provided. An employer should also provide employees with a health and safety policy statement.

Employees have a responsibility to take care of their own health and safety as well as the health and safety of those around them. Employees should co-operate with their employers in the good practices and promotion of health and safety at work.

Failure to comply with such recommendations or acts of a serious nature is likely to result in the loss of employment. Employees also face the possibility of prosecution following their actions!

IDENTIFYING HAZARDS IN THE WORKPLACE

Hazards and risks

The Health and Safety at Work Act covers all full-time and part-time employees and unpaid workers (such as work placements for students).

The Health and Safety Executive (HSE) is the body appointed to support and enforce health and safety in the workplace. They have defined the two concepts for hazards and risk:

THE MOST COMMONLY USED TERMS IN HEALTH AND SAFETY

TERM	DEFINITION
Workplace	Place of work
Accident	An unintended incident
Hazard	Something with the potential to cause harm
Risk	The likelihood of the hazard actually causing harm
Control measure	A measure to control the risk
EHO	Environmental Health Officer
PPE	Personal Protective Equipment
PAT	Portable Appliance Testing (portable electrical products)
Electric shock	The shock received if the body comes into direct contact with an electricity source
Evacuation route	A planned route to leave a building or premises in the case of emergency (e.g. fire)
Occupational health	Health at work
Manual handling	Lifting procedures – very important to protect the back
Noise	The volume and type of sound that people may be exposed to
Report	Usually a written document e.g. a record of an incident or situation/recommendations for improvements
Harassment	Unwanted behaviour which makes the receiver feel uncomfortable or threatened. Harassment can be of a verbal, physical or sexual nature.

1 A hazard is something with the potential to cause harm

2 A risk is the likelihood of the hazard's potential being realized.

Two examples of this are as follows:

1 A light bulb that requires replacing is a hazard. If it is one out of several it presents a very small risk. However, if it is the only light within a 'walk-in' cold room, it poses a high risk.

2 A stockpot full of hot stock being moved from one kitchen to another using a trolley presents a potential hazard. The pot could fall off completely or could spill over during transit causing spillage onto clothes, scalding and creating a wet and slippery floor surface. Therefore it is high in risk.

The main causes of slips, trips and falls

The likelihood of someone slipping, tripping or falling in the workplace is increased by a number of factors. Poor design can lead to such problems. For example, an unexpected step, whether up or down, could lead to a loss of balance and a fall. The risk of this happening is further increased if there is no signage to warn people of this unexpected hazard or if the signage is not obvious or unclear.

A clean and tidy environment without obstructions and clear signage helps to minimize such accidents.

Other examples include:

Lighting and ventilation – Poor lighting restricts vision and as such potential hazards will not be as obvious. Poor ventilation can lead to someone overheating, causing dizziness and even fainting.

Dangerous working practices – For example, not drying wet floors after a spillage or leaving items in areas that are inappropriate (poor storage practices).

Distraction or lack of attention – For example, not looking where you are going increases the likelihood of a collision, trip or fall.

Working too quickly – During a busy service, chefs and front-of-house staff often work at a much faster pace than usual. With everyone working at greater speed, the likelihood of a collision, trip or fall increases. In such situations, concentration and communication are vitally important.

Ignoring rules and working practices – Many restaurants operate a work flow system between the restaurant and kitchen. This includes a route in to the kitchen from the restaurant and another route from the kitchen back to the restaurant. If everyone follows this, there will be a good work flow and it is unlikely that there will be a collision as staff will always be walking in the same direction. If this working practice is broken and someone chooses to walk in the opposite direction, the likelihood of an accident is increased significantly.

Not wearing the correct 'Personal Protective Equipment' (PPE) – The employer must provide:

- protective gloves when washing pots and pans
- masks and goggles when cleaning stoves and ovens with hazardous substances
- provide staff changing and correct storage facilities.

The employee has a responsibility to comply with the policy of wearing PPE at all necessary times and report any defects in the PPE to the employer.

HEALTH & SAFETY

Physical/mental state – we are less likely to slip, trip or fall when we are fresh in our minds and concentrating on the tasks ahead.

The main injuries caused by manual handling

Working in hospitality and catering, and particularly kitchens, often involves manual handling to some degree. In kitchens, items come in many shapes and sizes, various temperatures, from frozen to boiling, and different weights. All have the potential to cause injury if not handled correctly. The main injury, and perhaps the most severe, is the damage that poor manual handling techniques can have on the back and spine. Other injuries associated with manual handling include:

- muscular injuries
- fractures
- sprains
- cuts and bruises.

Correct lifting and handling procedures

Maximum load

The maximum load a person can handle will depend upon individual strength at the time. If in any doubt do not attempt the task; seek advice from your supervisor. Always take into account your size, general health, and in particular any unnatural movement needed such as twisting or reaching if possible.

Sequence of lifting boxes

Stand with your feet apart

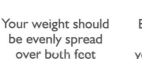

Your weight should be evenly spread over both feet

Bend your knees slowly keeping your back straight

Stand with your feet apart

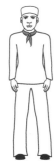

Tuck your chin in towards your chest

Get a good grip on the base of the box

Bring the box to your waist height keeping the lift as smooth as possible

Keep the box close to your body

Proceed carefully making sure that you can see where you are going

Lower the box, reversing the lifting procedure

HEALTH & SAFETY

Where there is any possibility of risk, break a load into smaller items, e.g. liquids and loose items can be put into smaller containers. This is particularly the case with trolleys when transporting many items, e.g. make trolleys lighter by increasing the number of journeys.

HEALTH & SAFETY

- Do not handle any load if the floor or the item is damp or slippery.
- Do not store anything other than light loads above shoulder height.
- Do not store liquids or sharp items or anything remotely heavy above eye level.
- Make maximum use of legs, keep the back as straight as possible and avoid twisting or bending forward.

Health considerations

- Report any medical condition (high blood pressure, osteoporosis, etc.) to your supervisor before handling heavy loads.

Protect yourself

- Wear the protective clothing provided. Wear sturdy footwear.
- If you feel that you require protective clothing and footwear then raise this with your supervisor.
- Spillages are your responsibility. If you spill anything, or come across a spillage or wet floor, you must either clean it up yourself or arrange for someone else to clean it. Ensure that warning notices are posted in the interim.

The main ways in which equipment can cause injury and the control measures to avoid injury

Injuries can happen in many ways. For example:

By entanglement or entrapment – This could happen by getting caught up in a mixing machine while it is in operation. People sometimes get tempted to move something or push a piece of food that may have been displaced back towards the centre of the mix. If such actions take place whilst the machine is switched on, the consequences can be extremely unpleasant.

By impact – The safe storage of items is essential in the kitchen environment. Equipment is regularly stored on racks, shelves and even hooks. This can often be at quite a height. If items are not stored properly and become unbalanced, there is significant potential for them to fall causing injury to anyone in their path.

Ejection – Ejection refers to items flying out unexpectedly. For example items of food or pieces of broken or loose equipment, a loose blade or screw in a mixing machine could fly out when switched on.

Faulty equipment – Faulty equipment presents a serious risk of injury. If equipment is not in good condition, performance will suffer and it will not function as it should. Damaged electrical equipment is particularly dangerous and should not be used.

Improper use of equipment – All equipment is designed to be used in a certain way. Manufacturers of equipment often provide user guidelines to demonstrate how a piece of equipment should be used. If guidelines or training in the safe use of equipment are ignored, the likelihood of an accident is increased significantly.

Any equipment that is faulty should be reported immediately and removed to avoid potential injuries.

HAZARDOUS SUBSTANCES

There are many hazardous substances used in the kitchen environment. Such substances include cleaning chemicals, cooking liquids, gas as well as the gels and spirits that are sometimes used to maintain the temperature in hot buffet containers.

The Control of Substances Hazardous to Health (COSHH) Regulations (1999)

Control of Substances Hazardous to Health (COSHH) is a workplace policy that is relevant to everyday working practices. Chemicals that are toxic such as detergents are hazardous and present a high risk. They must be stored, handled, used and disposed of correctly in accordance with COSHH.

Any substance in the workplace that is hazardous to health must be identified on the packaging and stored and handled correctly.

Hazardous substances can enter the body via:

- The skin
- The eyes
- The mouth (ingestion)
- The nose (inhalation).

The COSHH Regulations were consolidated in 2002 and employers are stated as being held responsible for assessing the risks from hazardous substances and for controlling the exposure to them to prevent ill health. Any hazardous substances identified should be formally recorded in writing and given a risk rating. Safety precaution procedures should then be implemented and training given to employees to ensure that the procedures are understood and followed correctly.

Hazardous substances are usually shown through use of symbols

The main causes of fire and explosions

Fire can be started from a number of sources. However, fire needs three separate elements to survive.

1 Fuel   2 Air (oxygen)   3 Heat.

Should any one of these elements be removed, ignition cannot take place.

The main causes of fire in kitchens arise through the following:

- Electricity and electrical faults
- Gas leaks or a build up of gas
- Smoking and cigarettes that have not been put out properly
- The ignition of oils, liquids and other flammable substances
- Misuse of tools and equipment with a naked flame.

With this in mind, it is essential that flammable materials should be stored safely and securely in a locked fireproof cupboard. Gas canisters should be kept stored away from direct sunlight and any other direct heat source.

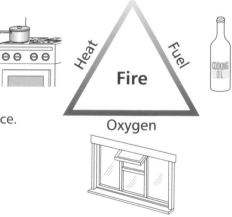

ACTIVITY

Think of several potential causes of fire in the kitchen. How could each of these be prevented?

In the event of a fire it is essential that no-one is placed at risk and that the emergency alarm is operated as soon as possible to alert others. The emergency services should also be contacted as fast as possible. Fires can spread quickly and easily, so it is important to leave the building at once, closing doors to prevent the spread of fire and report to the identified fire assembly point.

A new fire law came into force on 1 October 2006. The new law is called the Regulatory Reform (Fire safety) Order 2005. It replaces all the previous legislation relating to fire, including fire certificates which no longer have any validity. This law is applicable to England and Wales only. Northern Ireland and Scotland have their own similar legislation.

This new legislation puts the responsibility for fire safety onto the employer being the 'responsible person'. The 'responsible person' will have a duty to ensure the safety of everyone who uses their premises and those in the immediate vicinity who may be at risk if there is a fire. Anyone responsible for premises must carry out a fire safety risk assessment. The fire and rescue service will carry out inspections and failure to comply could lead to enforcement action or even prosecution.

Fire risk assessments will include:

- Identifying and removing any obstacles that may hinder fire evacuation.
- Ensuring that suitable fire detection equipment is in place.
- Making sure that all escape routes are clearly marked and free from obstacles.
- Testing fire alarm systems regularly to ensure they are in full operational condition.

All staff must be trained in fire and emergency evacuation procedures for their workplace. The emergency exit route will be the easiest route by which all staff, customers and visitors can leave the building safely. Fire action plans should be prominently displayed to show the emergency exit route.

Fire extinguishers are available to tackle different types of fire. It is important that these are checked and maintained as required.

The causes of fire and extinguishers to choose

Fire can be caused and started by many factors, different portable fire extinguishers are used to fight small fires, remember you should only use these if you have received training. Fire extinguishers are predominantly red with a colour label or band around the top identifying their contents. Also found on the fire extinguishers is a symbol and letter indicating the type of fire the extinguisher can be used for.

Fire blankets may be used to smother small localized fires such as a frying pan or burnt sugar pan. Fire blankets are also used to wrap people in if their clothes catch fire.

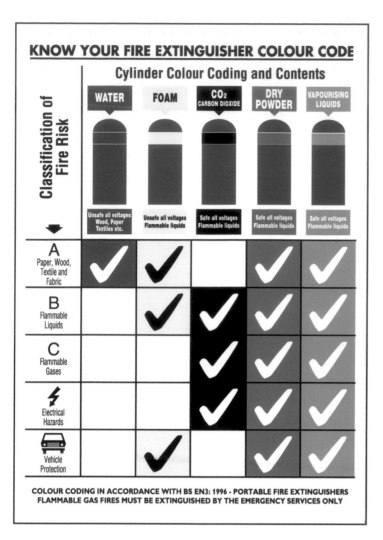

The dangers associated with electricity

If a person comes into direct contact with electricity, the consequences can be severe. Direct contact is referred to as an electric shock and the severity of an electric shock ranges from a short, sharp jolt to death!

It is also recommended that certain staff within an organization are trained to check cables, flex and plugs to ensure that the basic principles or electric circuitry in portable appliances are safe. This is referred to as 'Portable Appliance Testing – abbreviated as PAT'.

Emergency procedure

In a case of fire or emergency, the following sequence must be followed:

- Raise the alarm
- Switch off any source of power (if safe and possible to do so!)
- Call for help (first aid, emergency services)
- Evacuate.

CHEF'S TIP

Productivity refers to the amount of (good quality) work that a person can do in a specific time. For example, a highly skilled chef will be able to produce good quality results in the preparation and cooking of food in the same time that someone with low skill level will be able to produce a lower quality results and in lower quantity.

HEALTH & SAFETY

Examples of PPE include:
- Gloves to protect hands from cleaning chemicals
- Goggles to protect eyes from substances that will cause damage to eyesight.

FOLLOWING HEALTH AND SAFETY PROCEDURES

Health and safety is critical to our wellbeing! It can literally mean the difference between life and death and all that comes between.

The main reasons for working in a healthy and safe manner are to:

- Prevent accidents and injuries
- Maintain health
- Increase productivity.

The functions of Personal Protective Equipment (PPE)

Personal Protective Equipment should be issued as a last resort. This may sound strange, but before issuing equipment to protect, all other possible solutions for carrying out the task in a way that does not require such equipment should be explored. For example, if using a cleaning chemical that requires a mask to be worn, is there another product available that will perform the task but does not require the use of a mask as the same danger is not present?

Responsibilities for the use of Personal Protective Equipment

This is quite simple! Employers must provide staff with PPE when their role involves working in situations or with substances where PPE is deemed necessary.

Employees must use the PPE provided and comply with policy covering this issue. An employee must also report any faults or defects on the PPE to the employer.

Hazards and incidents that require reporting

To promote health and safety, it is important that any related issues or problems are reported to the appropriate person (e.g. supervisor or manager) so that remedial action can be taken.
Hazards can originate from a number of sources. For example:

- Problems with buildings or equipment (e.g. through damage or misuse)
- Ill health (e.g. dermatitis, infectious diseases)
- Environmental issues (e.g. excess noise or heat)
- Abuse (e.g. mental or physical).

Signage in the kitchen environment

Safety signs are used in the kitchen and surrounding areas to help identify hazards, obligatory actions and prohibited actions for all staff, customers and visitors.

Yellow – warning signs to alert people to various dangers such as slippery floors and hot water. Yellow signs also provide a warning of hazards, e.g. 'Corrosive substance'.

Blue – mandatory signs to inform everyone what they must do in order to progress safely through a certain area. Usually this would indicate the need to wear protective clothing.

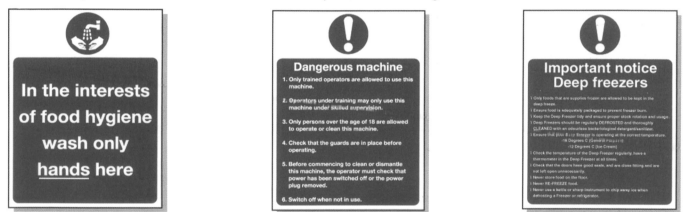

Red – prohibition signs are designed to stop persons from certain tasks in a hazardous area, such as no smoking or no access. Red signs also represent fire fighting equipment, such as a fire hose.

Green – escape route signs, designed to show fire and emergency exits to staff, visitors and customers. Green is also the colour used to identify first aid equipment.

Assessment of knowledge and understanding

1 Describe three reasons for working safely.

i) _____ ii) _____

iii) _____

2 List four potential causes of slips, trips and/or falls.

i) _____ ii) _____

iii) _____ iv) _____

3 List four potential benefits of following good health and safety practices.

i) _____ ii) _____

iii) _____ iv) _____

4 Describe the terms 'hazard' and 'risk'.

_____

_____

5 What is meant by the abbreviation 'PAT' as used in the context of health and safety?

_____

_____

6 Describe four points to be considered when lifting an item from the floor and taking it to another section of the kitchen.

i) _____ ii) _____

iii) _____ iv) _____

7 Name the three elements of fire.

i) _____ ii) _____

iii) _____

8 Identify the type of extinguisher that should be used in the following types of fire.

TYPE/CAUSE OF FIRE	EXTINGUISHER	LABEL COLOUR
Electrical fire		
Flammable liquids (e.g. oils)		
Solid material fire (e.g. wood)		
Vaporising liquids (e.g. gas)		

9 What is meant by the abbreviation 'PPE' as used in the context of health and safety?

_____

10 What is the procedure when dealing with electrical accidents and dangers?

_____

_____

4

Introduction to healthier foods and special diets

LEARNING OBJECTIVES

On completion of this chapter, learners will be able to:

- Identify the main categories of nutrients
- State the importance of nutrients in the diet
- Describe a range of foods within the main food groups and the key nutrients they contain
- Explain the importance of water and fibre in the diet
- Identify vulnerable groups of people and groups with special dietary requirements
- Describe the effects a lack or excess of nutrients may have with regard to health and wellbeing
- Identify foods that may cause allergies or intolerances
- List sources and content of current Government guidelines

Carbohydrates provide our greatest source of energy

CHEF'S TIP

Maltose – Maltose is the sugar that is found in cereal grains and is the sugar used in beer making. Maltose is not as sweet as sucrose.

CHEF'S TIP

Lactose – Lactose is the type of sugar that is present in milk. The amount of sugar present differs, depending on the type of milk being produced.

CHEF'S TIP

If you leave peeled and cut potatoes in water for a while, some of the starch from the potatoes will fall to the bottom of the bowl. It appears like a smooth, silky and waxy white substance.

NUTRIENTS AND THEIR IMPORTANCE

Nutrients are described as the parts of foods that help the body to perform and maintain bodily functions. This includes our movement, sight, growth and repair. Nutrients are broken down into five main categories: *carbohydrates, fats, proteins, vitamins* and *minerals*. Their main characteristics are described in the following:

Carbohydrates

Carbohydrates provide our greatest source of energy. Some carbohydrates are important in maintaining a healthy gut as you will see later in the section referring to dietary fibre. Carbohydrates consist of three main chemicals: carbon, hydrogen and oxygen.

Carbohydrates can be split into three sub-groups. These groups are called *sugars, starches and dietary fibre*.

Sugars

There are many different types of sugar, the most obvious being the sugar that we use to sweeten tea and coffee or when making cakes and biscuits, etc. Beyond this are a number of other forms of sugar.

Sucrose is the proper name for the sugar that we would add to tea, coffee, etc. Sucrose can also be found in fruits and vegetables and in high quantities in sugar cane and beet.

Starches

Starches have a different structure to sugars but are made up of many forms of simple sugars. Starches are not soluble in water (unlike sugars) but become much easier to digest once cooked. Starches are present in many types of food but are particularly high in cereals, rice and root vegetables.

Other products that are high in starch include flour and various products made from flour, such as pasta and bread.

Dietary fibre

Dietary fibre is a very important form of starch. Unlike sugars and starches, dietary fibre cannot be digested and does not provide the body with energy. However, dietary fibre is considered to be a very important part of a balanced diet playing a number of important roles in the diet.

■ Dietary fibre aids digestion and promotes bowel action, removing waste products from the body.

■ Dietary fibre helps to control the digestion of nutrients and the way nutrients are processed.

■ Dietary fibre also adds bulk to the diet, reducing the feeling of hunger and the desire to eat.

Fats

Fats have many functions in the human body and are naturally present in many of the foods we eat.

Fats come from animals, vegetables or cereals, seeds and nuts. They are referred to as saturated or unsaturated. Saturated fats are usually found in animal products whereas unsaturated fats are usually associated with vegetables, seeds and nuts.

Fats perform a number of functions within the body:

- Fats are capable of producing energy for the body in potentially greater quantities than carbohydrates (sugars and starches).
- Fat provides protection for the vital organs. Our vital organs are mostly within the chest and stomach area. Some of our organs, but particularly the kidneys, have a thick layer of fat surrounding them to protect them from impact and other potential damage.
- Fats help to stabilize our body temperature.

Proteins

Proteins are very important to the body as they are the major part of the cells that actually form the body. It is essential that we have a good supply of proteins In our diet as living beings. The following points describe the main functions of proteins.

Growth

As we grow from birth into adulthood, our bodies are constantly changing and developing.

Repair

Throughout our lives, the cells making up our bodies need to be replaced as they die. The lifespan of cells ranges from about a week to a few months. It is also to be expected that we will get injured from time-to-time as we go through life, which causes damage to our cells. As the major part of our cell structure, proteins need to be present in order for the body to repair itself in such cases.

To carry out bodily functions

Throughout life our bodies perform millions of tasks. This is happening every second of our lives in our thoughts, actions and in the functions required to stay alive.

A secondary source of energy

Any excess protein in our diet is converted into carbohydrate or fat as it cannot be stored for use at a later time. As this is not the main function of protein, it is referred to as a secondary source of energy.

CHEF'S TIP

We also use fats and oils in many cooking processes and as an ingredient within recipes. The main difference between fats and oils is in their condition at room temperature. At an ambient temperature, fats are solid whereas oils will be liquid.

HEALTH & SAFETY

Although fats are a requirement within our diets, there is a great deal of concern with regard to the links between excess fat consumption and problems with obesity (being overweight) as well as other health issues such as heart disease.

To provide the body with amino acids

Proteins are made up of acids called amino acids, which are very important to our bodily functions. Some of the amino acids are referred to as *'essential amino acids'*. Because the body is unable to produce these acids by itself it has to rely on them being supplied through the foods we eat.

Vitamins

As far as we are aware, there are 13 vitamins required by the body in order for it to function properly. In comparison to carbohydrates, fats and proteins, vitamins form a much smaller structural part within the foods we eat. Vitamins perform two major functions in the body.

■ To control growth and repair of the body
■ To control the functions of our body cells

Minerals

As far as we are aware, there are 18 minerals required by the body in order for it to function properly. Minerals are present in a vast range of foods and form a tiny structural part within the foods we eat. Minerals perform many functions in the body:

Minerals form the major structure of our bones and teeth

Minerals found in our bones and teeth include calcium, magnesium, phosphorus and fluorine.

Minerals help to carry out bodily functions

These actions are produced through various chemical reactions, through the production of enzymes and hormones. The enzymes and hormones are produced by proteins but assisted by minerals to release energy in order for the body to function.

Minerals help to control the levels of fluids held in the body

The body is approximately 60–65 per cent water. It is important to control the level of fluids in the body.

HEALTH & SAFETY

Without water a human can only survive for a few days.

FOOD GROUPS AND THE KEY NUTRIENTS THEY CONTAIN

It is important that our diet includes the full range of nutrients in the quantities required for us to enjoy a healthy life. One way to look at the balance in our diet is to place foods into groups, linked to the nutrients contained within those foods.

As you can see, the majority of nutrients are found in the groups of fruit and vegetables, breads and cereals, milk and dairy products and meat and fish. The main food groups are classified as follows:

FOOD GROUP	EXAMPLES OF FOODS	NUTRIENTS PRESENT
Fruits and vegetables	Fruits Fruit juices Vegetables Pulses (peas, beans, lentils)	Carbohydrate Dietary fibre Vitamins – C group Minerals Carotene Protein (from pulses)
Breads and cereals	Breads Cereals (e.g. rice, cous-cous) Breakfast cereals and porridge Pasta Flour and associated products	Carbohydrate Dietary fibre Vitamins – B group Minerals Protein
Milk and dairy products	Milk Cheese Cream Yoghurt Butter Eggs	Protein Carbohydrate Fat Vitamins – A & D Minerals – calcium
Meat and fish	Meat Poultry Offal Fish Shellfish	Protein Fat Vitamins – A, B group, D Minerals - iron
Fatty foods (non-dairy)	Foods containing animal fats (Suet, lard, dripping) Vegetable oils Vegetable suet Many convenience foods – Fast foods (burgers, fried foods)	Fat Vitamins A & D
Sugary foods	Confectionery – sweets, chocolate, biscuits, cakes, soft drinks, carbonated sweetened drinks Preserves and jams	Carbohydrate Fat

Drinks are also a form of nutritional intake and should be considered in the same way as food. Alcoholic drinks, in particular, have an impact on our bodies if consumed on a regular basis. As well as the health implications and potential organ damage from regular and excessive consumption of alcohol, there is also the impact from the levels of carbohydrate consumed. Excess levels of carbohydrate can be converted to fat and may result in the body becoming overweight.

WATER AND FIBRE IN THE DIET

Water is one of the most important substances in life and without it we would not survive for very long. A significant percentage of our bodies, approximately 60–65 per cent, is water. Without water, a human being can only survive for one or two days, whereas without food, we can survive for a number of weeks.

Water needs to be replaced regularly due to going to the toilet, breathing and sweating. We also lose large quantities of water when we are ill through being sick and diarrhoea. It is therefore extremely important that we consistently drink water to keep our bodies hydrated and provide the organs with enough water to function properly. It is recommended that we drink eight glasses of water throughout the day.

Water performs many functions in the body. The following points describe these functions.

To assist the body in removing waste products

It is very important that waste is removed from the body. If waste is not removed, it could start to release toxins (poisons) which could cause organ damage or sickness.

To control body temperature

Water helps to control our body temperature through sweating. When our bodies get hot or overheat, water is released through our pores to bring our temperature down to a more comfortable level.

To transport oxygen and nutrients around the body

Nutrients, enzymes and hormones are dissolved in water, allowing nutrients to be transported to the many cells around the body.

To supply minerals directly to the body

Water contains minerals naturally, although the amounts of minerals can differ according to where the water came from.

To act as a lubricant

Water helps to lubricate certain areas around the body, particularly in the workings of the eyes and eyelids. Water also helps to ensure that our joints are flexible, allowing free movement.

Dietary fibre

Dietary fibre cannot be digested as with other foods, although it will soften through cooking. When eaten, it is broken down mechanically by our teeth and swallowed but it is not broken down any further beyond this stage. Dietary fibre promotes the removal of waste from the body and provides a feeling of being 'full', satisfying our hunger and reducing the likelihood of overeating. Many recent findings recommend that we should aim to reduce the amounts of sugar, fat and salt in our diets and increase the quantities of dietary fibre. All dietary fibre comes from vegetables, fruits and cereals. Animal products contain no dietary fibre.

To increase our consumption of dietary fibre, the following recommendations are suggested:

- Eat wholemeal or granary bread
- Use wholemeal flour in place of white flour
- Eat wholegrain cereal products or bran enriched cereals
- Eat wholemeal pasta and wholegrain rice
- Eat plenty of fruit of vegetables
- Eat plenty of pulses and lentils.
-

VULNERABLE GROUPS AND SPECIAL DIETARY REQUIREMENTS

As people we have individual differences between one person and the next. Human beings carry with them personal features and their nutritional needs will differ according to a whole range of circumstances, including age, height, size, lifestyle, occupation, as well as hereditary factors.

However, at key stages and under certain circumstances, our nutritional needs will change. The following points highlight the vulnerable groups that have particular nutritional requirements.

Babies and young children

In the first six months of life, babies survive on milk to provide all of their nutritional requirements. Although this is an extremely important time for development, at this stage in life a baby will not be using vast amounts of energy. In fact, a great deal of time is spent sleeping and eating!

As children continue to develop and grow their nutritional requirements grow as well. By the time that they start school, their nutritional needs increase rapidly, particularly the need for calcium, protein and iron. Children are also particularly active during this time, demanding lots of nutrients to keep the body functioning. They are not fully grown so will not eat the quantities of an adult. They should, however, eat smaller amounts regularly throughout the day to keep up their energy levels.

Teenagers

As children move into their teenage years, the body is going through a great deal of physical change and growth. This can also be an emotional time for young people so it is important that a well balanced diet is followed, supplying the body with the nutrients required.

Pregnancy

During pregnancy, a woman is supporting the growth and development of her baby. It is vitally important that her nutritional intake is enough for the higher levels of energy and nutrients required.

Once the baby is born, the mother may breast feed the baby during the first months of its life and this will be the main source of food for the baby. Therefore, the mother will again need higher levels of nutrients to support the baby's growth as well as her own wellbeing.

The elderly

During the later years of life, the body generally starts to slow down and requires less energy. Appetite also tends to get smaller as we get older. Despite these facts, the nutritional requirements for the elderly remain high to support good health and wellbeing. As with children, it is recommended that smaller meals are eaten regularly throughout the day to ensure adequate levels of nutrients, particularly calcium and iron.

People suffering from ill health

People suffering from ill health can often lose their appetite and their immune system and energy levels are likely to be lower than usual. In such circumstances, it is important that the body gets the nutrients it requires to function and make its recovery to health.

People with special dietary requirements

In modern times we live in a society of many cultures and lots of people are more aware and concerned about the nutritional content of food and its origin. As far as special dietary requirements are concerned, people may follow a particular diet for a specific reason. This may be due to religion, personal preference, moral or health reasons or because of allergies or intolerances.

There are several reasons why some groups do not eat meat:

Vegetarian

Vegetarians do not eat any meat, meat products or fish. Some vegetarians do eat dairy products. These are called lacto-vegetarians. However, some do not eat dairy products and they are known as vegans.

Religion

In many religions, eating meat is forbidden. Many of the religions in India and the eastern world are vegetarian. As more people travel and relocate around the world, religions such as Hinduism and Buddhism are becoming more widespread throughout the western world.

Personal preference

Some people simply dislike the texture or flavour of meat and fish and choose not to include these foods in their diet.

Health

There has been a great amount of research into the consumption of meat and meat products, the levels of saturated fat they contain and the impact this has with regard to obesity, high levels of cholesterol and heart related illnesses. Many people in poorer countries do not have access to meat in the quantities that we are used to in the western world. It was through comparison of diet that it was first realized that a largely vegetarian diet, high in dietary fibre and nutrients, was much healthier than a diet high in saturated fats. It is for this reason that some people have opted for a vegetarian diet.

Allergies and intolerances

Some people may be allergic to eating meat or fish or it may cause them discomfort or unpleasant side effects. In this situation, the removal of meat and fish from the diet is more of a necessity than a preference.

The effects of a lack or excess of nutrients

A lack or excess of food and the nutrients within food is called 'malnutrition' in the forms of 'under-nutrition' or 'over-nutrition'.

The major concern is that both under-nutrition and over-nutrition have clear links to health problems. The tables below provide a summary of some of the health problems related to a lack or excess of certain nutrients.

Under-nutrition

NUTRIENT UNDERSUPPLIED	CONSEQUENCES WITH REGARD TO HEALTH
Protein	Water retention, muscle wastage, ulcers, hair loss
Carbohydrate	Weight loss, lack of energy, low immune system
Fat	Weight loss, lack of energy, low immune system
Dietary fibre	Constipation, bowel disorders, bowel cancer
Vitamin A	Potential blindness, hydration problems
Vitamin B1	Nervous disorders
Vitamin B2	Growth, irritable skin, cracks in skin
Vitamin B6	Sickness and depression, eczema, irritability
Vitamin B12	Mental problems, anaemia, blood disorders
Vitamin C	Scurvy, depression, fatigue, blood loss, bruising
Vitamin D	Rickets
Niacin	Cuts in the skin, mental problems, depression, diarrhoea
Iron	Fatigue, lack of strength, lack of energy
Calcium	Rickets
Trace elements	Associated with poor health and development

Over-nutrition

NUTRIENT OVERSUPPLIED	CONSEQUENCES WITH REGARD TO HEALTH
Carbohydrate	Tooth decay caused by eating sugar Overweight Diabetes caused by eating too many sugary foods over a long time
Fat	Overweight Heart disease, heart attack, high blood pressure, angina, all are linked to a diet high in fat, particularly saturated (animal) fats
Salt (Sodium chloride)	High blood pressure and heart problems

HEALTH & SAFETY

Allergies can cause 'anaphylactic shock' which is the way the body reacts to foods it rejects. A major concern with anaphylactic shock is that the reaction gets stronger each time the body is exposed to the food concerned. In extreme cases the throat closes leaving the person unable to breath.

FOODS THAT MAY CAUSE ALLERGIES OR INTOLERANCES

It is possible for any food to cause an allergy or intolerance in an individual as we are all unique in our bodily make up. However, there are certain foods that more commonly cause allergies. The most frequent food causing an allergic reaction is the peanut and peanut products. It is advised that young children are not introduced to peanuts, partly due to the risk of allergy but also to avoid choking.

People who are aware of allergies are provided with medicine to counteract the effects of the shock. Depending on the severity of the shock, the time in which a person needs to receive the antidote will shorten. It is therefore essential that foods associated with allergies and intolerances are clearly labelled so that people know what ingredients they contain. Other foods that commonly cause food allergies include alcohol, seafood, fish, fruit, flour, cow's milk and cereals.

An intolerance may not be so immediately dangerous as an allergy but will cause discomfort and potential illness through repeated exposure. For example, diabetes has links to the long-term eating of foods that are high in sugar. Diabetes refers to the body's inability to produce enough insulin to control the levels of sugar in the blood. Without intervention, this could be fatal.

CHEF'S TIP

Another common intolerance can be to gluten, a substance formed from proteins found in wheat and rye. If gluten is eaten over a period of time, people suffering from an intolerance to gluten are likely to suffer damage to the small intestine eventually causing a condition called **coeliac** disease.

CURRENT GOVERNMENT GUIDELINES

■ *The British Nutrition Foundation*

■ *Department of Health*

■ *Ministry of Agriculture, Food and Fisheries*

■ *The Food Standards Agency*

■ *The National Advisory Committee on Nutritional Education – NACNE*

  A committee of experts examining the links between health and diet

■ *The Committee on Medical Aspects of Food Policy – COMA*

  A committee examining the links between heart disease and the diet among other nutritionally related issues.

Assessment of knowledge and understanding

1   How many amino acids are there and how many of these acids are classified as 'essential'?

_____

2   List the main functions of the following nutrients.

CARBOHYDRATE	FAT	PROTEIN	VITAMINS	MINERALS
1.	1.	1.	1.	1.
2.	2.	2.	2.	2.

3   Provide two reasons why dietary fibre is so important in the diet.

i) _____   ii) _____

4   What is meant by the term 'balanced diet'?

_____

5   Why is water so important in the diet?

_____

_____

6   Provide three reasons why it is advisable to reduce the amount of sugar we eat in the diet?

i) _____   ii) _____

iii) _____

7   List two reasons why someone might choose to follow a vegetarian diet.

i) _____   ii) _____

8   Which of the following foods would a person suffering from coeliac disease have to avoid?

■ Milk   ■ Fruit

■ Bread   ■ Alcohol

■ Seafood

9   Why are young children and pregnant women referred to as vulnerable groups with regard to nutritional intake?

_____

_____

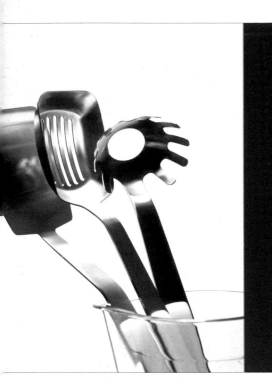

5

Introduction to kitchen equipment

Unit 105 Introduction to kitchen equipment

LEARNING OBJECTIVES

On completion of this chapter, learners will be able to:

- State the factors in selecting equipment and utensils for use
- State how to use equipment and utensils correctly and safely
- Identify associated hazards with using, cleaning and storing equipment and utensils
- State how to carry out routine care and storage of equipment and utensils
- Identify the different types of knives and cutting equipment and their uses
- State the importance of correct and safe use of knives and cutting equipment
- Describe how to clean, maintain and store knives and cutting equipment
- Identify relevant age restrictions specific to the use of cutting equipment.

FACTORS REQUIRED IN SELECTING EQUIPMENT AND UTENSILS

Equipment is designed with a purpose in mind. For example, scales were designed to weigh, refrigerators to keep food cold and ovens to cook food. Occasionally, we can be tempted to use equipment for the wrong purpose, perhaps because it seems convenient at the time or possibly due to a lack of experience and knowledge. It is when equipment is used incorrectly that the final result can be affected or accidents can happen.

Equipment comes in all shapes and sizes and is designed to be used for certain tasks. For example, many frying pans have a non-stick surface so that foods, including delicate foods such as eggs, can be cooked at fairly high temperatures without them sticking to the surface. This makes it much easier to handle and move foods without the risk of breaking or damaging them through having to use harsh movements. However, a frying pan would not be suitable for making soup due to its wide and shallow surface area; a much deeper pan would hold the amount of liquid required. There is also no requirement for the ingredients used in making the soup to be in direct contact with the surface area of the pan, as there is when shallow frying foods.

HOW TO USE EQUIPMENT AND UTENSILS CORRECTLY AND SAFELY

The following tables cover these two learning objectives:

■ Identifying associated hazards with using, cleaning and storing equipment and utensils

■ How to carry out routine care and storage of equipment and utensils.

CHEF'S TIP

There is a term 'A bad workman blames his tools', which to some extent is true. A chef with poor skills and/or approach will not perform a task very well regardless as to the quality of his or her tools and equipment.

HEALTH & SAFETY

It is much easier to perform tasks if the equipment being used is of high quality and suitable for the task in hand. For this reason, it is essential that aspiring chefs learn to handle, maintain and care for their knives and equipment at an early stage of their learning and development.

VIDEO CLIP
Demonstration of a selection of large and small equipment

TYPE OF EQUIPMENT	SAFE USES	ASSOCIATED HAZARDS	ROUTINE CARE AND STORAGE
Conventional oven 	The temperature in the oven chamber is thermostatically controlled and the burners at the top of the oven can be set to provide a low or high heat. It has many uses including baking, roasting, stewing, braising and frying.	If the oven is powered by gas, it is very important that the gas is ignited once turned on. Ovens should be fitted with a flame failure device to prevent gas spillage and the risk of explosion.	
Fan assisted oven (convection) 	A fan built in to the cooking chamber circulates hot air evenly through the oven, resulting in faster cooking times. Good for baking and roasting due to the accuracy and even nature of the temperature.	When cleaning, it is important that it is allowed to cool down sufficiently to avoid burns. Appropriate personal protective equipment, should be worn when using cleaning chemicals.	

TYPE OF EQUIPMENT	SAFE USES	ASSOCIATED HAZARDS	ROUTINE CARE AND STORAGE
Combination oven 	Can be used for many purposes. It can be used as a convection oven, a steamer or a combination of both. It has computerised control which can control temperature and humidity. It also has the capacity to hold food at a specified temperature without additional cooking or drying. It can be used to prove and bake, braise and stew, roast, grill, steam, fry, hold hot foods and a combination of the above. Modern combination ovens can record their history and use for hazard analysis.	Foods often have to be placed into or removed from the oven at height. Great care and attention is required when performing such tasks. If the oven is being used as a steamer or in combination mode, it is also important that heat and steam are released slowly before attempting to place or remove items from the oven.	Modern combination ovens have a self cleaning programme to ensure the oven stays in very hygienic, safe and efficient condition.
Microwave 	Cooks food by disturbing the water molecules within foods. The microwaves energize these molecules and this reaction produces heat, which in turn cooks the food. A microwave, if not used correctly, can have the potential to dry foods out and produce undesired textures. A microwave is very good for reheating foods that have already been cooked.	Microwaves will deflect from metal surfaces and cause small explosions within the oven chamber. Metal should never be used in a microwave.	It is essential that any spillages or spluttering from cooking are cleaned up immediately to prevent cross-contamination or bacterial growth.
Induction hob 	An energy saving and safety conscious invention. The hob will only heat up when a pan with a magnetic base is in direct contact. When contact is broken that heat retracts very quickly.	Reduces many of the hazards associated with conventional cooking methods. For example there is virtually no chance of burning from direct contact with an induction hob. Induction equipment tends to be very easy to clean.	Induction equipment tends to be quite expensive and the utensils have to be suitable (magnetic).
Solid top	The solid top is made of one large burner and a complete solid metal hob. A solid top provides an efficient use of surface area and pans can be moved around the cooking area to points where the heat is most suitable for the speed of cooking required (i.e. very hot in the centre and cooler at the edges).	Some solid tops, particularly those powered by gas, have removable rings in the centre of the plate. The rings, due to their thick metal structure are very heavy. Move and replace the rings carefully to avoid them falling. The surface also stays hot for a long time after it has been turned off.	Gas powered ovens should have flame failure devices to ensure gas does not leak. Thermostats need to be checked.

HOW TO USE EQUIPMENT AND UTENSILS CORRECTLY AND SAFELY

TYPE OF EQUIPMENT	SAFE USES	ASSOCIATED HAZARDS	ROUTINE CARE AND STORAGE
Grill 	The heat source is underneath the food and food items are placed on the grill bars above the heat. This type of grill produces the enhancing grill lines on foods reflecting where the food has been in contact with the bars. Due to the desired outcome when grilling food in this way, gas is usually the preferred heat source as this produces a flame. Barbeques or charcoaled fuelled grills will produce very similar results.	Care has to be taken when placing and removing food items on the grill. The use of sturdy tongs is recommended to protect the hands from burning. It is also necessary to be aware of flames rising if fats and/or oils drip onto the naked flame.	For catching grease and cooking liquids also needs to be cleaned at the end of the cooking process.
Salamander 	A salamander is also a type of grill. However, the heat from a salamander comes from elements above the food rather than below the food as in the case of the flame grill. It is important that grills are operating at the correct temperature when the cooking process begins.	Salamanders are often placed at chest height or above. Therefore, it is essential that care is taken when placing and removing items to and from the grill. A thick cloth that is in good condition and is clean and dry, is also required when handling grilling trays during cooking using a salamander.	Salamanders also have a tray to catch grease. This needs to be emptied appropriately and cleaned using hot water and cleaning chemical (detergent).
Pressure steamer	Steam is the vapour that is produced by boiling water. A steamer, in whichever of its formats, uses this vapour to cook food items. Pressure steamers have the capacity to increase the pressure within the steaming chamber and therefore increase the temperature.	The main hazard associated with the use of a steamer is scalding. When a steamer door is first opened, the steam will escape from the chamber and out into the open air. It is advised that the door is opened slightly at first while standing behind the door itself. Once the main body of steam has dispersed, the food items can be safely removed.	The cleanliness of a steamer is vital. The water held within the steamer itself needs to be changed on a regular basis. All shelving needs to be cleaned after use to ensure a hygienic chamber.

TYPE OF EQUIPMENT	SAFE USES	ASSOCIATED HAZARDS	ROUTINE CARE AND STORAGE
Deep fryer 	Potentially one of the most dangerous pieces of equipment in the kitchen. A deep fryer consists of a vessel which contains a depth of oil that will surround foods once they are placed into the vessel. The oil in a deep fryer reaches very hot temperatures (up to 200°C). Deep fryers contain a thermostatic control to avoid over heating to a point where the oil would catch fire. A deep fryer also has a 'cool zone' below the heat source. This is designed to catch any particles of food that fall away from the main item.	Placing items into a deep fryer can be quite a hazardous activity. Food items should never be thrown into a deep fryer or dropped from a height. This would cause splashing and the potential for a nasty accident. When changing the oil in a deep fryer, it is essential that it is allowed to cool first, and that suitable containers are in place to capture the oil.	The oil in a deep fryer needs to be kept as clean as possible to extend its life. Food debris should be removed to prevent spoilage and oil should not be overheated unnecessarily.
Refrigerator 	A refrigerator's main function is to keep food items cold and keep them in good condition for use. A refrigerator should function between 1°C and 5°C, a temperature that will not start to freeze foods but will prevent bacterial growth and spoilage for a period of time.	Refrigerators are used to store a whole range of products. Therefore, it is essential that good storage practices are followed to ensure that cross-contamination from one product to another is avoided.	Temperatures should be closely monitored on a daily basis and all food items stored in a refrigerator should be clearly labelled and dated.
Hotplate 	Designed to keep plates and other service equipment hot for service periods. This equipment should be heated to a point that is manageable for staff to handle but also keep food in its primary service condition.	Although hotplates and heated lighting are designed primarily to maintain temperature rather than increase it, the elements and bulbs used are extremely hot and would cause a nasty injury if they ever came into direct contact with the skin.	They should be emptied and cleaned on a regular basis to provide a clean and hygienic environment.

TYPE OF EQUIPMENT	SAFE USES	ASSOCIATED HAZARDS	ROUTINE CARE AND STORAGE
Bain-marie 	Bain-marie translates to mean 'water-bath'. The function of a bain-marie is to keep food items, particularly foods high in liquid content, such as soups, sauces and stews, hot during the service period.	It is important to monitor the amount of liquid that is present in a bain-marie. During the time that a bain-marie is functioning, water is being heated and will gradually vaporize (evaporate). This could cause the heating element to burn out, causing potential damage to the heating element and also a risk of fire.	A bain-marie should be monitored while in use to ensure that it has enough water. Once the service period is finished, the bain-marie should be switched off and emptied carefully. Once this is complete, the bain-marie should be cleaned thoroughly.
Proving cabinet 	A proving cabinet is designed to provide a warm and moist environment in which dough products can prove (rise). The temperature in a proving cabinet is between 30°C and 40°C. The ideal temperature for yeast to ferment is around 37°C. This environment will allow the yeast to ferment and develop the gluten in the flour to produce dough capable of rising to provide an airy and springy product.	Modern proving cabinets are often plumbed into a plumbing source removing the need to ensure that water is always present in the cabinet. Older proving cabinets may require a manual feed which will have to be monitored while the cabinet is in use.	Proving cabinets are not ovens and should not be exposed to the conditions that an oven receives. It is still important that the cabinet and its shelves are kept clean and hygienic for use.

SMALL EQUIPMENT AND ITS USE IN THE KITCHEN

PICTURE	TYPE OF EQUIPMENT	USE
	Scales	Used to accurately weigh ingredients for specific recipes.
	Measuring jug	Used to accurately measure volumes of liquids (water, wine, stock, milk, etc.).
	Liquidisers	Used to blend foods into liquids – soups and sauces, for example.
	Blenders	Blenders are similar to liquidizers but are usually larger and have additional functions – shredding vegetables, for example.
	Mixers	Mixers come in a variety of sizes. Mixing machines are used for making dough (e.g. bread) and other mixes (e.g. cakes).
	Pestle and mortar	A pestle and mortar is used to pound herbs and spices into pastes or purees. Oil or vinegar is sometimes used to help this process.
	Rolling pin	The main use of a rolling pin is to roll out pastry into the required shape. A rolling pin is sometimes used to roll out dough, when making Chelsea buns, for example.
	Spider	A spider is used to remove items (such as vegetables) from saucepans or deep-fried items from a deep-fryer. In both examples, the spider catches the food with the water or oil draining back into the cooking vessel.
	Slice	A slice is used to lift items safely from a tray. The slice has been designed to provide a very thin, usually square or rectangular platform, which slides between food items and the tray.

PICTURE	TYPE OF EQUIPMENT	USE
	Ladle	A ladle is used to serve or add liquids, such as stocks, soups and sauces.
	Whisk	Whisks are designed to add air and mix liquids and batters together. For example, a whisk is used when aerating egg whites to make meringues.
	Cutlet bat	A cutlet bat is normally square or rectangular and made of sturdy metal. It is used to batten out meats to make them flatter and more even. An example of a product where a cutlet bat would be used is a pork escalope.
VIDEO CLIP Using a cutlet bat to prepare pork escalopes		
	Saucepans	Saucepans come in many different sizes and can be made of many different metals (stainless steel, copper, alloys – a mixture of metals). Saucepans play a massive part in the kitchen and have many uses.
	Sauté pan	Sauté is a method of frying and the term literally means to jump or toss. The process of 'sauté' is often applied to cuts of meat or poultry, 'Sauté of Chicken', for example.
	Griddle pan	A griddle pan is normally finished with a non-stick coating and has raised sections inside the pan itself to form lines of contact. When foods are placed into the pan, it is the raised sections that come into contact with the food, producing the griddled lines associated with this method of cookery.
	Wok	The wok is associated with Oriental cookery. It is round and deep and usually made of a steel based alloy. The metal surface of a wok is thin and therefore conducts heat very quickly.
	Bowls	Bowls come in many shapes and sizes and are used for many different purposes. One of the main uses of bowls is to mix foods, vinaigrette or mayonnaise for example. As the majority of bowls used in the professional kitchen are made of stainless steel, they can be used for hot and cold items both safely and hygienically.
	Cooling racks	Cooling racks are usually square or rectangular and are designed to provide a flat cooling point for baked items. The 'mesh' type design and raised feet on the cooling rack provides items placed upon it a complete circulation of air.
	Moulds	Moulds come in countless shapes and sizes. Foods that are placed into moulds are intended to take on the shape of the mould. It is essential that moulds are cleaned properly to prevent cross-contamination or any bacterial growth. Moulds are used when making mousses (sweet and savoury), egg custard dishes, ice creams as well as moulding foods for presentation (rice for example).

PICTURE	TYPE OF EQUIPMENT	USE
	Sieves	Sieves are a very fine form of strainer. A sieve can be designed for dry goods, for sieving flour or cocoa powder, for example. Other sieves are designed for wet goods such as soups or sauces. The purpose of a sieve is to (1) aerate dry goods such as flour removing any unwanted particles or clusters during the process; or (2) to pass liquids (soups and sauces) where any items used as flavourings (e.g. mirepoix, bay leaves) are not intended to be served.
	Strainers/Colanders	A strainer has similar properties to a sieve but tends to be larger in size and has larger holes. A strainer would be used to capture items such as boiled vegetables once they are cooked.

DIFFERENT TYPES OF KNIVES AND CUTTING EQUIPMENT AND THEIR USES

Knives have many different purposes and have been designed accordingly. Knives come in different shapes and sizes and a chef should know which knife to use for the job in hand. Beyond this, a chef needs to know how to use the knife selected safely and efficiently and also how to maintain the knife.

The following table identifies the various types of knives and other cutting equipment and their uses.

PICTURE	TYPE OF EQUIPMENT	USE
	Paring knife	A paring knife is a small, multi-purpose knife used for small jobs such as 'topping and tailing' vegetables, removing skins from onions and preparing small fruits.
	Turning knife	A turning knife has a very small curved blade. This is designed to 'turn' vegetables into a barrel shape for presentation purposes. Mushrooms can also be 'turned' although the process is different. In this example, small reverse cuts/slices are made into the top of the mushroom producing a unique style of presentation.
	Filleting knife	A filleting knife has a medium length blade that is narrow and flexible. It is designed to be flexible so that it can bend while running along the bone structure of fish, particularly flat fish.
	Boning knife	A boning knife has a short to medium blade that is pointed at the end. A boning knife should be strong and rigid, not flexible like a filleting knife. The point is designed to get close to bones and cut away the meat.
	General chefs' knife	A general chefs' knife is a multi-purpose knife. It can be used on many different commodities such as vegetables, fruits as well as items such as meat and poultry. The knife can be used across a variety of cutting techniques including chopping, dicing, shredding and slicing.

PICTURE	TYPE OF EQUIPMENT	USE
	Palette knife	A palette knife is used for two main purposes. The first is to turn items over during the cooking process, for example, sautéed potatoes. Also used for lifting food from the pan to the plate.
		The second use is spreading. This could be butter onto bread, cream onto a cake or pâté on top of a canapé. It is usually quite long, although they vary quite a lot in length, and is flexible in order to get underneath food items. The blade of a palette knife is also rounded and therefore not designed for cutting purposes.
	Carving knife and fork	A carving knife usually has a long, thin blade. The edge of the knife should be very sharp to ensure neat, accurate and efficient cutting.
		A carving fork is usually a two-pronged fork that is substantially larger and stronger than a standard fork. It is designed to support meats, etc., during the carving process.
	Serrated edged knifes	Serrated edged knives are designed to slice certain foods and therefore have a long thin blade to assist in the sawing type motion required when slicing. A serrated knife cannot be sharpened.
	Saws	Saws are used mostly in butchery. A saw is used to saw through bones when breaking carcasses and large cuts of meat down into smaller joints.
	Food processors	Many food processors come with an assortment of attachments that are used to grate, slice and chop food items extremely quickly.
	Mincer	A mincer is used to pass meat, fish and other items such as offal through small holes, and in so doing produce a mince of the food being processed.
	Mandolins	A mandolin is used for manual slicing. It is made up of a flat platform with an adjustable blade. This is used by running an item of food, such as a potato, down the platform. The blade half way down the platform can be adjusted to different widths and will slice a piece of the food item as it passes the blade. This can be set to slice items such as potatoes at a regular thickness for a hot pot. A mandolin can also be set to slice items that are wafer thin. Mandolins have different sorts of blades, some will produce a criss-cross effect. As a mandolin is a manual device, extreme care and attention is required to ensure that hands are not in danger when slicing.
	Graters	Graters are used to roughly shred foods. Graters often come with four different edges (one on each side) to produce course or finer gratings.

VIDEO CLIP
Using a mandolin to prepare vegetable cuts

PICTURE	TYPE OF EQUIPMENT	USE
	Peelers	Peelers are used to remove the outer skins from hard fruits and vegetables.
	Corers	Corers are used to remove the core (the seeded and fibrous area) from fruits such as apples and pears. Corers have a long circular blade that penetrates through the core of the fruit. As this is pushed down, it encases the core and locks it inside the cutter. As the corer is retracted, the core from the fruit is removed.
	Can openers	In professional kitchens can openers are usually table mounted and more robust. The blade is connected to a long handle which, when pushed down, breaks the seal in the can. The handle is then pulled down and turned to rotate the blade around the can until it can be removed. It is very important to take care, the cut in the metal makes a very sharp and often jagged edge, which could cause a nasty cut.
	Scissors	Scissors are an essential piece of equipment for a chef. Scissors used to cut the fins from fish need to be strong and robust to break through the bones without buckling. Scissors are also used for other tasks such as cutting string used for tying.
	Cleaver	A cleaver is a very heavy knife that is designed to cut through large bones.
	Gravity slice	A gravity slice is an electrical appliance that provides uniform cutting, portion control and a virtually waste-free method of cutting. For example, a gravity-feed slice will cut thin slices of ham in exactly the same thickness according to its setting.
	Steels and sharpeners	A sharpening steel is made of a long, thin, circular and slightly ridged metal. As the blade of a knife runs up and down the steel at a slight angle, the edge of the knife is sharpened.
		Sharpening stones are used when the edge of the knife is lost. A steel would not be sufficient to retrieve the edge of the knife as it is designed to increase the sharpness.

VIDEO CLIP
Using a cleaver

THE CORRECT AND SAFE USE OF KNIVES AND CUTTING EQUIPMENT

Knives are particularly dangerous pieces of equipment if used incorrectly. However, they are an essential item for a chef as well as being equipment that a chef must master and control in order to become efficient and skilled within this profession.

Well organized and efficient chefs will work methodically and clean as they go. They will also clean, sharpen and handle knives throughout their working day. When placing knives on the table for use, it is good practice that the knife is placed in a parallel position to the chopping board, with the blade pointing inwards towards the board.

Hold the knife to the side of the body and with the blade of the knife pointing to the floor.

Safe practice for carrying a knife

Here you are!

Thanks!

Offer the knife to the receiver, who should have the handle pointing towards him or her, and the blade of the knife pointing towards the floor.

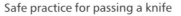

Safe practice for passing a knife

The condition of a knife has a massive impact on the finished product and the effort and energy that is required by the chef to prepare foods.

When a sharp knife is used to make a cut, regardless of the food item, the sharpness of the blade will penetrate through the food neatly and following the direction of the knife. The chef should be controlling the direction of the knife rather that having to use force to push the knife through the food to make the cut.

A blunt knife, however, produces a much more difficult scenario. In this case, because the blade is not sharp, it will not easily penetrate the food being cut and the chef has to increase the power being placed into the cut in order for the knife to get through the food. This will not only produce a poor quality cut but the chef is having to use much more energy and force to create a finished item that is inferior to the one cut using a sharp knife.

CLEANING, MAINTAINING AND STORING KNIVES

Knives are one of the most important kitchen items because of their direct contact with foods. Therefore, a knife has to be clean and in a hygienic condition before it is used. Modern knives are usually made of stainless steel or a steel based alloy. Handles are usually manufactured from an easy-clean, waterproof handle. Generally, the more expensive handles are 'riveted'. This is where the steel section of the knife continues from the blade, through the handle of the knife and two to three riveted sections come out from the handle at 90°. This forms part of the handle itself and makes it very secure.

The less expensive knives on the market tend to have moulded handles. In this case, the metal section of the knife continues from the blade to the handle but the handle is moulded around the handle section with a plastic or rubber based material. The handles on such knives are not as strong as those riveted to the handles and are generally not as well made, hence the difference in price.

There are many 'Oriental' style knives on the market. The metal base of the knife is actually formed into a handle itself, making the knife one continuous piece rather than a blade with a handle attached.

Care has to be taken when cleaning knives. Knives should be washed in hot, soapy water and then rinsed in clean hot water. **When cleaning the blade of a knife, it is essential that the blade of the knife is pointing away from your hand.** A sharp blade will easily cut through a cloth and into your hand or fingers if this rule is not followed. The same rule applies if you dry a knife – the blade must always point away from the hand drying the knife.

Maintaining knives in good condition is important for a number of reasons. There is the initial cost of buying knives. To maintain knives on a regular basis a steel is used. Occasionally, a carborundum stone can be used if the knife is starting to lose its edge. A stone usually has a coarser edge than a steel and will take more of the surface of the blade away. Care has to be taken to ensure that a rough edge is not created by uneven application across the stone. For safety reasons, when using a stone, the blade of the knife should always be pointing away from the body.

Sharpening a knife using a steel

There are two main methods used to sharpen a knife using a steel. However, the angle at which the blade runs along the steel remains the same.

VIDEO CLIP
Sharpening knives with steels

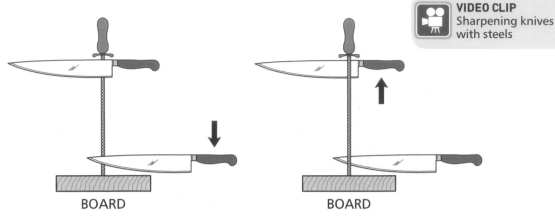

In the first method, the steel is placed downwards vertically onto a board. Holding the steel in one hand and the knife in the other, place the base of the knife at the base of the steel (just below the handle). Run the knife down the steel until the tip of the knife reaches the tip of the steel. This should be performed at an angle between 30° to 40°.

Once the tip of the knife has reached the tip of the steel, the knife should be moved so that the opposite side of the knife (tip) of is placed at the same angle on the other side of the steel (tip). This time the knife should run up the steel until the base of the knife reaches the base of the steel. Once this stage is reached, run the knife back down the steel from base to tip and then switch sides again. Repeat this about ten times on each side.

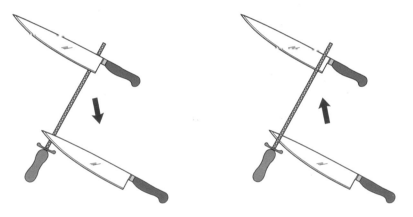

In the second method, the steel is held pointing upwards at approximately 45°. With the other hand, the knife is run down the steel. In this method, the base of the knife starts at the tip of the steel working downwards until the tip of the knife reaches the base of the steel. As in the previous example, this is done at an angle between 30° and 40°.

The knife is then moved to the alternate side of the steel and runs back up the steel from the tip of the knife and base of the steel to the base of the knife at the tip of the steel. Once this is reached the knife runs back down the steel before switching back to the original side again. Repeat this about 10 times on each side.

AGE RESTRICTIONS SPECIFIC TO THE USE OF CUTTING EQUIPMENT

Under health and safety legislation (law), young people have to be protected from potentially dangerous equipment. In a kitchen, this includes items such as electric gravity slicing machines. Such pieces of equipment should therefore not be used or cleaned by anyone less than 18 years old. For those more that 18 years old, full training should be provided to ensure that the equipment can be used and cleaned safely.

Assessment of knowledge and understanding

1 Provide three reasons why it is important to select the right piece of equipment for the job in hand.

i) _____

ii) _____

iii) _____

2 How does an induction hob save energy?

_____

3 Which methods of cookery can be performed using a combination oven?

_____

4 What is the difference between a salamander and a flame grill?

_____

5 What is the purpose of the 'cool zone' in a deep-fryer?

_____

6 Why would you want a 'spider' in the kitchen?

_____

7 Name three food items that could be 'turned'.

i) _____

ii) _____

iii) _____

8 What features and qualities would you look for in a filleting knife?

_____

9 Why would a 'mandolin' be useful in the kitchen?

_____

10 Why is it safer to use a sharp knife rather than a blunt knife?

_____

11 Name two ways in which a knife can be sharpened.

i) _____

ii) _____

12 Name one piece of equipment that you should not use or clean until you are over 18 years old and have received training.

_____

6

Introduction to personal workplace skills

Unit 106 Introduction to personal workplace skills

LEARNING OBJECTIVES

On completion of this chapter, learners will be able to:

■ Identify the correct uniform for work and the reasons behind it

■ Describe the importance of personal hygiene and appearance, highlighting examples of poor practices

■ State the importance of punctuality, attendance and good time management

■ Identify the communication skills used in teams and the factors that make a good team in the workplace

■ Describe the importance of knowing your own limitations and asking for help and assistance

■ State the importance of effective communication with customers

■ Highlight some of the potential barriers to effective communication.

THE CORRECT UNIFORM FOR WORK AND THE REASONS BEHIND IT

VIDEO CLIP
Showing correct uniform and personal appearance

Chef's Jacket

The chef's jacket is designed to protect both the food from the chef and the chef from the physical dangers of the kitchen. Originally made of cotton and linen, the materials have evolved into modern, lightweight textiles. It is double-breasted to protect the chest and stomach from the heat from ovens and stoves, and from burns and scalds. It acts as a barrier and gives a few vital extra seconds to protect its wearer should a spillage of hot liquid occur onto the upper body. The sleeves should be worn to the wrist for protection to the arms from burns.

Trousers

These are generally made of lightweight cotton or mixed material and Teflon coated fabric. They should not be worn tight-fitting to the leg as this creates a hazard if a spillage occurs and improve comfort during work in a kitchen.

Apron

Any difference in colour can be relevant to the operation but it must be worn at full length to protect the legs (always to below the knee). It is one of the most important items of protection. If a spillage of hot liquid occurs it is the first line of protection. It should be tied at the front to allow for quick release.

Necktie

The original use of the necktie was to mop the brow due to the lack of ventilation and the heat generated by solid fuel stoves. A system of coloured neckties can identify departments or seniority within the workplace, allowing for an assumption of ability based on a quick visual inspection.

Chef's hat

The tall hat, known as a Toque, has always epitomized the stature of the chef. Traditionally an apprentice cook would wear a skull cap and graduate to a Toque when they reached a position of Chef de Partie. Nowadays even some Head Chefs prefer the skull cap. The main function of the hat is to stop loose hair falling into the food and help absorb perspiration on the forehead. However, when the hair is worn beyond collar length it cannot be contained in a hat. In this case a hair net should be worn.

Safety shoes

Shoes should be of a sturdy design with non-slip soles and steel toe-caps. If clogs are preferred then they too should be protective and have a back strap to prevent slipping. The colour is usually dictated by the workplace. An important element is that footwear should be comfortable and give support to the chef who will be on their feet for many hours.

The wearing of trainers and non-specialist shoes should be prohibited.

Kitchen cloths

Kitchen cloths must be clean, dry and undamaged. They provide important protection between the hands and the sometimes very hot equipment that chefs handle on a regular basis.

CHEF'S TIP

Uniforms must be changed on a shift-by-shift basis. The clothing should be of an easily washable material and generally all chef attire is white in colour to show when clothing has been soiled, thus when it needs to be changed.

THE IMPORTANCE OF PERSONAL HYGIENE AND APPEARANCE

The hospitality and catering industry is expected, and rightly so, to prepare and serve food in very clean and hygienic conditions. The people working in the industry therefore have a personal and professional responsibility to present themselves properly and practice hygienic methods of work.

It is vital that a chef maintains a high standard of personal hygiene. Bodily cleanliness is achieved through daily showering or bathing. This removes stale sweat, dirt and bacteria which are the causes of body odour. An anti-perspirant or deodorant may be applied to the underarm area to reduce perspiration and thus the smell of sweat. Clean underwear should be worn each day. In terms of personal hygiene, the following points should be considered.

CHEF'S TIP

Cuts and abrasions on hands should be covered with a clean, waterproof, blue coloured dressing to minimize the risk of secondary infection. Disposable gloves may be worn for additional protection.

Care of hair

Hair should be kept clean by washing on a regular basis. As a chef, hair should be covered by a hat. Longer hair should be tied back and wrapped in a hair-net to avoid loose hair from falling, potentially, into food being prepared. From a customer perspective, hair should be neat and tidy in a style that is appropriate for a customer focused industry.

Care of mouth and teeth

There are many germs within and around the area of the mouth. Therefore it is essential that the mouth does not come into contact with utensils or hands that will come into contact with food.

It is important that we keep our breath fresh and it is also advisable that we should visit the dentist regularly to maintain healthy teeth and gums.

VIDEO CLIP
Washing hands
correctly

CHEF'S TIP

Wash your hands with a liquid gel from a sealed dispenser. Soap should be discouraged because bar soap can accumulate germs when passed from hand-to-hand. Disposable paper towels or warm-air hand dryers should be used to dry the hands.

To ensure good health and safety practice some employers insist on the use of plastic disposable gloves when preparing food items, although it must be remembered that when wearing gloves, they should be changed with every task to prevent cross-contamination.

CHEF'S TIP

Plastic disposable spoons should be used to taste food while preparing and cooking and then disposed of immediately, using a new spoon for each tasting.

Hands and nails

As chefs, the hands are used constantly in the preparation and cooking of food. It is therefore essential that they are kept clean. Hands and everything that has been touched are covered with bacteria, although most of these are harmless, some can cause ill health. Hands must be washed regularly and frequently, particularly after visiting a toilet, before commencing the preparation of food and during the handling of food. They should be washed using hot water with the aid of a nail brush and an antibacterial gel or liquid.

Our nails have the potential to harbour dirt, grime and therefore bacteria. With this in mind, nails need to be kept short and clean. From a customer perspective, if a chef or the person serving food had dirty nails, there would be a question about the safety of the food in terms of the bacteria present and this may be enough to put the customer off eating the food at all. It would certainly not promote the hygienic practices of the establishment concerned.

Nail varnish should not be worn!

SOME EXAMPLES OF POOR PRACTICE

Smoking

Smoking is not only proven to be bad for your health; it is also an unhygienic activity for a food handler. During the act of smoking, the hand regularly touches the lips as the cigarette is placed and removed from the mouth. During this action, the fingers are picking up bacteria from the mouth, which could potentially be passed onto the food.

Chewing

The act of chewing while at work does not create a professional image. Chefs, by the nature of their work, also need to taste the dishes they are making on a regular basis to ensure that the quality of food being produced is of the required flavour, texture and seasoning, etc.

Eating and drinking in the food preparation area

Although a chef should 'hygienically' taste foods being prepared to check quality, he or she should not eat and drink in food preparation areas during working times. This should be left for break times.

In working areas, if water is provided, this should be supplied in plastic glasses or bottles.

Wearing uniform outside the premises

Wearing uniform outside working premises not only looks unprofessional and unhygienic to customers, it potentially brings bacteria and dirt from the outside environment into the kitchen. This should be avoided at all times, unless it is required in the case of an evacuation or similar.

PUNCTUALITY, ATTENDANCE AND TIME MANAGEMENT

Punctuality and attendance at work are vitally important. For example, chefs are continuously working against the clock, making sure ingredients are prepared, and that meals are served on time. Lateness reduces the amount of time to get ready, as there is no way that the service time can be put back to accommodate a chef's poor timekeeping.

Non-attendance at work simply makes this problem even worse as this will put pressure on the other members of the team to cover for the missing person. However, it must be noted that people miss work for genuine reasons, such as illness or for personal reasons. In such cases, it is normal for the person to be covered by temporary cover. This could be someone within the organization or a temporary contracted person from an agency.

The key points of punctuality, attendance and good time management are as follows.

Dependability

As a chef you will normally work as part of a team. Your colleagues (team-members) will be relying on you to do your job. Each person has a role to play in the overall performance of the team, regardless of position (rank) or experience.

Contractual expectation of employers

When you secure a position within an organization, your employers will expect you to perform to that position and meet the requirements of your contract of employment. If you are regularly late or absent from work without a valid reason, you will be breaking the conditions of your contract and will be at risk of losing your job.

Expectation of colleagues

Your colleagues will expect you to perform your role in a professional manner. Your contribution at work will have an affect on the way that the team operates. Interpersonal relationships can be placed under pressure and sometimes break down if there are feelings that one member of the team is not pulling their weight. This obviously would have a negative impact on the way that the team would function.

CHEF'S TIP

When handling or preparing food, blue plasters should be used so that they are easily identifiable when lost. These dressings can feature an internal metal strip that allows them to be detected by electro-magnet equipment and metal detectors in large food production units.

CHEF'S TIP

Most organizations have set procedures to report illness. It is important that this is followed and that you report any absence as early as possible, so some arrangement can be made.

CHEF'S TIP

As you progress through your career, your working history follows you. Therefore, it is much better to leave a job on good terms and with a positive reference. This will increase your chances of securing future positions and develop routes of progression and promotion during your career.

Courtesy

Punctuality, regular attendance and good time-management are traits that you should try to develop. It is courteous for us to become reliable and not let our colleagues down.

Working to deadlines and meeting targets

Working to realistic deadlines is an important factor for a chef, especially during a busy luncheon or dinner service. Doing this effectively depends on the skills of estimating how long the task is going to take and being able to prioritize jobs. Once that is achieved, it may be helpful to set intermediate deadlines related to relatively short tasks.

The ability to set shared targets and make plans is vital to successful teamwork. If there is no real planning, progression cannot be properly monitored and the team may not be able to learn from the experience. It is during these stages that team members can support each other and provide help where necessary to achieve the end result.

COMMUNICATION SKILLS IN TEAMS

When working in teams, good communication is vital for all members of the team to be clear on what has been done and what needs to be done. If communication breaks down, for whatever reason, quite often many other things will go wrong as a consequence.

Communication takes many forms. The following points describe the main factors associated with communication.

Speaking

Speaking is probably the most obvious form of communication and one that chefs rely on very heavily. For example, during a busy service period, chefs are constantly communicating to ensure that orders are being prepared on schedule. There may also be times when parts of a dish are being prepared by more than one chef. In this situation, chefs need to inform one another of progress so that the final dish comes together at the same time to ensure a high quality product.

Clarifying and confirming

The process of communication is at least a two way process. Even if a person speaks clearly, using good pronunciation and at a sufficient volume, it does not guarantee that the message has been received and/or understood. One way to show that the message has been received is to respond. This shows the other person that you have recognized that they are communicating with you.

CHEF'S TIP

Time management is an important skill for chefs working in the hospitality industry. In order to manage your time more effectively, you must have a realistic assessment of all the tasks required and then plan the workload accordingly.

CHEF'S TIP

As kitchens can be very busy places with lots of hustle and bustle and noise, it is important that verbal communications are clear. The clearer the message, the more likely it will be understood by the person receiving it.

Listening

Listening skills are crucial for effective communication and teamwork. They ensure that we obtain the right information from the right people and help us understand what information or support other people need to help them to work more effectively as a group.

CHEF'S TIP

How to be a good listener
- Clear your mind of other things
- Spend a few minutes thinking about the topic before the meeting or discussion
- Avoid distractions
- Recognize how you are feeling (interested? bored? tired? cross?)
- Remember you are there to learn what the other person has to say, not the other way round
- Focus on the speaker – look at them, nod, encourage, use non-verbal cues to acknowledge what is being said
- Show interest, even if you disagree
- Let the speaker finish what they are saying before you respond
- Ask questions to increase your understanding
- Confirm your understanding by expressing what was said in your own words, or summarizing. This is referred to as 'paraphrasing'.

These points show that you are being 'active' in listening to the person with whom you are communicating. This is called 'active listening'.

Always remember that a good listener aims to get a thorough understanding of what the other person is saying before starting to form an opinion.

Other forms of communication

Other forms of communication include telephone and via a written format (e.g. email, memorandum or letter). The telephone is a fast and effective way of communicating. For example, detailing specific requirements or orders to a supplier can be achieved quickly by talking to the supplier directly on the telephone.

With the arrival of information technology and email it is now easier than ever to communicate in writing and attach relevant documents. Suppliers can now usually accept orders electronically via email which makes it easier to see potential mistakes in the order or provide a greater sense of clarity.

Non-verbal and verbal communication

To become effective in communication such as speaking and listening, you should have an understanding of non-verbal communication (NVC), or body language.

Non-verbal communication can take many forms:

- Touch: greetings, agreements, apologies, goodbyes
- Posture: sitting or standing straight, leaning forward or back
- Proximity: distance between people, personal territory

CHEF'S TIP

When using the telephone, your face cannot be seen and it is important to consider your tone of voice and to speak clearly.

CHEF'S TIP

It is important to be aware of cultural and gender variations in the meaning of some gestures, posture and facial expressions.

- Dress: clothes, hair, appearance
- Eye contact: indicates interest and attention or the opposite
- Hand gestures: agreement, disagreement, impatience, welcome
- Facial expression: shows emotion and provides feedback

When using verbal communication

- Briefly express your appreciation of the speaker, e.g. 'That was a really interesting point'.
- Briefly summarize the point made by the speaker, e.g. 'I was particularly interested in what you said about' …
- Ask your question, if you need to, write it down and read it out and try to make it clear, concise, relevant, informed and non-aggressive.

WHAT MAKES A GOOD TEAM?

A team is made up of a group of individuals contributing to the work of the group as a whole. There is a phrase 'A team is only as good as its weakest link'. This is true to an extent but teams are usually made up of people with different skills and experience.

A good team has to have direction so that it knows where it is going and what has to be achieved. Leadership is an important aspect here in providing a good example to others as well as the vision and support required to motivate other members of the team to perform to the desired standard.

Good team work increases creativity and makes the most of the available range of skills and knowledge. It also helps to improve understanding, communication and a sense of shared purpose, which overall will improve efficiency.

KNOWING YOUR OWN LIMITATIONS AND WHEN TO ASK FOR HELP

Knowing your own limitations is not showing a weakness in your ability. In fact, it shows a strength! As a chef, you are regularly working with foods, some of which can be very expensive. It could be costly to make mistakes in their preparation if they are then unusable.

In such cases where there is doubt over the way to prepare or cook certain food items, it is advisable to ask for assistance and let somebody demonstrate how to complete the task successfully. The same applies to the use of equipment. If you are unsure how a piece of equipment works, it is much better to ask than to run the risk of potentially damaging the equipment or possibly injuring yourself.

It is always better to ask! It may seem hard at the time, and you may feel that you are disturbing your supervisor, but they would prefer to help you than for you to make mistakes which could be costly or dangerous.

COMMUNICATION WITH CUSTOMERS

Customers are the lifeblood of a catering operation. Without customers, there is no business and therefore no need for the staff making up that business. It is essential that customers are treated well and enjoy their experience.

The catering world is very competitive and customers' expectations are getting higher all the time. Nearly all organizations have some sort of customer care or service policy and some have staff that are dedicated specifically to customer services.

This demonstrates the importance that is placed on customers and the revenue (money) that they spend when using the services of a catering organization. The staff within an organization represents that organization and are the front line of contact with the customers they serve. For example, a hotel can have the most impressive reception area, bedrooms and swimming pool, but if staff do not perform to the customers' expectations, the customer is likely leave the organization disappointed.

A vast amount of money is spent by catering businesses trying to attract customers to use their services and much research is performed to study the ways in which customers behave. All of this time and investment is trying to gain new customers and keep existing customers. One negative experience can influence a customer enough so that they decide not to return to that organization and potentially tell their friends, family and acquaintances of their poor experience.

On the other hand, a positive experience is likely to encourage the customer to return in the future and they may inform friends, family and acquaintances of their great experience. Word of mouth recommendation from a neutral source is considered to be a very powerful form of marketing!

All staff, whether they are working in front of house or back of house operations, should be aware of the importance of customers. Many organizations will train their staff in customer service as part of their induction to the organization, regardless of their role within the organization. If everyone has a customer focus, the more likely it is that customers will receive good products and service.

The following points list some of the correct methods that should be used when dealing with customers.

Acknowledging the customer

It is very frustrating as a customer not to be acknowledged. Even if you are busy with another task or order, an acknowledgement of the customer will inform them that you are aware of their presence and that you will deal with them as quickly as you can.

Keeping the customer informed

Keeping customers informed of how their requests or orders are being processed helps to inform them of progress and the likely outcome. A lack of information can cause anxiety for the customer and perhaps the impression that their request has been forgotten or even lost. The fact that someone is taking the time to communicate is also reassuring and sends the message that care and attention is being taken.

For example, during a busy service, there could be a slightly longer waiting time than usual between the end of one course and the service of the next. A simple message to apologise for the slight delay and to inform the customer that their order will be arriving soon or within a few minutes will reassure them of the staffs' attention.

Providing the service or outcome

Essentially, it is the delivery of the service or product in a timely and efficient manner that is the ultimate expectation of the customer. The customer will also expect the product to be of good quality so that they consider the whole package of product and service is good value.

POTENTIAL BARRIERS TO EFFECTIVE COMMUNICATION

There are many barriers to effective communication. However, they can be overcome with effort and willingness from those involved.

The following points highlight some of the potential barriers to effective communication and recommendations as to how they can be overcome.

Verbal barriers

Verbal barriers can be present in many formats. If speech is unclear and almost impossible to hear, the chances of being able to understand what has been said are small.

In addition to this, within the catering industry, people of many different nationalities work together, and for some people, English is not always a first language. Imagine if you were working in a country using another language and the difficulties this could cause in communication.

Even people from the same country can speak in very different ways due to the dialect from the region. For example, someone from Scotland has a very different accent to someone from the south of England and this has the potential for misunderstanding.

It is important that we recognize that we need to maximize the potential for understanding in such situations. Speaking clearly and at a reasonable pace

CHEF'S TIP

Value and cost
Value should not be associated directly with cost. It is possible to spend a lot of money and be very happy with what has been received or experienced. It is also possible to spend a small amount of money and be disappointed!

increases the likelihood of understanding. Look directly at the person and try to avoid slang or colloquialisms (informal language) that people from other areas or countries may not have come across before.

Hearing and listening barriers

Not everyone has perfect hearing, in which case an appropriate solution will have to be found to overcome the situation. The person may be able to lip read, but he or she will need good sight of you speaking. The person may require you to speak up slightly and speak slower that usual. Whatever the situation, there is nearly always a solution provided that all parties concerned have the commitment and desire to overcome the problem.

Written barriers

Writing can cause difficulty as a method of communication. Ideally, it should be clear, simple and to the point. Written communication can break down for a number of reasons, including how words are spelt, the use of grammar and how legible the handwriting is. Other considerations include how the writing is presented and its structure.

Other barriers

There are many examples of how we can produce barriers in communication without speaking or writing. The way in which we present ourselves and act sends out messages to those around us, regardless of whether or not the message has been received as it was intended.

Our own personal level of confidence and experience can also provide a barrier to communication. A lack of confidence can make people withdrawn and shy. Limited experience may prevent a young or new member of staff from performing well if they have not had sufficient training to prepare for the situations they are faced with. Although these examples are fairly common, the customer still expects to receive the service or product they are paying for. It is down to the organization and the teams within the organization to train and develop new or inexperienced people to perform to the required standard.

Body language sends out a multitude of signals, so it is extremely important that people are aware of the potential of their actions. Showing enthusiasm and interest to a customer will provide them with confidence of your attention and increase the likelihood of a clear route for communication.

Other barriers to effective communication can arise from the physical or mental state of a person at a specific time. For example, if someone becomes intoxicated (drunk), their mood can be difficult to measure. People react differently under the influence of alcohol, sometimes by becoming giggly and continuously laughing, or becoming upset and even violent. Whatever the reaction, communication is affected as a consequence.

CHEF'S TIP

In the hospitality and catering industry, personal appearance is very important. This is the case across all areas, whether front or back of house. If staff look clean, smart and professional, this communicates a professional image.

Assessment of knowledge and understanding

1   List three functions of a chef's uniform.

   i) _____   ii) _____

   iii) _____

2   How often should a chef change his or her uniform? Explain the reasons behind your answer.

   _____

   _____

3   As a chef, why is it important to keep nails short and clean?

   _____

   _____

4   Provide two reasons why a blue plaster should be used to cover small cuts and grazes.

   _____

   _____

5   Why should drinking from glass containers be avoided when working in the kitchen?

   _____

   _____

6   Provide three reasons why good timekeeping is important.

   i) _____   ii) _____

   iii) _____

7   List four types or methods of communication.

   i) _____   ii) _____

   iii) _____   iv) _____

8   List four traits or characteristics of a good listener.

   i) _____   ii) _____

   iii) _____   iv) _____

9   Describe why it is considered important for all staff to be aware of the importance of customers.

   _____

   _____

10 Provide three examples where communication can break down.

   i) _____   ii) _____

   iii) _____

7

Prepare and cook food by boiling, poaching and steaming

Unit 107 Prepare and cook food by boiling, poaching and steaming

LEARNING OBJECTIVES

On completion of this chapter, learners will be able to

- Describe the methods of boiling, poaching and steaming
- Identify foods that can be boiled, poached and steamed
- Identify the liquids that are used to boil, poach and steam
- Select suitable techniques associated with boiling, poaching and steaming
- Describe associated products that are made when boiling and poaching
- List the quality points to look for in food that has been boiled, poached and steamed
- List the general safety points to follow when boiling, poaching and steaming food

BOILING

What is boiling?

Boiling is the cooking of food by placing it into a prepared liquid, which is at, or brought to, boiling point. This can be achieved by using a variety of different liquids including water, stock, milk and a range of infused cooking liquids, for example, water enhanced with herbs, spices and vegetables.

In certain cases, such as with an egg, boiling changes the structure of the egg making it more pleasant to eat. The process also helps to ensure that the egg is safe to eat by destroying harmful bacteria such as salmonella.

THE METHODS AND EQUIPMENT USED TO BOIL FOODS

The equipment normally used to boil foods is quite standard in the kitchen. This includes saucepans of varying sizes, stockpots and bratt pans.

It is very important that the correct size of pan is selected to cook the food being boiled. If the pan is too small, it will be difficult to place foods in and remove them from the liquid. It could also be dangerous as the liquid could overflow when the food is placed into it. It may also be difficult to ensure that the food is always covered with the liquid as there may not be enough space within the pan for the food items and enough liquid to cover them. If the pan is too big, it will be an uneconomical and wasteful use of equipment, space and liquid.

There are two methods used to boil food. These are as follows:

1 The food is placed into cold liquid and brought to the boil. Once the liquid has reached boiling point, the temperature is reduced to a simmer as described above. For example, when cooking potatoes, they are usually placed in cold water and brought to the boil. New potatoes are the exception to this rule. They are placed into boiling water.

2 The food is placed into boiling liquid. At this stage the cool or ambient temperature of the food entering the liquid will normally reduce the temperature of the liquid temporarily to below boiling point. The liquid is then heated back to boiling point and then reduced to a simmer.

Foods that are suitable for boiling

The most common type of food associated with boiling is vegetables. Many vegetables can be boiled, although it is important that they are not boiled for too long as overcooking vegetables leads to a loss of vitamins and nutrients and can also make the vegetables soggy and unpleasant to eat.

CHEF'S TIP

Simmering describes a gentle boiling motion. As more energy is applied to the boiling process, the liquid will boil more rapidly and severely. If the motion of the liquid is too harsh, it could damage the food being boiled. Therefore, when boiling food, care and attention is required to control and check the heat applied and movement of the liquid.

ACTIVITY

Excluding the examples given, name five other vegetables that are suitable for boiling

1 _____
2 _____
3 _____
4 _____
5 _____

Other foods that are commonly boiled include eggs, pasta, pulses and grains. When cooking pasta, pulses and grains, the liquid is partially absorbed in the cooking process, improving the texture of the food and at the same time making it more digestible and easy to eat.

Certain cuts of meat and poultry, particularly tougher and generally cheaper cuts of meat are also suitable for boiling. This is similar to the way that the meat is cooked by braising or stewing as the meat is cooked slowly in moist surroundings. This helps to break down the muscular structure and connective tissue, making the meat tender to eat.

The advantages of placing food into cold liquid and bringing to the boil

- The process of bringing the liquid to the boil can help to extract flavours from the food and also help to make food tender

- It is less likely to damage the shape and structure of the food as the liquid is not moving rapidly at the beginning of the heating process

- Bringing a liquid to simmering point can help to clarify the cooking liquid if impurities are removed from the surface in the process.

The advantages of placing food into boiling liquid

- This will prevent the reaction that causes the loss of vitamin C in vegetables

- It will help to retain the colour when cooking green vegetables such as broccoli, fine green beans and cabbage. The addition of salt to boiling water will help to retain the colour in green vegetables.

VIDEO CLIP
Boiling pasta

CHEF'S TIP

Blanching vegetables and pasta. Blanching refers to the cooking of the food item followed by rapid cooling, normally in iced water, to stop the cooking process. This is referred to as 'refreshing'. When the vegetables or pasta are ready to be served, they are placed back into boiling water, not with the intention of cooking the food any further, just to re-heat. Ideally, pasta should be cooked and served immediately, although this is not always practically an option due to pressures of service, etc.

CHEF'S TIP

Some people prefer not to refresh pasta in water for any length of time as this will make the pasta swell and decrease the eating quality. Another alternative is to cook the pasta until almost cooked (still with a fairly firm bite) and strain, leaving it to cool without the addition of water. A little olive oil will help prevent the starch in the pasta from sticking to itself. The pasta can then be reheated as appropriate when required, whether in boiling water, in a pan with oil, or through a sauce.

Step-by-step: **Blanching pasta (spaghetti)**

STEP 1 Add the pasta by spreading it into a saucepan containing deep, salted boiling water

STEP 2 Test to see if the pasta is cooked by removing some with a spoon. The pasta should cooked through but retaining a 'bite' referred to as 'al dente'

STEP 3 Once cooked, the pasta should be drained and served.
Tip – If a little of the pasta water is retained, this will help prevent the pasta from sticking. A little olive oil can also help to prevent sticking as well as adding a delicate flavour

CHEF'S TIP

When cooking lentils with an acid ingredient, such as tomatoes, either allow extra cooking time or add the tomatoes at the end of the recipe, as the natural acid will prolong the cooking process.

CHEF'S TIP

The term 'impurities' refers to any dirt or grease that becomes a by-product during the cookery process.

CHEF'S TIP

The soup could either be eaten with the vegetables left as they were originally cut, as in a broth, or placed into a liquidizer or food processor and made into a puree.

ASSOCIATED TECHNIQUES WHEN BOILING

■ *Soaking* – Most dried beans and pulses need to be soaked before cooking. Split lentils do not always need to be soaked before cooking but you need to follow instructions carefully to ensure that they can be cooked without soaking.

■ *Skimming* – During the boiling process, the food/s being boiled may produce some impurities in the form of froth or foam rising to the surface. This is very common when making a soup or a sauce. If the impurities are not removed, they will go back into the liquid due to the natural movement of the boiling motion. This could result in the liquid going cloudy or greasy and the flavour being spoiled.

Removing impurities from a liquid is quite a simple process. As foam or froth rises to the surface of the simmering liquid, stir the liquid from the centre with the base of a suitably sized ladle. The foam will then move to the edge of the pan. Using the ladle, but this time from the lip of the cup of the ladle, move the ladle around the edge of the pan to remove the froth from the liquid and discard (throw away in a safe and hygienic manner).

■ *Refreshing, storing, reheating and serving* – In the professional kitchen, it is essential to be well prepared for service periods when large numbers of customers will be served in short spaces of time. Taking the preparation and cooking of vegetables as an example, if you tried to cook and serve vegetables as customers requested them (to order), you would create a great deal of hard work for yourself and would find it very difficult to cook, hold at temperature and serve the vegetables in prime condition.

To achieve these aims, the practice of blanching, refreshing and storing for service is used. The vegetables can then be reheated and served very quickly.

Associated products as a result of boiling

It is important to note that there are very common products made as a result of boiling. The most common products made by this process are soups and sauces.

Soups

When making a soup, it is common practice for the ingredients to be cooked in the liquid that will make up the soup itself. For example, if you were making a vegetable soup, the flavour would depend on the quantities of the vegetables used. For instance, in the case of a mushroom soup, the main ingredient would be mushrooms but it is likely that other ingredients such as onion, leek, celery and even potato could be used in smaller quantities to develop the flavours and texture of the soup. Herbs and spices would also add delicate flavours.

Sauces

Sauces are offered with many dishes. They make a huge difference to a dish, making it moist and adding a lot of flavour. A good sauce also adds to the eating quality and enjoyment of the dish as well as helping to digest the food.

Sauces can be made from many bases including stock, wine, milk and, as in the case of a tomato sauce, the food item itself. In most cases, sauces will be simmered for the time it takes to develop the flavours and consistency looked for in the finished sauce.

Cold sauces, such as vinaigrette and mayonnaise are made without cooking process. Cold sauces are referred to in the unit on Cold Food Preparation.

CHEF'S TIP

Consistency in sauce making refers to the thickness and texture of the sauce. A good consistency is found in a sauce that is neither too thick nor thin. This often depends on personal preference and the type of sauce.

Step-by-step: **Making a cartouche**

STEP 1 Take a sheet of greaseproof paper

STEP 2 Fold it in half lengthways

STEP 3 Fold in half again

STEP 4 Keeping all the 'open' ends facing the same direction, fold in half again from the corner.

STEP 5 Repeat this process once or twice more depending on the size of the cartouche

STEP 6 Measure the size of the item you are going to cover by placing the point of the folded cartouche in the centre of the item. Add a little extra to your measurement to go up the edge of the pan or bowl being covered

STEP 7 Cut or tear along the line of your measurement

STEP 8 Unfold to produce a cartouche that fits the size of the item you are covering

POACHING

What is poaching?

Poaching is the cooking of foods by placing them into a prepared liquid which has been heated to boiling point and then lowered, just below boiling point, to a very gentle simmer. Foods can be poached using a variety of different liquids including water, stock, wine, milk, stock syrup and a range of infused cooking liquids, for example, water enhanced with herbs, spices and vegetables.

The liquid will also help to develop flavour and texture. In some cases, the poaching liquid is reduced to become the sauce to be served with the poached item of food. A practical example of this is 'Smoked haddock Florentine'.

Step-by-step: **Poaching smoked haddock**

STEP 1 A fillet of smoked haddock with the poaching ingredients, milk, white peppercorns, parsley stalks and bay leaves

STEP 2 Place the haddock, skin side down, in to the infused milk (milk with the parsley, stalks, etc).
Tip – Use a wide and fairly shallow saucepan when poaching. This will provide easy access to place and take out the food items being poached

STEP 3 Place a buttered cartouche on top of the poaching liquid and bring the poaching liquid to a gentle simmer

STEP 4 Poach the fish gently for 5 minutes and then remove carefully using a fish slice

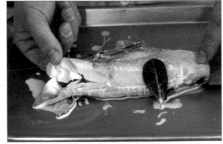

STEP 5 Place on a tray and gently brake down the fillet into the natural flakes

STEP 6 Fill a shallow ring with some lightly sautéed spinach and top with flakes of the poached haddock

METHODS AND EQUIPMENT USED TO POACH FOODS

The equipment normally used to poach foods is a shallow or deep-sided poaching pan. It is important that the pan is quite wide to allow foods to be poached together at one level (rather than on top of one another) and also to allow easy access to place and remove the items of food being poached.

There are two methods used to poach food. These are as follows:

1 The food is placed into a shallow poaching liquid. In this situation, the food is placed into the minimum amount of liquid. In some cases, the poaching process is started on the top of the oven and then finished by placing the whole pan into a medium oven between 170°C and 180°C. This temperature will keep the poaching liquid just below boiling point. Foods cooked by shallow poaching often use the poaching liquid as the base for the sauce that is served with the food item being poached.

2 The food is placed into a deep poaching liquid. For example, an egg is poached in simmering water which is three or four times as deep as the shelled egg. A poached egg can be blanched, refreshed and reheated for service in a similar way to the way that vegetables are reheated for service.
The sequence below demonstrates an egg being poached.

VIDEO CLIP
Deep poaching salmon

Step-by-step: **Poaching an egg**

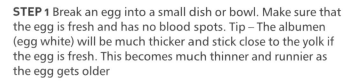

STEP 1 Break an egg into a small dish or bowl. Make sure that the egg is fresh and has no blood spots. Tip – The albumen (egg white) will be much thicker and stick close to the yolk if the egg is fresh. This becomes much thinner and runnier as the egg gets older

STEP 2 Using a shallow poaching pan, fill two thirds full with water and bring to the boil. Whisk or swirl the boiling water, this will encourage the white to surround the yolk. Tip – The addition of vinegar to the poaching liquid will help to coagulate the egg white and keep this surrounding the yolk as it poaches

STEP 3 This picture shows the egg white surrounding the yolk as it poaches. Usually, a poached egg is cooked until the egg white is firm and the yolk is left soft

STEP 4 Once the egg is sufficiently cooked, remove the egg carefully using a perforated (slotted) spoon. Tip – if the egg is to be served at a later time, it can be refreshed and stored by placing it into ice-cold water

Foods that are suitable for poaching

 **ACTIVITY**

Other foods that are commonly poached include fruits, fish and chicken.
In the categories below, research two dishes that are poached.

TYPE OF FOOD	DISH EXAMPLE	
Eggs	1	2
Fish	1	2
Chicken	1	2
Fruit	1	2

 **VIDEO CLIP**
Poaching fruit

Step-by-step: **Poaching a pear in red wine**

STEP 1 The ingredients for poaching a pear in red wine –
(red wine, sugar, cinnamon stick, star anise and the pears)

STEP 2 Carefully peel the pears

STEP 3 Place the pears into the poaching liquid, ensuring
that the liquid covers the pear and bring to a gentle simmer
(A slightly deeper saucepan can be used in this instance)

STEP 4 Poach the pears until cooked (this will depend on
how ripe they are) and remove using a perforated (slotted)
spoon

Step-by-step: **Poached chicken breast**

STEP 1 Prepare a white mirepoix (chopped onions, leek and celery) and gather aromatics (parsley stalks, peppercorns, bay leaves and sliced garlic)

STEP 2 Place the mirepoix and aromatics into a poaching pan, bring to a gentle simmer and then carefully place in the skinned chicken breast

STEP 3 Cover with a cartouche and poach until cooked through

STEP 4 Once cooked, remove the chicken breast with a slotted slice and use as required

VIDEO CLIP
Poaching a whole chicken

ASSOCIATED TECHNIQUES USED WHEN POACHING FOODS

A number of techniques help to achieve a good quality and consistent finished dish when poaching foods. These are as follows:

- *Cutting into uniform size* – Cutting to uniform size helps to ensure that food items cook evenly in the same amount of time. Accurate cutting helps with portion control, making sure that enough portions are produced. Presentation is also improved by accurate and uniform cutting skills.
- *Tying* – Tying helps to make sure that foods stay in the required shape while they are poached. Tying food items also makes it easier to handle the food during the whole cooking process.

- *Folding* – As in tying, folding food items such as fish fillets helps the items stay in the required shape. Folding can help to make the thickness of the food items more even, allowing the food to cook in an even time. Presentation can also be improved if the food has been folded neatly.

- *Draining* – When poaching, as the food is placed in a liquid, it is important that the food is dried properly before it is served. If the food is not dried properly and is being served with a sauce, the poaching liquid would appear separately from the sauce or possibly make the sauce thinner.

- *Reducing for sauce* – With some poached dishes, the liquid is strained and reduced in volume by boiling it rapidly. It can then be used as the base of the sauce to be served with the poached item of food.

- *Holding for service* – Once the food item is cooked, there may be a period of time before the item is served. For example, this could be the time that it takes to prepare the sauce. It is very important that the food is kept hot and in good condition during this time. As many poached foods are quite delicate, this has to be done carefully so that the food remains in prime condition.

STEAMING

What is steaming?

Steaming has a major difference to boiling and poaching. When steaming, the food is cooked by placing it in the steam produced as a by-product (side-effect) of boiling water. This produces an atmosphere of moist or wet heat. Some steamers are designed to capture the steam and increase the pressure and temperature within the steamer itself. This enables the food to be cooked faster.

Steaming food changes the texture of the food making it pleasant to eat. The process also kills harmful bacteria making the food safer to eat.

METHODS AND EQUIPMENT USED TO STEAM FOODS

There are two main methods of steaming. Which method is used will determine the type of equipment that is used. This is described below.

A Chinese bamboo steamer

1 *Atmospheric or low-pressure steaming* – The food is cooked in the steam produced by boiling water. It is either in direct contact with the steam (the food is placed into the steam itself) or the process is indirect, and the food item is protected from the steam by a sealing it in a mould or container. The equipment required to steam food by this method is very basic. For example, a rack in a pan of water will make a good steamer (as long as the

rack is higher than the water level or else the food will cook in the water rather than the steam.) A Chinese bamboo steamer is also a low-cost way of producing a very good atmospheric steamer.

2 *High pressure steaming* – To cook food by this method, a high-pressure steamer is required. This is a purpose-built piece of equipment that will keep the steam within the steaming chamber. This increases the pressure within the chamber and also increases the temperature. In this situation, the food can be cooked more quickly than if cooked using an atmospheric steamer.

Modern high-pressure steamers have many features to control the temperature and pressure when cooking food. A high-pressure steamer is a much more expensive piece of equipment than anything required to steam by low pressure.

Foods that are suitable for steaming

■ Most vegetables can be steamed, particularly if using a high-pressure steamer.

■ Fish that can be poached are also suitable for cooking by steaming.

■ Sponge and suet puddings can be steamed to produce a light and moist texture.

Step-by-step: **Preparing cauliflower florets for steaming**

STEP 1 Place the cauliflower securely on a chopping board and, using a large knife, cut the root from the base of the cauliflower

STEP 2 Using a paring knife, trim the remaining leaves from the base of the cauliflower leaving the white florets of the cauliflower intact

STEP 3 Cutting squarely across each floret, cut into evenly sized florets

STEP 4 Place neatly onto a steaming tray and steam

ACTIVITY

In the categories below, research two dishes that are steamed

TYPE OF FOOD	DISH EXAMPLE	
Vegetables	1	2
Fish	1	2
Chicken	1	2
Sweet and Savoury Puddings	1	2

Step-by-step: **Steaming cod with lemon grass, fennel and tarragon**

STEP 1 The ingredients – loin of cod (trimmed central fillet), lemon grass, fennel, tarragon and olive oil

STEP 2 Slice the lemon grass lengthways and lightly crush using the back of the knife H&S Tip – Make sure the blade is pointing away from you

STEP 3 Slice the fennel lengthways

STEP 4 Place the lemon grass and fennel on to a steaming tray and add some fresh tarragon

STEP 5 Lay the cod on top of the aromatic vegetables, brush with olive oil and season lightly with salt and freshly ground white pepper. The cod is now ready to be steamed

STEP 6 Steam, according to size and shape of the fish, before carefully removing from the steamer

VIDEO CLIP
Steaming fish

ASSOCIATED TECHNIQUES USED WHEN STEAMING FOODS

A number of techniques help to achieve a good quality and consistent finished dish when steaming foods:

■ *Preparing the container or mould* – It is important that the container used to steam the food is in good condition and the right size for the job.

- *Greasing* – Lightly coating the inside of the mould with oil or fat will provide a non-stick surface to allow the food to come free from the mould when ready to be served.

- *Moulding* – This refers to the food being placed into the mould itself. It is important that the food is added evenly to take on the shape of the mould. A gentle tap of the filled mould onto a table can help the food to spread out around the mould.

- *Waterproofing* – Foods that are steamed in containers or moulds are usually sealed to prevent the steam (water vapour) from getting into direct contact with the food item itself. This is to enable the food item to be cooked by the steam without taking in the moisture and becoming soggy. To produce a waterproof seal, the mould is usually covered with greaseproof paper and kitchen foil. When covering, a fold in the centre of the paper and foil will allow room for the food (such as a steamed pudding) to expand.

- *Traying up* – Sometimes many items may be needed to be steamed at the same time. For example, if serving an individual steamed pudding as a dessert for 30 covers, 30 moulds would need to be filled and covered. Rather than placing each mould individually into the steamer, it would be much easier and more efficient to place the moulds onto a tray and steam the puddings together in one batch.

- *Loading* – This refers to the moulds, or trays of moulds, being placed into the steamer. When working with steam, it is very important that you keep a safe distance from the steam itself. Steam can produce a nasty scald if in direct contact with skin. Particular attention is required when opening the doors of high-pressure steamers. When opening, the steam from the chamber will pump out from the door. Therefore, it is good practice to stand away from, or behind, the door to let the steam out before removing the moulds or trays from the steamer.

CHEF'S TIP

As some items, such as sweet steamed puddings, will rise during the steaming process, it is important that the mould is not filled to the top. In this situation, the mould would be filled about two thirds of the way up the mould to allow space for the sponge to rise.

VIDEO CLIP
Steaming sweet puddings

ASSOCIATED TECHNIQUES USED WHEN STEAMING FOODS

Step-by-step: **Steamed sponge pudding**

STEP 1 The ingredients and basins for producing steamed sponge puddings – Plain (soft) flour, butter, eggs, castor sugar, baking powder (Note – Self raising flour can be used – this flour already has the raising agent added so the baking powder would not be necessary)

STEP 2 Cream the butter and sugar together in a suitably sized bowl

STEP 3 Beat the eggs in a separate bowl and add the creamed mixture gradually whilst continuing to beat. Tip – Adding the eggs gradually should prevent the mixture from curdling

STEP 4 Mix the baking powder with the flour and sieve into the butter, sugar and egg mix. Fold this in gently using a large metal spoon.

STEP 5 Line the pudding basins by brushing with melted butter and finely coating with flour. This will prevent the cooked puddings from sticking to the basins when removing to serve.

STEP 6 Using two spoons, as shown, place the sponge mix into the pudding basins leaving some room at the top of the basins for rising

STEP 7 Prepare a suitably sized cartouche, brush one side with melted butter and make a fold in the centre of the cartouche as shown. The cartouche will protect the sponge mixture from moisture in the steamer and the fold will allow the mixture to rise

STEP 8 Place the cartouche, butter side down, over the basin and secure by typing with a piece of string or elastic band

STEP 9 Place in the prepared steamer and steam until cooked (approximately 40 minutes for a pudding of this size)

STEP 10 Once cooked, remove from the steamer, untie the string and carefully peel off the cartouche

STEP 11 To serve, demould the puddings by releasing from the basins as shown

STEP 12 Coat with an appropriate sauce (e.g. lemon, orange, etc.), garnish and serve

WORKING SAFELY

It is important to follow safe working practices when boiling, poaching and steaming food items.
The following points should be considered:

When boiling and poaching:

■ Use the right sized pan for the job in hand

■ Handle hot pans with care!

■ Make sure that handles from pans do not stick out from the stove!

■ Be careful when placing and removing items from the liquid!

When working with steamers:

■ Make sure that there is enough water in the steamer before turning it on.

■ Ensure that steam is released in a controlled manner!

Assessment of knowledge and understanding

1   Briefly describe the processes of:
Boiling _____
Poaching _____
Steaming _____

2   When boiling raw green vegetables, why are they placed into salted boiling water?

_____

3   Why is it important to cut vegetables into a uniform size when cooking them by boiling?

_____

4   Name three liquids that can be used as the base for a sauce.
i) _____   ii) _____
iii) _____

5   When making a sauce or a soup, why is it important to skim the impurities (foam and froth) from the top of the liquid?

_____

6   What is steam?

_____

7   What are the two main methods used to steam foods?
i) _____   ii) _____

8   Name a poached fish dish that uses the cooking liquid to make the accompanying sauce.

_____

9   Name a sauce that is made from milk.

_____

10 If poaching in the oven, at what temperature would you set the oven?

_____

11 When poaching or boiling, why is it important that pan handles are not left to stick out from the oven?

_____

12 If steaming food in a mould, how would you prevent steam from getting into direct contact with the food?

_____

13 If a fish can be poached, it can be steamed.   ☐ True   ☐ False

CHEF'S PROFILE

Name: HERBERT BERGER

Position: Chef Partner/GM

Establishment: 1 Lombard Street, Restaurant – Bar – Brasserie

Training and experience: Grand Hotel Zell am See and catering college Salzburg, Austria (apprenticeship).

■ **5 years Switzerland:** Sunstar Hotel Grindelwald, Grand Hotel National Luzern, Hotel Lausanne Palace, Derby Hotel Davos and others.

■ **Jersey:** St Brelades Bay Hotel.

■ **London:** Head chef Le Connaisseur, gained 1 Michelin star, senior sous chef The Connaught Hotel and Claridges; head chef at The Mirabelle, chef partner at Keats, gained red M Michelin, executive chef Café Royal overseeing catering for 21 banqueting rooms, five restaurants, gained Michelin star for the Grill room at the Café Royal.

■ **Present:** 1 Lombard Street, gained Michelin star for the restaurant.

Main responsibilities: Responsible for all aspects of running the business.

Best parts of the job: Running a very successful business and enjoying the benefits it brings to the whole operation; being surrounded by a very good professional team; being recognized by the customers as their favourite and best restaurant in the city.

Seeing young staff grow and develop and watching them succeed.

Providing a huge choice, cooking brasserie food as well as fine dining and being able to use the best and seasonal products available.

Continuously working on providing total 'hospitality', being proactive and always looking at ways to improve and grow.

Receiving great comments from our customers and the recognition by a Michelin Star.

Secrets of a successful chef: Cook with love, passion, care and respect – the rest follows automatically. Enjoy the challenge and think about what you cook!

Be determined, maintain consistency and use the best products only!
(rubbish in – rubbish out)!

Enjoy, develop and experience the pleasure of eating. This will help you cook great genuine food.

Recipe: Poached fillet of new season lamb with summer vegetables and minted broth.

Mentor or main inspiration: Many chefs and people have inspired me but the main inspiration is the enjoyment and pleasure one gets by eating good food and drinking amazing wine. From comfort food to fine dining, it is one of the greatest pleasures on earth.

A brief personal profile: Dining out, travelling, food markets, skiing and the arts.

CHEF'S RECIPE

Poached fillet of new season lamb with summer vegetables and minted broth

INGREDIENTS	4 PORTIONS
Pair of best ends of lamb, remove fillet and clean completely. Keep all trimmings and bones for stock (no fat)	1 pair
Asparagus tips	16 tips
Broad beans (shelled)	50g
Peas (shelled)	50g
Baby turnips	12 turnips
Baby carrots	12 carrots
Baby leeks	8 leeks
Small Jersey Royals	12 potatoes
Grellots or button onions	12 onions
Girolle mushrooms	50g
Stick celery (retain leaves for garnish)	1 stick
Mild virgin olive oil	4tbsp
Mint	1 small bunch

Method of work

Stock for lamb

1 Roast lamb bones and trimmings until golden brown.

2 Put in saucepan without the fat.

3 Cover with 3 pints of water and half a pint of white wine.

4 Add a bouqet garni (celery stick, carrot, garlic, 3–4 white peppercorns, leeks, bay, thyme, rosemary and parsley stalks).

5 Bring to the boil, skim and simmer gently for 3 hours.

6 Reduce to approximately 1½ pints.

7 Pass and skim, adjust seasoning.

8 Split stock into 2/3 and 1/3, retain the 2/3 for poaching the lamb, and pre-cook all the summer vegetables separately in the remaining stock.

To Finish

1 Season the fillets of lamb with salt and pepper.

2 Add the fillets to the stock and simmer gently (do not allow to boil) for 6–8 minutes – until pink.

3 Take out, leave to rest in a warm place for 5 minutes.

4 In the meantime, start to re-heat the summer vegetables.

5 Cut lamb into 4 portions and place in the middle of a deep plate.

6 Arrange vegetables around the lamb.

7 Flood bowl with stock.

8 Finish with pearls of mint oil (made from blending the mint and olive oil in a food processor and passing through a fine sieve).

RECIPES

Lemon tart filling *lemon curd*

Will fill 1 × 8 inch tart or 8–10 individual tartlets

INGREDIENTS	4 PORTIONS
Granulated sugar	450g
Grated zest of 2 lemons	
Freshly squeezed lemon juice	240ml
Large eggs	8
Large egg yolks	2
Unsalted butter cut into pieces	350g

Method of work

1. Place the sugar into a bowl. Grate the zest of lemon into it and rub together.
2. Strain the lemon juice into a non-reactive pan. Add the eggs, egg yolks, butter and zested sugar. Whisk to combine.
3. Place over a medium heat and whisk continuously for 3–5 minutes, until the mixture begins to thicken.
4. At the first sign of boiling, remove from the heat and strain into a bowl and cool.

Spaghetti Carbonara

INGREDIENTS	4 PORTIONS	10 PORTIONS
Spaghetti	400g	1kg
Salt		
Oil	1tbsp	8tbsp
Streaky bacon or pancetta (cut into lardons)	100g	875g
Egg yolks	4	10
Single cream	100ml	250ml
Parmesan cheese, freshly grated	75g	175g
Freshly ground black pepper		

Method of work

1. Spread the spaghetti and drop into a pan with plenty of rapidly boiling salted water.
2. Heat the oil in a fairly large frying pan, add the bacon and fry lightly over a medium heat until the fat has melted.
3. Remove the pan from the heat and set aside, keeping it warm.
4. In a separate bowl, whisk the egg yolks with the cream and half the parmesan cheese. Season generously with the pepper.
5. When the spaghetti is still firm to the bite (al dente), drain it and transfer it to the pan with the bacon.
6. Place over a medium heat and pour the egg mixture over it.
7. Stir quickly and turn off the heat. (Do not let this mixture boil as it will curdle the eggs!).
8. Serve immediately offering the remaining Parmesan cheese.

Béchamel and Mornay sauce

VIDEO CLIP
Making Béchamel sauce

INGREDIENTS	4 PORTIONS	10 PORTIONS
For the Béchamel sauce		
Butter	50g	125g
Plain flour	50g	125g
Milk	500ml	1250ml
Pinch of freshly grated nutmeg (optional)		
Salt and freshly ground white pepper		
For the Mornay sauce		
Egg yolk	1	3 small or 2 large
Double cream	100ml	250ml
Recipe Béchamel sauce	1	1
Freshly grated Gruyère cheese	25g	65g
Freshly grated Parmesan cheese	25g	65g
Salt and freshly ground white pepper		

Method of work

For the Béchamel sauce

1 Melt the butter in a saucepan over a low to medium heat.
2 Add the flour and mix to a paste (white roux).
3 Pour the milk in gradually (a small amount at a time), mixing constantly until it comes to the boil. The milk should bind well with the mix to form a smooth paste. This will become thinner as more milk is added.
4 Reduce the heat, cover with a cartouche and simmer gently, stirring occasionally, for at least 45 minutes. Béchamel sauce should not taste floury.
5 Remove the saucepan from the heat and season with salt, pepper and/or nutmeg.
6 If the sauce is too thick, add a little more milk. If too thin, return to the heat and add a knob of butter mixed with an equal quantity of plain flour. For a richer béchamel sauce, replace half the milk with the same amount of cream.

For the Mornay sauce

1 Beat the egg yolk with the cream in a small bowl.
2 When the Béchamel sauce is ready, remove the saucepan from the heat and stir in the Gruyère and Parmesan.
3 Stir in the egg yolk mix.
4 Season to taste with salt and pepper.
5 Use for poached eggs, fish dishes and gratins.

Pears poached in red wine

INGREDIENTS	4 PORTIONS	10 PORTIONS
Water	100ml	250ml
Red wine	300ml	750ml
Granulated sugar	125g	300g
Redcurrant jelly	1tbsp	3tbsp
Lemon – zested	1	2
Cinnamon stick	1	3
Firm pears (Williams/Comice)	4	10

Method of work

1 Place the water, wine, sugar and jelly in a saucepan and heat gently until the sugar has dissolved.

2 Add the lemon zest and cinnamon.

3 Peel the pears very neatly without removing the stalks.

4 Place upright in the pan and cover with a lid. The pears should be completely covered by the wine and water mixture, so choose a suitable pan.

5 Bring the liquid up to the boil and simmer until the pears are cooked. The pears should be a cherry-red colour and tender when pricked with a small sharp knife.

6 Remove the pears from the pan and allow to cool.

7 Reduce the wine liquid by boiling to a syrupy consistency and strain it over the pears.

8 Allow to cool, then chill in the refrigerator and use accordingly.

Poached eggs with cheese sauce and spinach *Florentine*

INGREDIENTS	4 PORTIONS	10 PORTIONS
Spinach	500g	1250g
Poached eggs	4	10
Mornay sauce	250ml	625ml

Method of work

1 Poach, refresh and reheat eggs as shown earlier in the chapter.

2 Remove the stems from the spinach.

3 Wash well in cold water until clean. Drain.

4 For larger leaves, blanch by placing in boiling salted water for 30 seconds and remove using a spider.

5 Refresh in iced water and squeeze dry into a ball.

6 To serve, place the spinach into a pan containing 50g heated butter.

7 Mix with a fork and reheat quickly without colouring.

8 Season lightly with salt and freshly ground white pepper.

9 Serve by neatly arranging the spinach on a plate.

10 Place the reheated eggs on top and coat each egg carefully with Mornay sauce.

Poached smoked haddock Florentine

INGREDIENTS	4 PORTIONS	10 PORTIONS
Smoked haddock	400g	1kg
Milk	500ml	1250ml
Bay leaves	2	5
Parsley stalks		
Bouquet garni	1	3
Studded onion (studded with 2 cloves)	½	1½

Method of work

1 Place the haddock into the milk (with herbs) and simmer gently for 5 minutes.
2 When cooked, take out of the milk and remove the backbone.
3 The flesh should now break into firm flaky pieces.
4 Retain the milk to make the Mornay sauce.

Steamed sponge puddings

Makes 10–12 portions

Basic Sponge

INGREDIENTS	10–12 PORTIONS
Individual moulds buttered and floured	12
Unsalted butter	200g
Castor sugar	300g
Eggs	4
Egg yolks	2
Self-raising flour	400g
Milk (if needed)	2–3tbsp

Method of work

1 Beat the butter and sugar until creamed.
2 Add the eggs and egg yolks gradually and continue to beat.
3 Fold in the sifted flour, adding the milk if necessary.
4 Spoon the mixture into the prepared moulds (¾ full) and cover with greaseproof paper (fold in the centre to allow for the rising pudding).
5 Steam for 40 minutes.

Steamed Treacle Sponge

Add a spoonful of golden syrup to the mix with a spoonful at the base of the moulds.

8

Prepare and cook food by stewing and braising

Unit 108 Prepare and cook food by stewing and braising

LEARNING OBJECTIVES

On completion of this chapter, learners will be able to:

- Describe the methods of stewing and braising
- Identify foods that can be stewed and braised
- Identify the most suitable equipment for stewing and braising
- Describe the techniques associated with stewing and braising
- State the points that require consideration when stewing and braising food
- List the quality points to look for in food that has been stewed and braised
- List the general safety points to follow when stewing and braising food

STEWING

What is stewing?

Stewing is described as pieces of food that are cooked slowly in a liquid. The liquid is then served as a sauce to accompany the food that has been stewed.

As stewing is a slow method of cooking, cheaper cuts of meat can be used with excellent, flavoursome results. When making meat-based stews for example, the cubes of meat are coated with the sauce that will eventually be served alongside the meat itself. This produces a moist environment and a gentle heat in which the connective tissues within the structure of the meat are slowly broken down, making the meat tender to eat. As this happens over a long cooking time the natural flavours and juices from the meat fall into the sauce, increasing its flavour. This is also true of any other food items that are added to the stew, some of which may have been added purely to release flavour, not to be served as part of the finished dish. Examples of this include a mirepoix, a rough cut of root vegetables (onion, celery, leek, carrot) used to flavour the dish rather than to be served as part of the dish. Additional flavours can be developed with herbs and spices. This can be achieved by adding a bouquet garni during the stewing process.

The methods and equipment used to stew foods

There are many varieties of stews and methods used to produce them. With meat-based stews, this includes stews where the meat is cooked within a pre-thickened sauce that will be served as part of the dish, such as ragout of beef or boeuf bourguignon. In other methods, the liquid used is thickened at the end of the cooking process. An example of this is a blanquette of lamb. There are also stews that are thickened naturally by the ingredients within the stew itself. An Irish stew provides a good example.

Other food items can also be made into stews. This includes fish, vegetables and fruit. Due to the structure of these items, the cooking time is much less than meat stew.

Examples of stews made from these food items include:

Vegetables – ratatouille
Fruit – stewed fruit or fruit compote
Fish – bouillabaisse (Level 2/3 dish)

 VIDEO CLIP
Making a bouquet garni

 **CHEF'S TIP**

Cooking liquids – In the production of many flavoured cooked liquids, such as stocks, soups or sauces, a package of herbs is often added during the cooking process to enhance flavours. This is referred to as a 'bouquet garni'. To make a bouquet garni, this can be achieved by wrapping the herbs, usually parsley stalks, bay leaf and thyme with the addition of a few peppercorns. This is then wrapped in either strips of leek or within a parcel of muslin, tied with string and placed carefully within the liquid during the cooking process. As the liquid is left to simmer, the delicate flavours are imparted and developed.

Step-by-step: **Ratatouille**

VIDEO CLIP
Making ratatouille

STEP 1 Place some olive oil into a suitably sized pan (e.g. sauteuse) and heat.

STEP 2 Add the onion and sweat for a few minutes before adding the garlic and peppers

STEP 3 Add the courgette and aubergine and continue to cook, stirring on a regular basis. Some chopped herbs (e.g. marjoram, basil, parsley) can be added to enhance the flavour.

STEP 4 If intended to serve as a vegetable stew, a few ladles of tomato coulis/pasatta (strained tomatoes) can be added at this point to provide a binding sauce.

STEP 5 Continue to cook, stirring gently

STEP 6 Just before serving, add some diced fresh tomato (concassé) and stir in gently

Step-by-step: **Stewing fruit**

STEP 1 Cut the plums from the core all the way around the stone, twist to split in half and remove the stone

STEP 2 Place the fruits to be stewed into suitably sized saucepans and add sugar

STEP 3 Add water – this will produce a syrup with the sugar when dissolved and heated

STEP 4 Heat the saucepans and gently stew the fruit

STEP 5 Apples being stewed with cinnamon and cloves added for additional flavour

STEP 6 Stewed plums, apples and blackberries

BASIC PRINCIPLES WHEN MAKING A STEW

The flowchart below shows the basic method for making a brown meat stew:

Using a medium to large saucepan, seal the meat by frying with colour

↓

Add mirepoix and continue to fry to gain colour

↓

Add flour and stir in

↓

Add tomato puree and stir in

↓

Gradually add the appropriately flavoured stock, stirring consistently

↓

Add bouquet garni and cover with a lid

↓

Cook slowly until the meat is tender
85°C to 90°C – simmering on the hob
160°C to 170°C – in a gentle moderate oven

Step-by-step: **Navarin of lamb**

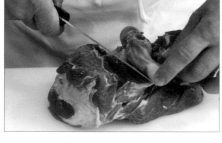

STEP 1 Carefully remove any bones (bone out) from the lamb. In this example, half a leg of lamb has been used

STEP 2 Remove any skin and excess sinew and cut or pull into the natural cushions(sections) of meat

STEP 3 This shows the natural cushions of meat next to the bone and skin

STEP 4 Cut the meat into fairly large dice

STEP 5 Lightly oil a frying pan, heat though and fry the diced meat quickly to brown the outside surface of the meat

STEP 6 Once browned, remove the meat with a perforated spoon and place into a bowl. Tip away any excess oil and deglaze the pan by heating the sediment (deposits) and adding some red wine. This will absorb the flavour from the pan into the liquid and maximize the flavour of the stew. Pour onto the meat placed into the bowl

STEP 7 Fry the mirepoix (carrots, onion, leek and celery) until browned.

STEP 8 Pour the browned mirepoix into the stewing pan, heat gently and stir in the tomato puree and flour

STEP 9 Pour in the wine from the meat and stir into the mixture until smooth. Continue to repeat this process but adding stock, stirring consistently until the liquid reaches the boil. At this point, the liquid should resemble the consistency of a sauce

STEP 10 Add the browned meat to the sauce and mirepoix and stir

STEP 11 Add a bouquet garni, and place a lid on top of the pan. Stew gently either on the hob or place in a pre-heated oven at 170°C until cooked (tender)

STEP 12 Once tender, remove the meat from the sauce and place into a clean pan. Strain the sauce through a chinois back onto the meat. This will remove the mirepoix and any other particles left in the sauce during the stewing process

STEP 13 Cook (e.g. sauté) any other garnishes, e.g. button onions, mushrooms, and add to the stew

STEP 14 Season with salt and freshly ground black pepper, adjust the consistency of the sauce, if necessary, and serve

Dishes cooked by stewing

- Ragout (brown beef stew) – sauce thickened at the beginning of the cooking process
- Navarin (brown lamb stew) – sauce thickened at the beginning of the cooking process
- Fricassée (white stew – chicken/veal) – sauce thickened at the beginning of the cooking process
- Blanquette (white stew – lamb/veal) – sauce thickened at the end of the cookery process.

Other examples include

1 Goulash (Hungarian influence – paprika) – beef

2 Curries – any meat or poultry

3 Irish stew – lamb

THE METHODS USED WHEN STEWING FOODS

Sealing

This describes the initial cooking to 'seal' in the nutrients, natural juices and flavours. This can be achieved to verifying degrees of colour.

Sealing with colour (browning)

In this situation the meat is placed into hot oil or fat so that it is sealed while developing good colour. This will also help to develop natural flavours. This is a requirement when making a brown stew.

Sealing without colour

When making a fricassée of chicken for example, the chicken is placed into moderately (gently) heated oil or fat. This will start to seal the chicken, which helps to retain the nutrients and natural juices as well as developing flavour, but without colouring. As a fricassée is a white stew, additional colour is not sought from the initial sealing process.

Blanching and refreshing

When making a blanquette, for example, the initial process involves the meat (lamb/veal) being placed into cold water which is brought to the boil. On reaching boiling point, the meat is refreshed by placing it under running cold water until all impurities have been washed away. The meat is now ready for the main cooking process.

The addition of liquid

Liquids can be added to stews at different points, for example a blanquette is made differently to a fricassée, ragout or navarin in that the sauce is thickened once the meat has been cooked. At this stage, the meat is strained from the liquid and, using a roux, made into a velouté sauce. This is then cooked out by simmering for approximately 30 minutes. The sauce is then corrected for seasoning and consistency before being passed through a fine chinois. This is then reheated and the meat is placed back into the sauce. The sauce is finished with cream or a liaison of cream and egg yolks.

Liquids – (for Stewing and Braising)

Stewing can take place using a variety of liquids. Liquids other than stock that are commonly used to stew foods include:

- **Stock syrup** – a water and sugar base that is often flavoured with other ingredients to infuse with the item being stewed. Examples include lemon, cinnamon and star-anise. A stock syrup would be used to stew fruits such as apricots and plums.

- **Wine** – the alcohol within wine is destroyed during the cooking process leaving behind its rich flavours. Wine makes an excellent base for a sauce and, when stewing, this is enhanced even more during a lengthy cooking process. A famous stew using red wine as its base is boeuf bourguignon. This stew uses red wine from the Burgundy region of France.

- **Beer and cider** – as with wine, the alcohol content is destroyed during the cooking process. Beer and cider also make very tasty sauces when used as a base in stews. Many regional dishes are produced using local beers and ciders. For example, in Devon and Cornwall (South West England), cider is often used in pork-based stews.

- **Sauce** – there are many ready-made sauces in which meats can be stewed. As with all ready-made or convenience products, this saves time but does not always produce a product of the same quality as when freshly made.

ASSOCIATED TECHNIQUES WHEN STEWING FOODS

- **Skimming sauces** – During the cooking process, impurities, grease and fat will rise to the surface of the sauce. It is good practice to remove such impurities to improve the overall quality of the sauce. If sauces are not skimmed, the impurities will be cooked into the sauce due to the natural movement of the liquid in the cooking process. This will reduce the quality and flavour of the finished sauce and potentially leave the sauce with a greasy finish.

- **Straining** – For a more refined presentation and to increase the balance of flavours and consistency, stews are often strained to separate the meat and vegetables from the sauce. The sauce is then adjusted to correct seasoning, consistency and flavours. Once this is complete, the meat is then returned to the heated sauce and is ready to serve. It is optional whether the mirepoix (root vegetables used primarily to flavour the stew) would be served or left out. Other garnishes, such as button mushrooms or neatly cut spring vegetables may be used to enhance the dish and add contrast.

- **Reducing** – Reducing a sauce will intensify the flavour and naturally thicken the sauce in the process. This is one method of adjusting a sauce once it has been strained. To achieve this, the sauce is placed over a high heat source (flame, hob) and boiled rapidly.

 **CHEF'S TIP**

It is very important that sauces to be reduced are not seasoned with salt and pepper until the reduction is complete. If seasoned in advance of reducing, the amount of seasoning will remain the same but in less liquid, making it too severe and potentially ruining the sauce.

■ *Enriching white stews* – To enrich and thicken the sauce of a white stew, a combination of egg yolk and cream can be added at the very last moment. This is referred to as a 'liaison'. It is good practice that a small amount of the hot sauce is added to the liaison and mixed before adding this back into the sauce.

Health and Safety Requirements

When making a stew, it is necessary to stir the food throughout the cooking process from the sealing and browning of meat to the production of the accompanying sauce. Therefore, selecting a saucepan of the appropriate size is essential to allow space for stirring without spillage or splashing.

Extreme care is required when moving a large saucepan, particularly when using the oven. Once removed from the oven, place the saucepan onto a suitable surface that is safe to check the sauce. If placing on the hob, make sure that it is not being placed on top of a fierce flame or heat. This would bring the stew to a rapid boil and potentially burn the base of the pan, catching the ingredients in this area and spoiling the flavour of the stew.

Take care when opening the lid of the saucepan when checking progress or finishing the stew as steam will escape and could cause scalding.

Always communicate with others in the kitchen when leaving hot saucepans on surfaces. It is very hard to identify the temperature of a saucepan by its appearance and a hot saucepan could cause a very nasty injury.

When stewing on the hob/range, ensure that the saucepan handle is not over a flame or direct heat source. If it was, this would become extremely hot and cause a nasty scald if touched by an unprotected hand.

 **CHEF'S TIP**

Once a liaison has been added to a sauce, the sauce cannot be allowed to boil as this would scramble the egg yolks and spoil the sauce. Therefore, it is recommended that the liaison is added at the latest possible moment before service.

CHEF'S TIP

Some kitchens use signage to communicate a hot pan. A small sprinkle of flour on the lid or handle is sometimes the method used to show that the saucepan is very hot.

CHEF'S TIP

It is also good practice to have saucepan handles directed inwards from the stove to avoid people colliding with them.

QUALITY POINTS TO LOOK FOR IN STEWED ITEMS

■ Main items are of even size (e.g. meat)

■ The appropriate colour is reached (e.g. for brown stews, the meat has colour/for white stews, the meat has been sealed without colour)

■ Food items are tender

■ There is a good ratio of sauce to items of food (meat, fish, fruit, etc.)

■ The sauce has a good consistency (not too thick or thin)

■ The sauce is not greasy

■ The stew has a good depth of flavour and is well seasoned

■ The stew is well presented at the correct temperature and in the correct, even portion sizes

Complete the following table stating the quality points that you would look for in the following stewed items.

ITEM/QUALITY POINTS	SIZE	COLOUR	TEXTURE	FLAVOUR/ TASTE	APPEARANCE/ PRESENTATION
Fricassée of chicken					
Navarin of lamb					
Bouillabaisse					
Fruit compote					

BRAISING

What is braising?

Braising is a very similar process to stewing. However, when braising, meat is usually left in joints or portion sized cuts rather than cut into pieces or dice, as it is when stewing. Braising always takes place in the oven and for the majority of the cooking time, the cooking vessel will have a lid on to seal in the liquids and flavours

THE METHODS AND EQUIPMENT USED TO BRAISE FOODS

Most meat-based braises follow the same basic steps. The meat or poultry is browned in hot fat. This helps to seal and develop flavour and retain nutritional values as well as providing an appetizing appearance. Aromatic vegetables (mirepoix) are usually browned as well. The cooking liquid is then added, which often includes an acidic element, such as tomatoes or wine. The pot is then covered and cooked in a gentle, moderate heat in the oven until tender. Often the cooking liquid is finished to create a sauce.

Braising meats also helps to kill harmful bacteria during the process, making the food safe to eat.

When braising commodities other than meat and poultry, the process is slightly different. This includes items such as vegetables (onions, leeks, celery), offal (sweetbreads, liver, oxtail) and rice.

For example, when braising vegetables such as onions and celery, the vegetable is usually blanched and then refreshed.

When braising foods it is important that the temperature of the oven is carefully controlled. A braised item should cook slowly in liquid that is barely simmering. The ideal temperature for braising is usually 160°C. Time is also

CHEF'S TIP

A bed of roots consists of vegetables such as carrots, leeks, celery and onions, normally sliced at an angle or into chunks to provide a large, flat cut, suitable to create a 'bed' for the item to be placed upon.

important to ensure that the item is cooked to the degree required without drying or burning. The structure of the item has to taken into consideration when braising. For example, a large item, such as a leg of lamb, will require a longer cooking time than smaller items, such as braised steaks. In addition to this, if the item is to be braised on the bone, this will also have to be taken into consideration. Checking the degree of cooking is essential during the braising process to ensure that the food remains in good condition and the cooking liquid is sufficient i.e. not dehydrating, boiling too rapidly, etc.

ASSOCIATED TECHNIQUES WHEN BRAISING FOODS

The techniques identified in stewing would also apply when braising. In addition to this, the following techniques are more applicable to braising.

- *Trussing and tying* – Trussing refers to the tying of poultry (chickens, ducks, etc.) to make them compact and to retain shape during the cooking process. This ensures that the bird will cook more evenly and presentation will be enhanced. Joints of meat are often tied to retain their shape during the cooking process. Joints are also tied when they have been boned out (had the bone removed). Examples of this include a boned and rolled shoulder or leg of lamb or silverside of beef.
- *Basting* – Basting refers to the regular spooning of sauce over the outside surface of the food item during the cooking process. This helps to keep the item moist and will enhance the colour of the item as it cooks.
- *Relaxing before carving* – Before carving meat or poultry, it is advisable to let it relax. This means that the meat or poultry can adapt to the change in temperature from the oven and its structure will begin to settle. Meat and poultry is very difficult to carve straight from the oven, not only due to its extremely hot temperature but because of the contraction of the muscle structure. Relaxing on a board in a hygienic and safe environment for up to 20 minutes will make the carving process much easier and therefore portion control and presentation much better.

ASSOCIATED PRODUCTS

Sauce

As with stewing, it is common practice that the braising liquid is served as a sauce to accompany the braised food item. This can be thickened at the beginning or the end of the cooking process depending on the recipe in question. For example, when braising steaks, it would be more likely that the sauce would be thickened at the beginning of the process whereas, when braising a joint of beef, a stock would be used as the braising liquid and this would be thickened towards the later stages of the cooking process.

QUALITY POINTS

- Not all cuts of meat are suitable for braising.
- As with stewing, it is the tougher and generally cheaper cuts that are particularly suitable for braising.

Step-by-step: **Braised rice**

STEP 1 The ingredients for braised rice – long-grain rice, onion, bay leaf, saffron (strands and ground), star anise and fresh thyme. Hot (boiling) stock is also required. A white chicken or a vegetable stock can be used.

STEP 2 Melt the butter (or oil) in a saucepan and then add the chopped onions. Fry gently until soft

STEP 3 If making a spiced variety, add the spices and herbs. If making plain braised rice, leave these ingredients out.

STEP 4 Stir in the additional flavourings to ensure an even coverage

STEP 5 Add the rice and stir in well to take on the flavourings from the onions and spices. This will also ensure the rice takes on the colour from the spices

STEP 6 Pour on the boiling stock to a ratio of two parts liquid to one part stock

STEP 7 Cover with a cartouche and place in a preheated hot oven (220°C) for 17–18 minutes

STEP 8 After this period of cooking, the rice will have absorbed the stock and no liquid should be left in the saucepan

STEP 9 Well braised rice should leave the grains individual and fluffy and will have taken on the additional flavourings from the spices (if used) and the stock

Whole braised items (multi-portion)

Upon removing the saucepan or braising vessel from the oven, the braised item will have to be taken out in order to carve it for service. This should also be planned before undertaking the task. Clean and appropriate tools should be used to remove the meat, such as a carving fork and spoon. This does not mean that the item is necessarily pierced with the fork as, ideally, it is preferable that the item retains its natural juices and flavours. Some of these would be lost if pierced, resulting in the potential loss of moisture and flavour.

Boards, knives and other small equipment should be clean and suitable for working with cooked meat products. Raw and cooked meats require different boards to avoid cross contamination from the raw to cooked food.

Step-by-step: **Braised celery**

STEP 1 Cut the root and tips from the celery. Wash and peel the outside of the celery before tying into portions

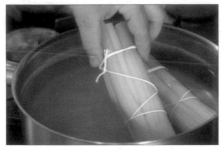

STEP 2 Blanch the celery in plenty of boiling salted water for approximately 10 minutes

STEP 3 Refresh by placing into ice-cold water

STEP 4 Sweat a mirepoix in a wide pan (large enough to fit the celery)

STEP 5 Add vegetable stock and a bouquet garni

STEP 6 Place the blanched celery into the stock and bring up to a simmer

STEP 7 Cover with a cartouche ensuring that the celery is submerged in the water

STEP 8 Cover with a lid and place in a medium oven (160°C) until tender

STEP 9 When cooked, remove with a slice. Remove the string, place into the serving dish or plate and strain the sauce into a clean saucepan

STEP 10 Dissolve some arrowroot or corn flour (starch) in a little cold water and stir to ensure that the starch is fully dissolved

STEP 11 Pour the arrowroot mixture gradually into the sauce, bringing the sauce to the boil each time until the correct consistency is achieved

STEP 12 Season the sauce with salt and freshly ground white pepper, pour over the celery and serve

Assessment of knowledge and understanding

1 Why it is important that meat is cut into even sized pieces when making a stew?

_____

2 Why is it important to use good quality stock when making a stew or braise?

_____

3 Identify four cooking liquids that can be used as a base for stews and braises.

i) _____ ii) _____

iii) _____ iv) _____

4 State two differences between a stew and a braise.

i) _____ ii) _____

5 What is the main purpose of a 'mirepoix' when making a stew or braise?

_____

6 What is the ideal oven temperature for cooking meat-based stews or braises?

_____

7 State the two ingredients that make up a liaison.

i) _____ ii) _____

8 Why is it essential not to allow a sauce to boil once a liaison has been added?

_____

9 Which cooking liquid would you associate with the production of a carbonnade?

_____

10 Name four commodities, other than meat or poultry, that can be braised.

i) _____ ii) _____

iii) _____ iv) _____

11 What type of heat is associated with braising?

☐ a. Convection ☐ b. Conduction ☐ c. Radiant ☐ d. Induction

12 Why is braising considered to be a nutricious cookery process in terms of healthy eating?

_____

13 Name four vegetables that can be braised successfully with menu examples.

i) _____ ii) _____

iii) _____ iv) _____

14 What steps could you take to ensure that meat did not dry out during the braising process?

_____

15 Name three pieces of small equipment that would be commonly used when braising foods.

i) _____ ii) _____

iii) _____

CHEF'S PROFILE

Name: ALAN BIRD

Position: Head Chef

Establishment: The Ivy Restaurant, I–5 West Street, London WC2H 9NQ

Training and experience:

1982–1986   West Lodge Park Hotel, Hertfordshire
Apprentice Chef for three years. Attended Southgate Technical College on part-time day release. Left as a Chef Tournant.

1986–1988   Goring Hotel, London
I joined the Goring as First Commis on the sauce section and was promoted to Chef Saucier in 1987. I gained 18 months experience in this position before leaving in 1988.

September 1988–August 1990   Simply Nicos, London SW1
I joined Simply Nicos as Chef De Partie on the fish section. I held this position until new premises were opened on May 1989 whereupon I was promoted to Sous Chef. In June 1990 I was promoted to Head Chef.

1990–1991   Andrew Lloyd Webber – I was personal chef to Mr Lloyd Webber.

1991–to date   The Ivy Restaurant, London WC1
I joined The Ivy as Sous Chef and became Head Chef in 1997.

Main responsibilities: I oversee the daily running of the following:

Creating, development, writing, costing and execution of Menus for the restaurant and private dining room.

Financial control of food cost/reporting.

Employment and recruitment of all kitchen staff.

Hygiene.

Health and safety.

Maintenance and upkeep of kitchen.

Best parts of the job: Cooking and being creative. Looking after your staff.

Secrets of a successful Chef: Be a good listener, work hard and do not be afraid to try different cooking techniques.

Recipe: Kedgeree

Your mentor or main inspiration: Mark Hix (Chef Director of Caprice Holdings)

A brief personal profile: Spend time with my family, travel, cooking demonstrations, mountain biking, movies and football

Kedgeree

INGREDIENTS	4 PORTIONS
For the curry sauce	
Butter	60g
Onion, finely chopped	½ onion
Garlic, crushed	1 clove
Fresh ginger, peeled and finely chopped	20g
Turmeric	1tsp
Ground cumin	1tsp
Curry powder	1tsp
Fennel seeds	10 seeds
Bay leaf	1 leaf
Pinch saffron threads	
Tomato purée	½ tsp
Fish stock	100ml
Double cream	250 ml
For the kedgeree	
Basmati rice	360g
Cumin seeds	1tsp
Smoked haddock fillet, lightly poached	350g
Salmon fillet, lightly poached	350g
Oyster mushrooms	300g
Eggs, poached	4 eggs
Chopped chives	15g

Method of work

1 For the curry sauce, melt 30g of the butter in a thick-bottomed pan and fry the onion, garlic and ginger without letting them brown.

2 Add all the spices and fry for another minute to release the flavours. Put in the tomato purée and fish stock and allow it to reduce by half.

3 Pour in the cream and simmer gently for 15 minutes.

4 Process the sauce in a blender, pass it through a fine strainer and check if it needs seasoning.

5 Wash the rice three times in cold water and cook it in plenty of boiling, salted water with the cumin seeds until it is al dente.

6 Drain it and return it to a pan off the heat with a lid on. (A little butter may be forked through it.)

7 To serve the Kedgeree, reheat the sauce and add the cooked, smoked haddock and pieces of salmon fillet. Meanwhile, sauté the oyster mushrooms in the remaining butter and add to the sauce.

8 Poach four eggs whilst reheating the rice.

9 Put the rice into a bowl, spoon over the fish then place a poached egg on top, sprinkle with chopped chives and serve.

RECIPES
Boeuf Bourguignon

INGREDIENTS		4 PORTIONS	10 PORTIONS
Stewing beef		500g	1250g
Dripping or oil		25g	65g
Onions		75g	175g
Carrots	} Mirepoix	75g	175g
Leeks		75g	175g
Celery		75g	175g
Flour		25g	65g
Tomato purée		1tbsp	2½tbsp
Red wine		750ml	1850ml
Bouquet garni		1	2
Salt and freshly ground black pepper			
Garnish			
Button onions		100g	250g
Button mushrooms		100g	250g
Bacon		100g	250g

Method of work

1 Cut any excess sinew and fat from the beef and cut into 1 inch cubes.
2 Season the meat and seal quickly in hot fat until browned and remove from the pan.
3 Fry the mirepoix to a golden brown colour before mixing in the flour.
4 Add the tomato purée and stir using a wooden spoon.
5 Gradually mix in the wine and bring to the boil.
6 Using a ladle, skim away any impurities.
7 Add the bouquet garni and replace the sealed cubes of meat.
8 Cover with a lid and simmer gently in the oven set at 160°C for 1½ to 2 hours (or until tender).
9 When cooked, place the meat into a clean pan, straining the sauce through a sieve into a separate pan.
10 Correct the consistency and seasoning of the sauce and pass on to the meat.

To prepare the garnish

1 Peel and trim the button onions before boiling for 10 minutes. Place in a frying pan with heated oil or butter and sauté until glazed.
2 Cut the button mushrooms in half and fry in a little oil or butter.
3 Cut the bacon into lardons (thin strips) and blanch by placing them into cold water and bringing them up to the boil. Refresh immediately, separating the lardons, before frying in a pan.

Note: Traditionally, heart shaped croutons are served with Boeuf Bourguignon. To achieve this, a stale loaf is carved into a heart shape and is then sliced. These slices are then fried in butter until crisp and lightly golden brown.

To serve

Place a portion of the beef dish on a plate or bowl and garnish with the glazed button onions, mushrooms, bacon lardons and croutons (if appropriate).

Braised celery

INGREDIENTS		4 PORTIONS	10 PORTIONS
Heads of celery		2	5
Onions		75g	175g
Carrots	Mirepoix	75g	175g
Leeks		75g	175g
Celery		75g	175g
Bouquet garni		1	2
White stock (vegetable/chicken)		250ml	600ml
Salt and freshly ground white pepper			

Method of work

1 Trim the celery heads and the root.

2 Peel the outside stalks and cut the heads to approximately 15 cm lengths.

3 Wash well under running cold water.

4 Place in a pan of boiling water and simmer for approximately 10 minutes. Refresh and rewash.

5 Place the mirepoix in a wide flat pan (e.g. sauteuse) and place the celery heads folded lengthways on top.

6 Barely cover with the stock and add the bouquet garni.

7 Cover with a buttered cartouche and a tight lid.

8 Bring to the boil and braise gently in the oven at 160°C until tender (approximately 1 hour).

9 Remove the celery from the pan, drain well and place in the serving dish.

10 Reduce the cooking liquor (an equal amount of jus can be added at this stage to enhance the flavour of the sauce. However, this would make the dish unsuitable for vegetarians).

11 Correct the consistency and seasoning.

12 Coat the celery with the sauce and serve.

Braised red cabbage

INGREDIENTS	4 PORTIONS	10 PORTIONS
Red cabbage, thinly sliced	600g	1.5kg
Red wine	80ml	200ml
Red wine vinegar	20ml	50ml
Onion, sliced	20g	50g
Unsalted butter	25g	65g
Brown sugar	10g	25g
Chicken stock	150ml	400ml
Clove	½	1
Peppercorns	25	60
Dessert apples, peeled, cored and sliced	1	2
Dry white wine	40ml	100ml
Salt and freshly ground pepper		

VIDEO CLIP
Braised red cabbage

Method of work

1 Season the cabbage with salt and pepper and marinate in the red wine and red wine vinegar for 4 hours.
2 Sweat the onion in the oil until transparent before adding the sugar. Sweat until well glazed.
3 Add the cabbage with its marinade and the chicken stock and transfer to a braising pan or dish. Wrap the clove and peppercorns in a piece of muslin and add to the cabbage.
4 Cover and braise at 170°C/325°F/ Gas mark 3 for 40 minutes, stirring occasionally.
5 Add the apple slices and white wine to the cabbage.
6 Braise for a further 30 to 40 minutes or until the cabbage is tender and all the liquid has evaporated.
7 Remove from the oven, take out the muslin bag and season to taste.
8 Serve

Braised steaks

INGREDIENTS		4 PORTIONS	10 PORTIONS
Stewing beef		500g	1250g
Vegetable oil		25ml	65ml
Onions		75g	175g
Carrots		75g	175g
Leeks	Mirepoix	75g	175g
Celery		75g	175g
Flour		25g	65g
Tomato purée		25g	65g
Brown stock		750ml	1750ml
Bouquet garni		1	2

Method of work

1 Cut away any excess sinew and fat from the beef.
2 Carefully slice into ½ inch thick steaks.
3 Season the steaks and seal quickly in hot fat until browned, then remove from the pan.
4 Fry the mirepoix to a golden brown colour before mixing in the flour.
5 Add the tomato purée and stir using a wooden spoon.
6 Gradually mix in the stock and bring to the boil.
7 Using a ladle, skim away any impurities.
8 Add the bouquet garni and replace the steaks in the sauce.
9 Cover with a lid and simmer gently in the oven, pre-set at 160°C for 1½ to 2 hours (or until tender).
10 When cooked, place the meat into a clean pan, straining the sauce through a sieve into a separate pan.
11 Correct the consistency and seasoning of the sauce and pass on to the meat.
12 Serve with appropriate garnishes and accompaniments (e.g. fresh noodles and vegetables).

VIDEO CLIP
Braised steaks

Fricassée of chicken

INGREDIENTS	4 PORTIONS
Chicken	1.5kg
Butter	50g
Vegetable oil	10ml
Flour	35g
Chicken stock	½ litre
Bouquet garni	1
Egg yolks	2
Cream or yoghurt	4tbsp
Salt and freshly ground white pepper	

Note:
Due to the fact that 1 chicken cut for sauté will provide 4 portions
(4 cuts from the leg and 4 from the breast), multiples for this recipe
will always have to be in 4.

Method of work

1   Cut the chicken for sauté and season with salt and pepper.
2   Place the butter in a sauté pan with a little vegetable oil and heat gently.
3   Add pieces of chicken in the order of thighs and drumsticks, followed by the two central breast pieces and the two half 'supremes'.
4   Cook gently on both sides without colouring and remove from the sauté pan, placing on a clean tray.
5   Mix the flour into the pan oils to form a paste (roux) and cook out carefully without colouring.
6   Gradually mix in the stock, stirring constantly to form a smooth and silky sauce.
7   Once sufficient stock has been added, bring to a simmer and skim off any impurities with a ladle.
8   Replace the chicken, add the bouquet garni and simmer gently until cooked.
9   Once cooked, remove the chicken and place into a clean pan.
10 Mix the egg yolks and cream in a small bowl. (This is referred to as a liaison.)
11 Pour a little boiling sauce on to the liaison and mix well.
12 Pour the liaison mixture back into the sauce and mix thoroughly. The sauce must not reboil at this stage or the egg yolks will curdle, spoiling the sauce.
13 Correct the sauce for seasoning and pass through a strainer over the chicken.
14 Reheat very carefully without boiling.
15 Each portion is made up of one piece of dark (leg) meat and one piece of light (breast meat). Serve with appropriate accompaniments and garnishes.

VIDEO CLIP
Fricassée of chicken

Irish stew

INGREDIENTS	4 PORTIONS	10 PORTIONS
Boneless lamb or mutton, cut into cubes (Boned shoulder or breast of mutton is ideal; however, lamb is probably more easily accessible)	800g	2kg
Potatoes, thinly sliced	800g	2kg
Onions, thinly sliced	3	8
Celery, cut into paysanne (small pieces)	100g	250g
Savoy cabbage, cut into paysanne (small pieces)	100g	250g
Leeks, cut into paysanne (small pieces)	100g	250g
Button onions	100g	250g
Chopped fresh thyme	1tbsp	3tbsp
Fresh flat-leaf parsley, chopped	2tbsp	5tbsp
Bay leaf	1	3
Salt and freshly ground black pepper		

Method of work

1 Arrange alternate layers of meat, sliced potatoes and onions in a flameproof casserole dish.
2 Season each layer with salt, pepper, thyme and parsley.
3 Add the bay leaf/leaves and pour in just enough water to cover.
4 Bring to the boil over a high heat, cover, lower the heat and simmer for ½ hour.
5 Add the remaining vegetables and continue to cook for 1 to 1¼ hours or until tender.
6 Skim off any impurities, correct the seasoning of the sauce and serve.

Gary Rhodes' beef and potatoes braised in Guinness

INGREDIENTS	4 PORTIONS
Olive oil for cooking	
Large onions, sliced	3
Pieces of chuck steak or braising beef	4 × 175g (6oz)–225g (8oz)
Flour for dusting	
Salt and pepper	
Guinness	440ml
Tablespoon muscavado sugar	1
Tin of beef consommé or stock	400ml
Large potatoes, peeled and halved	4

Method of work

1 Pre-heat the oven to 170°C 325°F / gas 3. Heat some olive oil in a large frying pan. Add the onions cook and over a moderate heat for a few minutes, until tender and golden brown. Transfer the onions to an oven-proof braising pot or casserole dish.

2 Toss the beef in the flour and season with salt and pepper. Heat a little more oil in the frying pan and fry the steaks until well coloured on all sides then transfer to the dish.

3 Pour the Guinness into the hot frying pan, stir to lift the residue from the base, sprinkle in the sugar. Add the consommé and simmer for a minute before pouring over the beef. Cover tightly with a lid and braise in the oven for 1½ hours. Add a little water if necessary to keep the meat covered with the liquor during cooking.

4 Add the potatoes and continue to braise for a further 1–1½ hours until the potatoes have absorbed and thickened the sauce and the beef is soft and tender.

Note: Serve the beef and potatoes with any green vegetable, such as steamed spinach or buttery cabbage. The sauce can be finished with chopped parsley.

Ratatouille

INGREDIENTS	4 PORTIONS	10 PORTIONS
Small aubergines (do not cut until required)	2	5
Courgettes, cut into cubes	2	5
Large onion, chopped roughly	1	3
Clove of garlic, crushed	1	3
Medium green pepper, deseeded and chopped into cubes	1	2
Medium red pepper, deseeded and chopped into cubes	1	2
Medium yellow pepper, deseeded and chopped into cubes	1	2
Tomatoes, blanched, peeled, quartered, deseeded and cut into large dice	6	15
Olive oil for frying		
Salt and freshly ground black pepper		
Chopped fresh basil	1tbsp	3tbsp

Method of work

1 Gently heat a little olive oil in a large heavy wide saucepan (sauteuse).

2 Add the onions and garlic and fry until translucent (see through).

3 While the onions and garlic are frying, cut the aubergines into cubes.

4 Add the peppers, aubergines and courgettes, cover and cook over a low heat for 25 minutes.

5 Add the tomatoes and continue cooking for a further 5 minutes. Serve sprinkled with freshly chopped basil.

VIDEO CLIP
Ratatouille

Note: A little fresh tomato sauce can be used to bind the vegetables together to produce a more 'stew' like dish. This would be added after the addition of the peppers, etc.

9
Prepare and cook food by baking, roasting and grilling

Unit 109 Prepare and cook food by baking, roasting and grilling

LEARNING OBJECTIVES

On completion of this chapter, learners will be able to:

- Describe the methods of baking, roasting and grilling
- Identify foods that can be baked, roasted and grilled
- Identify the most suitable type/s of equipment for baking, roasting and grilling
- Describe the techniques associated with baking, roasting and grilling
- State the points that require consideration when baking, roasting and grilling food
- List the quality points to look for in food that has been baked, roasted and grilled
- List the general safety points to follow when baking, roasting and grilling food

BAKING

What is baking?

Baking refers to foods that are cooked by placing them in a pre-heated oven. Food items to be baked are usually placed on a lightly oiled baking tray to prevent them from sticking during the cookery process. There are mats available which can sit on top of a baking tray and do not require the addition of oil. This is efficient in that it saves the chef a job, saves the cost of oil and promotes healthy eating.

Baked items have a variety of textures based on the type of food being produced. For example, a bread roll or loaf usually has a crust on the outside with a soft, light and airy texture to the cooked dough in the centre. On the other hand, a biscuit or pastry would have a firmer and snappier (shorter) texture, whereas when baking fruits and vegetables, such as an apple or potato, the skin would crisp while the centre would become moist and soft in texture.

The colour of baked items makes them pleasing to the eye and increases the desire to eat such items. For example, many breads and pastry products are light, golden brown in colour and crisp in texture. On the other hand, the egg custard in a baked crème caramel should be creamy in colour with a very soft, smooth and velvety texture.

THE METHODS AND EQUIPMENT USED TO BAKE FOODS

Many baked items require much preparation before they are baked. This is particularly the case when making fresh bread, pastry or baked egg custard dishes. The baking process is merely the cookery of the prepared item.

Step-by-step: **Baking a potato – 'Arlie'**

STEP 1 Clean the baking potato and score around the centre with a small sharp knife.

STEP 2 Place the potato onto a baking tray and bake in the oven until the potato is cooked. Tip – Use a small sharp knife to test to see if the potato is cooked. It should have little resistance beyond piercing the skin.

STEP 3 Cut the cooked potato in half lengthways

STEP 4 Using a spoon, scoop out the flesh from the potato

STEP 5 Using a scraper, press the cooked potato flesh through a drum sieve

STEP 6 Season the sieved potato with salt and freshly ground white pepper and enrich the potato mix with a little melted butter

STEP 7 The ingredients for the potato filling – chopped onions, quartered button mushrooms, diced chicken breast, lardons of pancetta (dry cured crispy bacon), thyme, cheddar cheese and double cream

STEP 8 Sweat the onions, add the chicken breast followed by the mushrooms, pancetta and thyme. Pour in the double cream and bring to the boil. The cream will thicken as it cooks. Once this is ready, add the grated cheddar

STEP 9 Place the empty potato skins onto a baking tray and fill the shells with the chicken based filling

STEP 10 Pipe the pureed potato neatly on top of the filling

STEP 11 An example of the filled potato and one with the potato piped on top

STEP 12 Gratinate under a medium salamander and serve

The preparation of equipment when baking products is very important. For example, having the oven pre-heated to the correct temperature is essential so that the product starts to cook as soon as it is placed into the oven. Failure to do this will have a damaging effect on the finished product.

The heat, when baking, is often described as a dry heat and sometimes referred to as convection. In this case the oven is assisted by a fan within the oven itself to circulate the heat evenly throughout the oven chamber. This helps to ensure that foods are cooked evenly.

Some baked products benefit from the addition of steam within the oven chamber. This is referred to as a 'humid' oven. In modern baking ovens, this facility is a built in feature. An example of a product that can benefit from the addition of steam is bread. In this instance, an injection of steam in the final stages of cooking produces a crusty surface to the bread.

Baking in a bain-marie

A third method of baking uses a water bath, referred to as a bain-marie. This is particularly good for egg based products, such as egg custards, and hot mousses, when a crust is not wanted. These types of products are usually moulded before they are cooked. The water is placed in a suitable tray and is there to protect the egg custard or mousse from burning, scrambling or drying.

Baking is a versatile method of cookery as there are so many products that can be produced using this method. This applies to both savoury and sweet products.

Step-by-step: **Bread rolls**

STEP 1 The ingredients to make a batch of bread rolls – strong flour, sugar, butter, fresh yeast, warm water (35–37°C), salt

STEP 2 Sieve the flour into a bowl and add the sugar and salt. Fold in the butter.

STEP 3 Place the yeast in a small bowl and cream in a little of the warm water

STEP 4 Make a well in the flour and pour in the creamed yeast. Allow this to start fermenting (Small bubbles will appear)

STEP 5 Mix the yeast into the flour and bring together to form a dough

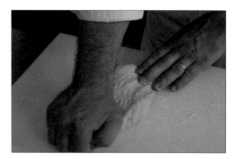

STEP 6 Place the dough onto a clean surface and knead to stretch the gluten. The dough should be slightly moist and elastic.

STEP 7 Form the kneaded dough into a ball and place into a clean bowl. Cover with a warm damp cloth and leave to prove, ideally in a proover. The dough should double in size

STEP 8 Proove the dough in a warm and moist environment (ideally a prooving cabinet) until the dough has doubled in size. This is referred to as the bulk fermentation time (BFT)

STEP 9 Once proven, take the dough from the bowl and gently knead to remove the carbon dioxide produced during the initial fermentation

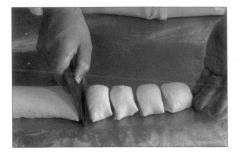

STEP 10 Roll into a log thin piece of dough and cut into evenly sized pieces of dough using a pastry cutter/scraper. These can be weighed to ensure evenly sized and weighted rolls.

STEP 11 Press each piece of dough firmly into a lightly floured work surface and shape into a roll by rolling in the palm of your hand

STEP 12 Place the moulded rolls neatly onto a greased baking tray and brush with egg wash (beaten egg with milk). Tip – The rolls can be shaped into knots, plaits, etc. at this stage if desired.

STEP 13 Sprinkle with seeds for additional flavour and to enhance appearance.

STEP 14 Bake in a pre-heated oven at 200ºC until cooked. The rolls should be light golden brown and sound hollow when tapped at the bottom of the roll. Place the cooked rolls onto a cooling rack to cool down.

ACTIVITY

Name a dish or item that is baked in the following categories:

CATEGORY	DISH/ITEM
Savoury dough product	
Sweet dough product	
Fruit	
Potato dish	
Sweet pastry	
Short pastry	
Savoury egg custard	
Sweet egg custard	

Step-by-step: **Crème caramel**

STEP 1 To make the caramel, place granulated sugar into a heavy saucepan (ideally a copper sugar pan) and dissolve in water. Bring this to the boil and cook until a light caramel is achieved

STEP 2 Once a caramel is achieved, stop the cooking process by placing the pan base into cold water. A little cold water can also be added to the caramel itself. Pour a little caramel into the base of the dariole moulds and leave to set.

STEP 3 Cut the vanilla pod in half lengthways and, using the tip of a small knife, scrape the tiny seeds from the pod

STEP 4 Place the milk into a saucepan and add the vanilla seeds and bring to the boil

STEP 5 The ingredients for making the egg custard – eggs, milk, sugar and vanilla

STEP 6 Beat the eggs and sugar together in a bowl

STEP 7 Once the milk has boiled, pour over the egg and sugar mixture whilst whisking to ensure even distribution and so that the eggs do not cook (scramble) as you add the hot milk

STEP 8 Strain the mixture through a fairly fine chinois to remove any bits of coagulated egg, etc. and then ladle on top of the set caramel in the dariole moulds

STEP 9 Place the moulds into a water bath (bain-marie) and bake in a low oven until set (150˚C for approximately 30 minutes)

STEP 10 Once the custard has set, remove the tray from the oven and carefully take each mould out of the bain-marie. Cool before serving

 **HEALTH & SAFETY**

Always have a thick, dry cloth to handle a hot the saucepan. Always stand back from the caramel when adding water as the caramel is likely to spit a little

ASSOCIATED TECHNIQUES WHEN BAKING FOODS

■ *Greasing* – Grease, usually oil or butter, is lightly brushed around the surface of the tray or tin to prevent food items from sticking.

■ *Marking* – Certain baked items are marked to aid presentation of the finished item. An example of this is shortbread. Marks can also provide an indication as to where the item should be cut, if being cut or split into portions.

■ *Loading* – This refers to the loading of the oven, making efficient use of the space available on the oven tray and of the shelves within the oven itself.

■ *Brushing* – Brushing baked items with egg wash, milk or sugar syrup will enhance the presentation and, in the case of the sugar syrup, sweeten the flavour of the item. Egg wash will enhance the colour of the item whereas the sugar will produce a shiny finish. Baked items are brushed at different stages of the cooking process according to the finish required. For example, to enhance the colour of a loaf of bread, it could be brushed with egg wash or milk in advance of cooking whereas to provide a shine to a fruit bun, the glaze would be brushed on at the end of the process.

■ *Cooling* – To prevent baked items from becoming soggy, they are placed onto cooling racks once they have been taken out of the oven. This will also help to stabilize the item, helping, for example, bread rolls to relax into their shape and pastry items to become crisp (short).

■ *Finishing* – This refers to the final steps to make the product as appealing as possible. Some baked items will benefit from dusting with icing sugar, whereas others, such as a fruit tartlet, will be enhanced by brushing with a glaze, such as apricot.

CONSIDERATIONS WHEN BAKING FOODS

Baking is quite a technical process. It is scientific in the way that the ingredients are proportioned and also in the way they are prepared. Both of these points will have an effect as to how the item will react when placed into heat. Any adjustment to the recipe, method of preparation, the temperature and cooking time will result in differences to the finished product – e.g. texture (light, heavy, soft, crisp, airy, tight), colour (light, dark), etc. This is why the following points are so important:

1 Pre-heat ovens to the temperature specified in the recipe.

2 Use a reliable set of scales and weigh ingredients accurately.

3 Prepare all other pieces of equipment required, such as bowls, mixing machines, spoons, trays and tins, cooling racks, etc.

4 Follow the recipe accurately, handling items according to instructions, e.g. kneading bread or lightly mixing pastry.

5 Have any finishing or decorative items ready to complete the process.

CHEF'S TIP

Avoid opening oven doors too often as this will reduce the temperature inside the oven and could affect the item being baked. It is also important that oven doors are not slammed closed as the air movement can have a damaging affect on more delicate items such as cakes and sponges.

QUALITY POINTS TO LOOK FOR IN BAKED ITEMS

■ Depending on the product being made, the desired finishes can be very different in colour, texture and flavour.

Step-by-step: **Apple tart**

STEP 1 The ingredients to make the apple puree (marmalade) – peeled and sliced apple, water, sugar, butter and ground cinnamon

STEP 2 Add all the ingredients to a suitably sized saucepan

STEP 3 Cook over a low to moderate heat, stirring constantly until the apple has softened. Using a wooden spoon, beat to a puree and cool

STEP 4 The ingredients to make the pastry – soft flour, butter, sugar and water. Note – for a richer pastry, egg can be used to replace the water

STEP 5 Sieve the flour and cut the butter into small dice. Lightly crumb these two ingredients together

STEP 6 Add the sugar and water (or egg) together and add to the crumbed mixture

STEP 7 Gently bring the mix together (do not knead!) and form into a ball. Wrap in cling film and leave in the refrigerator to relax

STEP 8 On a cool, lightly floured surface, form the pastry into a circular shape and gently roll out, turning by 90° after each roll

STEP 9 Check to ensure that the pastry is rolled enough to cover the base and sides of the flan ring

STEP 10 Roll around a rolling pin and then out and across the flan ring Note – the flan ring and baking tray should be lightly greased to prevent sticking

STEP 11 Push the pastry into the inside corners of the flan ring to take on the shape of the ring

STEP 12 Using a rolling pin, roll over the top of the flan ring. This will take off the excess pastry at the top of the ring

STEP 13 For a decorative finished effect, the edge of the pastry can be crimped between the fingers as shown
Note – At this stage the pastry can be partially or fully cooked by using a cartouche and baking beans to retain the shape of the pastry before finishing with the apple puree and sliced apples, etc. This would produce a very crisp pastry as a finished tart.

STEP 14 Fill with the apple puree

STEP 15 Peel and core some apple/s and slice neatly. Carefully arrange the sliced apple on top of the apple puree

VIDEO CLIP
Making pastry

STEP 16 Brush with some sugar glaze and sprinkle with a little more sugar

STEP 17 Bake in a pre-heated oven at 200°C until cooked. The sliced apples should lightly brown at the edge of each slice

ROASTING

What is roasting?

Roasting is one of the methods associated with the traditions of British cookery. Roast Beef with Yorkshire Pudding and Horseradish Sauce is known throughout the culinary world as a great British classic.

Roasting is the cooking of food in a dry heat with the addition of oil or fat. Roasting can take place either in an oven or on a spit, e.g. spit roasted pig. Roasting enhances the natural flavours in foods, particularly meats. The smell of roast beef or a roast chicken is very distinguishable and, for people who enjoy eating meat and poultry, this can certainly get the senses going and whet the appetite.

Roasting meats also helps to kill harmful bacteria during the process, making the food safe to eat. The usual process for roasting is to seal the outside of the food. Once sealed, the temperature is usually reduced to finish the cooking process without drying the surface of the meat.

Roasting as a process also enhances the presentation of foods. A roast chicken, for example, has an appealing light golden brown appearance. Roasted vegetables also achieve enhanced presentation. When roasting bell peppers, for example, the skin blisters and colours while the flesh naturally sweetens. Roasting is therefore an excellent process to enhance the presentation of foods while naturally developing their flavours.

CHEF'S TIP

When turning roast meats in the oven, do not puncture the flesh by inserting a carving fork. This will break the seal described in the text by puncturing the flesh, resulting in the loss of natural juices.

THE METHODS AND EQUIPMENT USED TO ROAST FOODS

There are two main methods associated with roasting.

1 Oven roasting 2 Spit roasting.

Oven roasting

The first method is roasting using a conventional oven or convection oven, in which the heat is distributed throughout the oven chamber to produce an even heat. In this example, food items are usually placed into a roasting tray with the addition of oil or fat. Depending on the items being cooked, the tray and oil might be heated before adding the food items. Roast potatoes provide a good example where the oil or fat would usually be heated first. This ensures that the potatoes immediately start to seal on the outside surface, frying in the heat of the oil. Once in the oven, this will produce a crisp surface to the outside of the potato while the heat from the oven will penetrate to the centre.

To prevent meat or poultry from frying by being in direct contact with hot oil or fat while roasting in the oven, a trivet can be used to provide a gap

VIDEO CLIP
Roasting a shoulder of lamb

Step-by-step: **Roast leg of lamb**

STEP 1 The ingredients for roasting a leg of lamb – leg of lamb, garlic, rosemary, vegetable/olive oil, vegetables for the trivet (carrots, onions, leeks, garlic)

STEP 2 With a boning knife, cut around the shin bone in a circular motion

STEP 3 Scrape the skin and flesh back away from the bone to expose the clean bone

STEP 4 Using a small, sharp knife, make small incisions into the flesh of the joint. Place small sprigs of rosemary into the incisions

STEP 5 Cut fine slices from the peeled garlic cloves and place a slice next to each sprig of rosemary

STEP 6 Wrap a piece of kitchen foil around the exposed bone to prevent it from burning during the roasting process

STEP 7 Prepare the trivet by cutting the vegetables into fairly large pieces as shown (mirepoix)

STEP 8 Cut the bulb of garlic through the centre and place in the centre of the trivet. Place the prepared leg of lamb onto the trivet

STEP 9 Brush the meat with oil and pour a small ladle of oil around the base of the roasting tray to prevent sticking. Season the lamb with salt and freshly ground black pepper and place in a preheated oven at 200°C

STEP 10 Throughout the roasting process, baste the meat by pouring the oil and roasting juices from the roasting tray back over the lamb. Do this every 15 to 20 minutes

STEP 11 Check the degree of cooking by inserting a temperature probe into the core of the meat

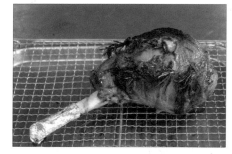

STEP 12 Once cooked, place the lamb onto a rack to relax in a warm environment for at least 10 minutes before carving. The core temperature of the meat will remain safe and this will allow the structure of the meat time to relax and become less tense (taut), making carving much easier and more efficient

between the base of the roasting tray and the item being cooked. A trivet could be in the form of a rack or vegetables, such as carrots, leeks, celery and onions, normally sliced at an angle or into chunks to provide a large, flat cut, suitable to provide a 'bed' for the item to be placed on.

When roasting foods it is important that the temperature of the oven is carefully controlled. Time is also important to ensure that the item is cooked to the degree required without drying or burning. The structure of the item must be taken into consideration. For example, a large item will require a longer cooking time that a small item. In the case of meat, if the item is to be roasted on the bone, this will also have to be taken into consideration. In addition, red meats can be cooked to various degrees from underdone, where the flesh will be pink, to cooked through (more thoroughly cooked) where the meat will be a darker colour. To check the degree of cooking, a temperature probe can be inserted into the meat to determine the temperature in the centre of the meat and provide an indication as to the degree at which the item is cooked.

(Please see page 201 for a checklist of beef cuts.)

CHEF'S TIP

Poultry refers to domestically reared birds for the purpose of eating. Examples include chicken, turkey and duck.

Spit roasting

Spit roasting usually involves larger items such as whole items (e.g. pig → hog-roast), cuts or birds (such as chickens) being placed onto a spit (large skewer) and rotated (continuously turned) over the heat source. This could be a radiant heat from electricity of gas bars or an open fire of wood or charcoal. Therefore, it can be an indoor or outdoor activity. This particular method of cookery is associated with a larger number of customers due to the size of the item being cooked; an outdoor celebration or festival, for example.

ASSOCIATED TECHNIQUES WHEN ROASTING FOODS

■ *Stuffing* – This refers to stuffing the meat or poultry. Stuffings can be made from a variety of ingredients, such as sausage-meat, vegetables, fruit, cereals and grains to provide a variety and contrast in flavours. It is important, particularly if using any meat products, that stuffing is

Step-by-step: **Roast chicken**

STEP 1 Roughly crush a few cloves of garlic

STEP 2 Peel the zest from a fresh lemon

STEP 3 Remove the wish-bone from the chicken and stuff the cavity of the chicken with the lemon and garlic

STEP 4 Place a trivet of vegetables into a roasting tray. Place the prepared chicken on top of the trivet and baste with vegetable oil. Season the chicken with salt and freshly ground black pepper

STEP 5 Roast the chicken in a pre-heated oven at 200°C, basting on a regular basis and turning the chicken throughout to ensure that the legs of the chicken are sufficiently roasted.

STEP 6 Once cooked, place the chicken onto a rack to relax in a warm environment for at least 10–15 minutes before carving. The core temperature of the chicken will remain safe and this will allow the structure of the chicken time to relax and become less tense (taut), making carving much easier and efficient

 VIDEO CLIP Roasting a chicken

thoroughly cooked before serving. A safe way to cook stuffings, particularly when serving with poultry (chicken), is to cook the stuffing separately. The stuffing can then be carved and served alongside the meat.

■ *Trussing* – Trussing refers to the tying of chickens to make them compact and retain their shape during the cooking process. This ensures that the bird will cook more evenly and presentation will be enhanced. Traditionally, poultry was tied with string using a trussing needle to pierce the chicken in key places to hold the bird tightly together. Poultry in current times is often trussed with elastic bands, especially if it is purchased for the domestic (household) market.

■ *Tying* – Joints of meat are often tied to retain their shape during the cooking process. Joints are also tied when they have been boned out (had the bone removed). Examples of this include a boned and rolled shoulder or leg of lamb or silverside of beef.

■ *Basting* – Basting refers to the regular spooning of fat or oil and cooking juices over the outside surface of the food item during the cooking process. This helps to keep the item moist and will enhance the colour of the item as it cooks. Fat within the meat itself will melt and pour away from the meat during the roasting process. This will assist in keeping the meat moist but it is also beneficial because the fat content is reduced.

■ *Relaxing before carving* – Meat and poultry is very difficult to carve straight from the oven, not only due to its extremely hot temperature but because of the contraction of the muscle structure. Relaxing on a board in a hygienic and safe environment for approximately 20 minutes will make the carving process much easier and therefore portion control and presentation are improved.

TABLE OF TEMPERATURES

	RARE	MEDIUM	WELL-DONE
Beef Sirloin, topside/ top rump, rib, silverside, brisket	20 mins per 450g/½kg(1lb) + 20 mins Approximate internal temp: 60°C	25 mins per 450g/½kg(1lb) + 25 mins Approximate internal temp: 70°C	30 mins per 450g/½kg(1lb) + 30 mins Approximate internal temp: 80°C
Lamb Loin, shoulder, leg, rack, shanks, breast		25 mins per 450g/½kg(1lb) + 25 mins Approximate internal temp: 70–75°C	30 mins per 450g/½kg(1lb) + 30 mins Approximate internal temp: 75–80°C
Pork Loin, shoulder, leg, belly, hock		30 mins per 450g/½kg(1lb) + 30 mins Approximate internal temp: 75–80°C	35 mins per 450g/½kg(1lb) + 35 mins Approximate internal temp: 80–85°C

ASSOCIATED PRODUCTS

Gravy or jus

During the roasting process, roasting juices and sediment (deposits) from meat and poultry will be captured in the roasting tray along with oils and fats. Once the meat or poultry is removed from the roasting tray to relax, the natural juices and sediment should be retained to enhance the flavour of the accompanying sauce. However, the fats and oils need to be removed or the sauce would be greasy and oily. These fats and oils naturally rise to the surface and will be found on top of any natural roasting juices. Therefore, if the roasting tray is tipped at an angle, all the liquid will slide to the lowest point in the tray. At this point it will be possible to carefully spoon off the oil and discard.

The tray is now ready to make a gravy or jus to accompany the roasted meat or poultry. This is usually achieved by the addition of a suitably flavoured stock and reduced. The liquid would then be strained to remove any sediment and adjusted in terms of seasoning, colour and consistency (thickness).

Accompaniments

Most roasted meats are enhanced by accompaniments such as mustards. However, certain roast meats are traditionally associated with a particular accompaniment which is thought to aid digestion or specifically enhance the meat. An example of this is roast beef and horseradish sauce.

Health and safety requirements

When roasting, the roasting tray should be of a suitable size for the job in hand. This will allow easy access to the food without causing difficulties that could lead to an accident. A roasting tray that is too large will burn in the empty spaces. This would impair and spoil the accompanying sauce if the roasting tray used to produce the sauce using the natural roasting juices and sediment. The meat itself may also get tainted by burnt fumes.

ACTIVITY

Match up the following roast meats with the traditional accompanying sauce

Roast pork	Bread sauce
Roast turkey	Apple sauce
Roast lamb	Horseradish sauce
Roast beef	Mint sauce
Roast duck	Cranberry sauce
Roast chicken	Orange sauce

QUALITY POINTS

- Not all cuts of meat are suitable for roasting. Cuts that are particularly high in muscle and fat will toughen during the process and will be chewy and potentially unpleasant to eat. However, fat is a requirement during the roasting process in order for the meat or poultry to remain moist. This is why it is particularly important that regular basting takes place when cooking lean joints and poultry.

- When sealing meat, it is recommended that external seasonings are added after the initial sealing process has taken place. This will prevent a delay in the browning of the item. Once the item is coloured sufficiently, it should then be seasoned lightly with salt and pepper to enhance the flavour.

Upon removing the tray from the oven, the roasted item will have to be removed from the tray. This should also be planned before undertaking the task. Clean and appropriate tools should be used such as a carving fork and spoon. This does not mean that the item is necessarily pierced with the fork as, ideally, it is preferable that the item retains its natural juices and flavours. Some of these would be lost if pierced resulting in the potential loss of moisture and flavour.

Raw and cooked meats require different boards to avoid cross contamination from the raw to cooked food.

GRILLING

What is Grilling?

Grilling is the cooking of food items by radiant heat. This refers to the heat source transferring heat directly towards the food item being grilled.

THE METHODS AND EQUIPMENT USED TO GRILL FOODS

There are three main processes applied when grilling foods. The first is grilling where the heat source is above the food and is referred to as grilling by salamander.

Contact grill

True grill (flame grill/barbeque)

The second method of grilling is where the heat comes from beneath the food item. Examples of this method include a barbeque, whether fuelled by charcoal, wood, gas or electricity, and char-grills which are often used in restaurant kitchens. These grills are sometimes referred to as 'true grills'.

The third method of grilling is where the food item is place between the sources of heat. Examples include a contact grill where an item such as a chicken breast could be placed between the plates of the grill. This type of grill is currently popular in the domestic market as it involves very little use of fat. In addition to this, any fats or oils that come away from the food during the cooking process are drained away leaving a very lean cooked product.

CHEF'S TIP

If using wooden kebab skewers, it is recommended that they are soaked in water for a few hours to help prevent them from burning during the grilling process

Grilling by salamander

As with most other cookery processes, it is important that the salamander is pre-heated before cooking commences. Salamanders are fitted with a transferable shelf usually consisting of a rack or grill bars and a tray. These can sometimes be in one contained unit or the shelf can be separate from the tray. In this situation, as an item is being grilled, any fats or liquids that come away from the food fall between the gaps in the rack or bars and are collected by the tray underneath.

With items such as kidneys or bacon, it may be more appropriate to place them on a tray to grill them, as these items could potentially fall between

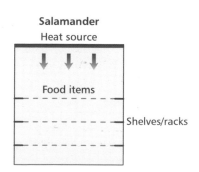

Salamander

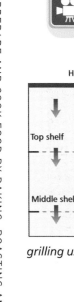

the gaps if placed on bars. In this situation, it is important that such items are placed on a tray that is suitable for catching fats and other liquids as they will inevitably come out of the food during the cooking process, i.e. a tray with a lip.

When cooking large but fairly delicate items such as whole fish, the use of a double wired cage is often used. This enables easy handling of the fish, particularly when turning, and will help to hold the shape of the fish, preventing it from curling under the heat and burning.

Salamanders are also used for 'flashing' food. This refers to a short, intense period where items can be placed under the salamander to raise the temperature of the item concerned. Great care is required in this situation as, if left too long, the food item could potentially burn, dry out and lose eating quality. The second purpose would be to 'gratinate' foods. This is when food is placed under the salamander to brown, providing an attractive glaze to the dish, e.g. cheese lightly browned (gratinated) on the top of a dish of pasta.

The radiant heat generated from a salamander is hotter towards the top of the grill, where it is closer to the source of the heat, becoming less hot the further away from the heat source. Therefore, if an item is to be cooked very quickly, it should be placed on a shelf close to the top of the salamander. On the other hand, if the item requires cooking for a longer period, it should be placed on a shelf nearer to the bottom of the salamander. The power of the heat source can also be controlled in a similar way to a control on a gas or electric hob, i.e. the size of the flame or the heat of the ring.

VIDEO CLIP
Cooking lamb cutlets under a salamander

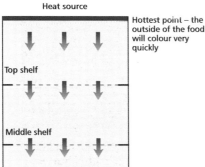

Heat source

Hottest point – the outside of the food will colour very quickly

Top shelf

Middle shelf

grilling using a salamander

Grilling by true grill (char-grill)/barbeque

Once again, it is very important that these types of grills are pre-heated so that food items begin to cook immediately on contact. When using these grills, food items are usually placed directly onto the bars above the source of the heat. Some grills, such as a barbeque may have shelving options to raise or lower the height of the food. Fixed grills, as found in many restaurant kitchens, will not have this option and it will require the skill, knowledge and experience of the chef to place the food item on the grill according to how it is to be cooked. Although different parts of the grill will be hotter than others, it is possible to reduce the source of power (gas or electricity) by reducing the input, although the bars will retain their heat for a long time.

VIDEO CLIP
Grilling steaks on a charcoal grill

These types of grills leave the distinctive 'grill lines' on food often in a criss-cross pattern where the food has been turned. Food cooked in this way will also have the distinctive flavour of grilled food, particularly if barbecued as the charcoal or lump-wood produces a smoky flavour that is transferred into the food. The flavour is also enhanced as natural fats, oils and juices fall from the food and onto the heat source, resulting in a flame being produced and shortly catching the food (flame grilled). If this process is controlled, this produces a very pleasant and unique taste to the item being grilled.

When grilling in this manner, the bars on the grill (or the food itself) are usually lightly oiled to prevent the food items from sticking.

A true grill

Step-by-step: **Preparing kidneys for grilling**

STEP 1 A tray of lamb's kidney's

STEP 2 From the side of the kidney, use a small, sharp knife to cut into the centre of the kidney

STEP 3 Using a pair of kitchen scissors, cut away the fatty tissue in the centre of the kidney

STEP 4 Repeat this process with the remaining kidneys

STEP 5 Using cocktail sticks, secure each kidney by inserting two cocktail sticks at 90° from one another across the kidney

STEP 6 Place onto a lightly greased tray, brush the kidneys with melted butter and season with salt and freshly ground black pepper. Grill as required

Step-by-step: **Preparing vegetable kebabs**

STEP 1 Cut the peppers in half and remove the stalk and seeds

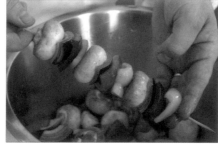

STEP 2 Cut the peppers into large dice

STEP 3 Remove the stalks from the mushrooms

STEP 4 Cut red onions into quarters, remove the root and cut each quarter in half

STEP 5 Mix the vegetables together in a bowl. Lightly oil (olive) and season with salt and freshly ground black pepper. Neatly skewer the vegetables alternately onto kebab skewers

STEP 6 Place onto a lightly oiled grilling tray and place under the grill (salamander) until cooked

Grilling is also considered to promote healthy eating as it requires very little in terms of additional ingredients. Natural fats within the food items themselves also melt during the grilling process and fall from the food naturally reducing the fat content of the finished item.

Foods suitable for grilling

Grilling is a particularly intense method of cooking in that items are usually cooked at high temperatures for a fairly short amount of time. Therefore, commodities such as meat have to be of high quality and low in muscle and connective tissue. These are referred to as the prime cuts of meat. Poultry, particularly breasts of poultry and cuts free from bone are most suitable for grilling as they are low in muscular structure. However, it is possible to grill a chicken on the bone if it has been prepared correctly (e.g. spatchcock). In this situation, it is important that the grilling process is closely monitored to ensure that the chicken is sufficiently cooked without drying out or burning.

A cut of meat high in muscular structure would retract (tighten) when exposed to the heat from the grill and become tough and unpleasant or difficult to eat.

Other suitable meat items include bacon, sausages and other mince-based meat products such as burgers and grill steaks. Certain offal are also suitable for grilling due to the structures of the items concerned.

Due to its delicate structure most types of fish are suitable for grilling. Obviously, larger fish, such as a tuna or salmon would have to be cut down into, for example, a darne (fish steak) or supreme (cut from the fillet), whereas it is possible to grill smaller fish such as sardines, mackerel and small trout from whole.

Many vegetables are also suitable for grilling, particularly tomatoes, mushrooms, courgettes, bell peppers and aubergines. Other vegetables, particularly ones with less water content would tend to dry and burn, so would be unsuitable for grilling as the initial method of cookery. Examples include French beans (haricots verts), cauliflower, broccoli, corn and potatoes. However, once these items are cooked, it is perfectly feasible that they could be sauced and placed under the grill to gratinate.

ASSOCIATED TECHNIQUES WHEN GRILLING FOOD

■ *Batting out* – Batting out refers to the use of a meat bat to make the item of meat even in thickness and also to break down connective tissue in the meat itself, making the item concerned more tender to eat. This process usually involves the item being placed between two sheets of cling film for protection before the bat is used in a firm motion until the item is of the shape and size required. In this situation, the item will naturally become wider and longer but thinner and this is dependent on the degree to which the bat is used.

■ *Oiling, greasing and basting* – To prevent items from sticking to grill bars or racks they are often lightly oiled or greased before cooking. It is also advisable that the grill bars themselves are lightly oiled before and after use. If food sticks to a grill bar, the point of contact will rip the surface away from the food as it is lifted and remain stuck to the grill bar. Food that is low in natural fat can continue to be lightly oiled throughout the grilling process to ensure that it retains a moist external surface and does not dry out. This process is referred to as basting.

■ *Traying up* – Food items, such as bacon, sausages and tomatoes, would usually be placed on lightly oiled or greased trays if they were being grilled under a salamander, when preparing multiple breakfasts, for example. When traying up, it is important to consider space for turning items and making full use of the space at hand. Items that have been floured, such as fish fillets, or crumbed (pané) such as a chicken supreme, would also be placed on lightly oiled trays before being placed under the salamander.

■ *Marinating* – To impart additional flavours to foods which are to be grilled, they can be soaked in what is referred to as a marinade. A marinade is usually a flavoured liquid into which food items, such as meat, poultry and fish, may be placed to absorb the flavours concerned. This process can take some time and will increase in strength the longer the food is left in the marinade. Marinades can be produced from bases of wine, vinegar, yoghurt and oils to name but a few possibilities. They can also be flavoured with herbs and spices to add another dimension to the flavour of the item being grilled. Chicken breast, for example, is quite commonly marinated as it absorbs flavours well and this can completely transform its flavour. A marinade can also help to break down the connective structure within meat, making it more tender to eat once cooked.

CONSIDERATIONS WHEN GRILLING FOODS

Shelf position

Shelf position is particularly important when grilling foods. The closer food is to the heat source, the faster it will cook as the heat will be more intense. However, the thickness of the food item also has to be taken into consideration. If the food item was very thin, such as a fillet of plaice or an escalope of chicken, the time it would take to seal the outside of the food would usually be sufficient for heat to go through to the centre of the food. This would ensure that the item is cooked through while retaining moisture and a pleasant texture. If such items were placed towards the bottom shelf of the grill, where the heat would not be so intense, by the time the outside of the item was sealed, the item would, in all probability, be dry and much less pleasant to eat.

On the other hand, when cooking a thicker item such as a fillet steak, consideration has to be taken as to where the steak would be placed within the

DEGREE OF COOKING	APPEARANCE OF THE STEAK
Rare	The steak is well sealed on the outside. Once the steak is cut open, the internal meat is not cooked through with almost raw meat towards the centre of the steak.
Medium-rare	The steak is well sealed on the outside. Once the steak is cut open, the internal meat is undercooked with meat that is red in colour towards the centre of the steak.
Medium	The steak is well sealed on the outside. Once the steak is cut open, the internal meat is very slightly undercooked with meat that is pink towards the centre of the steak.
Well done	The steak is well sealed on the outside. Once the steak is cut open, the internal meat is cooked through showing no signs of red or pink meat towards the centre of the steak.

salamander or grill. This is because red meats can be cooked to varying degrees and still remain safe to eat. For example, when ordering a fillet steak in a restaurant, it would be customary that you would be asked how you would like the item to be cooked.

Time and temperature are therefore key considerations when grilling foods. The structure, size and, in some cases, degree of cooking, has to be taken into account when grilling foods.

Health and safety considerations when using a salamander

Moving items in a salamander

As food items are grilled, they will release fats and natural juices. These will fall onto the grilling tray and will become very hot. Therefore, it is essential that trays are moved carefully so that these liquids are not spilled causing injury. The tray itself will also become very hot so a clean, thick and dry oven cloth should be used to hold the tray and protect the hands.

Placing items on top of a salamander

When a salamander is in use, the top casing will become extremely hot. This is not always visually clear as there is no flame evident and the surface will not change colour to indicate a rise in temperature. Therefore, this space should not be used for storage and contact should be avoided.

SMALL EQUIPMENT OFTEN USED WHEN GRILLING FOODS

The following items are often used when grilling foods:

- Tongs – use to turn items to ensure even cooking, for example, sausages, burgers, steaks or chicken
- Palette knives – used to slide under items such as fillets of fish
- Slices – for larger items such as small whole fish
- Skewers – to secure food items when grilling kebabs.

Assessment of knowledge and understanding

1   Link the following types of grill with the correct description

Char-grill/barbecue	Items are cooked under the heat source
Salamander	Items are cooked between the heat source
Contact grill	Items are cooked over the heat source

2   What type of heat is associated with grilling?

a) Convection ☐   b) Conduction ☐   c) Radiant ☐   d) Induction ☐

3   If you were asked to grill a steak rare, would you . . .

a) Cook the steak for a long time under intense heat ☐

b) Cook the steak for a short time under low heat ☐

c) Cook the steak for an intermediate time under medium heat ☐

d) Cook the steak for a short time under intense heat ☐

4   Name the degrees in which a steak may be cooked.

a)_____ b) _____ c) _____ d) _____

5   Why is grilling considered to be a healthy cookery process?

_____

6   Which type of grill would produce the 'char' lines on food items?

_____

7   Name four vegetables that can be grilled successfully with menu examples.

i) _____   ii) _____

iii)_____   iv) _____

8   What steps could you take to ensure that a cut of chicken did not dry out during the grilling process?

_____

9   What are the main reasons for marinating food items before grilling?

_____

10 Name three pieces of small equipment that would commonly be used when grilling foods.

i) _____   ii) _____

iii)_____

CHEF'S PROFILE

Name: STAS ANASTASIADES

Position: Executive Chef and General Manager of Milsoms, Associate Director of Milsom Hotels

Training and experience:

1987–88	Kitchen Porter at The Pier at Harwich
1988–90	The Pier kitchen and day release at Colchester Institute (apprentice)
1990–92	Morosani Post Hotel, Davos, Switzerland (Chef de Partie, Pastry)
1992–93	Dedham Vale Hotel, Dedham (Sous Chef)
1993–95	The Pier (Sous Chef)
1995–96	Le Talbooth (Senior Sous Chef)
1996–99	Stour Bay Café, Manningtree (Head Chef)
2000–01	Sabbatical – travelling on world food tour
2001	Head Chef, Milsoms
2002	Executive Head Chef & General Manager at Milsoms
2005–present	Ditto above and Associate Director of Milsom Hotels

Main responsibilities: Ongoing food development. Liaising with chefs throughout the company. Developing a group food culture by taking chefs to markets, restaurants and producers. Over-seeing the day to day running of milsoms. Establishing and working with group suppliers.

Best parts of the job: Diversity of the role. Constant challenges. Realizing people's full potential in the workplace

Secrets of a successful chef: Have some backbone.

Eat out whenever/wherever you can.

The best role models are real people that you know personally; not television or media personalities.

Don't follow the money; follow the most beneficial course of employment and the money will often follow.

Absorb trade journals and recipe books, use and cook from them; don't just read them.

Recipe: Colchester Natives

Mentor/inspiration: Several people have been inspirational with their love of food. When I was growing up, the day was all based around the dining table. My late mother was an excellent, albeit rather experimental, cook. My Ya-Yia (Cypriot grandmother) was an amazing pastry chef and I can always remember there being something wonderful to eat.

When I embarked on a career in the kitchen, Chris Oakley from The Pier at Harwich spent so much of his time making sure we learnt and understood the foundations of good technique and cooking; he was the most inspirational of head chefs.

I also found much inspiration from travelling around the world and experiencing some amazing restaurants and styles of cooking and this will continue to inspire me.

The late Gerald Milsom had an infectious love of food, people and of the industry. We would spend endless hours discussing food, ingredients and their origins, which really developed my thought process and how I approach my work.

I am fortunate to have Paul Milsom, Managing Director of Milsom Hotels, as my mentor. He has driven me to achieve milestones and goals in my career I would not have thought possible five or so years ago.

Personal profile: I enjoy tennis, eating out, staying in great hotels, music, reading the Sunday papers, cooking for friends and travelling.

Baked oysters with creamed chard and Gruyère cheese

INGREDIENTS	SERVES 2
Colchester Native oysters	12
Finely chopped shallots	6tbsp
Butter	100g/4oz
Splash of Noilly Prat vermouth	
Head of chard, washed and finely sliced	
Flour	1½tbsp
Double cream	100ml/4floz
Dijon mustard	2 tsp
Pinch cayenne pepper	
Pinch nutmeg	
Grated Gruyère cheese	75g/3oz
Maldon sea salt	

Method of work

1 Sauté 3 tablespoons of shallots in 50g of the butter over a low heat until golden, add vermouth and chard

2 In a heavy pan, sauté the remaining shallots and butter over a medium heat for 3 minutes or so, add the flour to make a roux and cook for a further 5 minutes, then add the cream, Dijon mustard, nutmeg and cayenne. Season to taste with salt and pepper

3 Open the oysters and disconnect from shell, reserve the best half of each shell and discard the other.

4 Put a spoonful of chard mixture in each shell, top with oyster, finish with Dijon sauce and sprinkle with the grated gruyere cheese

5 Place the oysters on a layer of Maldon sea salt in an oven proof dish and bake until golden brown and bubbly.

Preparation time: 20 minutes

Cooking: 20 minutes

Since Roman times Colchester oysters have been famed for their quality (and their mythical aphrodisiac properties!) Even if you are a die-hard traditionalist who believes that oysters should be eaten raw this dish is certainly worth a try.

Not suitable for freezing.

RECIPES
Apple tart

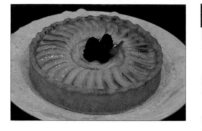

INGREDIENTS	8 PORTIONS
For the apple tart	
Sweet paste (see below)	200g
Sugar	100g
Apples (Granny Smith, Braeburn, Bramley's)	500g
Apricot glaze	
For the sweet paste	
Unsalted butter (cut into small pieces)	280g
Icing sugar	70g
Large egg yolks	2 eggs
Plain (soft) flour	350g
Double cream	2tbsp

Method of work

For the sweet paste

1 Place the icing sugar into of a food mixer.
2 Add the butter and toss.
3 Cream the butter and sugar mixture until the sugar is no longer visible, scraping down the sides of the bowl as you work.
4 Add the egg yolks gradually and blend again, scraping the bowl as before.
5 Add half the flour and mix until the paste becomes crumbly.
6 Stop the machine and add the remaining flour and mix until the dough forms into a ball.
7 Shape, wrap and chill until firm.

For the pastry case

1 Line a flan ring leaving excess pastry to overhang. Dock the base to prevent rising and leave to relax for 30 minutes.
2 Line with a cartouche or cling film and baking beans and bake at 200°C for 10 minutes. Take out, remove the baking beans and continue to bake for a further 5 minutes.
3 Take out, remove the cartouche and allow to cool.
4 Carefully slice off the overhanging pastry by cutting away from the tart along the line of the flan ring.

Apple purée

Reserve the 2 best-shaped apples and make the remainder into a purée by completing the following.
1 Peel, core and slice the apples.
2 Melt 25g of butter in a pan.
3 Add the apples and sugar. Stir well, place a lid on the pan and cook until the apples are soft.
4 Remove the lid and cook while stirring to evaporate any excess liquid and intensify the flavour.
5 Pass through a sieve or liquidiser.
6 Allow to cool.

To finish

1 Place the apple purée neatly into the flan case.
2 Peel and quarter the remaining apples.
3 Cut the apple quarters into neat thin slices and lay carefully on the apple purée overlapping each slice. Ensure that each slice points to the centre of the flan, joining the pattern up neatly.
4 Sprinkle a little sugar on the apple slices and bake the flan in a moderately hot oven (200°C/410°F/Gas mark 6) for 10–15 minutes.
5 When cooked, remove the ring and place carefully onto a cooling rack.
6 Brush all over with hot apricot glaze (including the sides of the pastry).

Bread rolls *(Yield 32–40 rolls)*

INGREDIENTS	32–40 ROLLS
White rolls	
Strong plain flour	1kg
Fat (lard or oil)	50g
Yeast	35g
Milk powder	25g
Salt	20g
Caster sugar	10g
Water	1050ml at 37°C
Wholemeal rolls	
Wholemeal flour	1kg
Lard	50g
Yeast	35g
Salt	20g
Sugar	10g
Water	1300ml at 37°C

Equipment

Large Hobart mixer with
Hook attachment
Proover
Baking sheet lined with silicon paper
Oven set – 230°C/450°F

Method of work

1 Sieve flour onto paper.
2 Rub in fat.
3 Dissolve the yeast in half the water.
4 Dissolve milk powder, salt and sugar in other half of water.
5 Add BOTH liquids to the flour in one go.
6 Using a mixing machine, mix on speed No I for 5 minutes to achieve a smooth dough
7 Cover with cling film and leave to prove for 1 hour. (Double in size.)
8 Knockback to expel the carbon dioxide.
9 Scale into 50g rolls, keeping covered at all times.
10 Roll, shape and place on silicon covered baking sheet in neatly spaced staggered rows.
11 Egg wash carefully and prove until double in size.
12 Bake at 230°C/450°F) for 8–10 minutes (with steam).

Alternatives (suitable for white bread dough)

Tomato and basil bread – Replace half the water with tomato juice, add fine chopped sun-dried tomatoes and dried basil after the 'knockback'.

Olive and walnut bread – Replace lard with olive oil (add to salt, sugar etc) add chopped walnuts and sliced olives after the 'knockback'.

Caramel creams *Crème caramels*

INGREDIENTS	4–6 CARAMEL CREAMS	10–12 CARAMEL CREAMS
For the caramel		
Granulated or cube sugar	200g	400g
Water	10ml	20ml
For the cream		
Eggs	4 eggs	8 eggs
Castor sugar	100g	200g
Milk	600ml	1200ml
Vanilla pod (or drop of good quality vanilla essence)	1 pod	2 pods

Method of work

For the caramel

1 Using a strong small saucepan (e.g. a lined copper pan), dissolve the sugar in the water and bring to the boil.

2 Cook quickly until a light caramel colour is achieved, cleaning the sides of the pan with a pastry brush soaked with clean water.

3 Remove from the heat and add a few drops of water and shake thoroughly. This will help to avoid the caramel from setting to a hard texture.

4 Pour the prepared caramel into the base of dariole moulds and allow to set.

VIDEO CLIP
Making caramel creams

For the cream

1 Mix the eggs and sugar in a bowl.

2 Bring the milk and split vanilla pod or essence carefully to the boil.

3 Strain and whisk onto the egg and sugar mixture.

To cook

1 Place the prepared moulds in deep trays.

2 Fill to just below the brim with the egg custard mixture.

3 Pour warm water into the tray about half way up the height of the dariole moulds.

4 Carefully place into the oven, set at 150°C and bake until set. (approximately 30 minutes).

5 Once set, carefully remove from the oven and remove the dariole moulds from the tray.

6 Once cool, turn out onto plates and serve. The caramel will naturally run down the set custard to provide its own caramel sauce.

Plain scones

INGREDIENTS	12 SCONES
Medium strength flour	500g
Baking powder	30g
Pinch of salt	
Butter	100g
Caster sugar	100g
Milk	568ml
Vanilla essence (to taste)	

Oven temperature set at 220°C

Method of work

1 Sieve the flour, baking powder and salt into a bowl.
2 Cut the butter into small cubes and rub into the flour mixture as finely as possible.
3 Make a bay in the centre, place the sugar into the bay and dissolve using the vanilla flavoured milk.
4 Gradually mix the flour mixture into the milk.
5 Continue mixing until equally blended, but avoid overmixing.
6 Place the mix onto a lightly dusted surface and form into a ball.
7 Gently roll out until ½ inch thick and cut into individual scones using a scone cutter.
8 Place on a lightly greased baking tray and egg-wash.
9 Rest for 15–20 minutes before baking until the tops of the scones are golden brown (approximately 15–20 minutes).
10 Once cooked, place on cooling wires and allow to cool.

Stilton and onion tartlets

INGREDIENTS	10–12 TARTLETS
For the pastry:	
Unsalted butter	120g
Plain flour	250g
Salt	¼tsp
Egg, lightly beaten	1 egg
Milk (if required)	1–2 tbsp
For the filling:	
Large onions	3 onions, (about 750g)
Butter	50g
Sunflower or light vegetable oil	2 tbsp
Salt	
Plain flour	2 tbsp
Grated Stilton	250g
Double cream	450ml
Eggs	3 eggs, lightly beaten
White pepper	

Method of work

To make the pastry:

1 Cut the butter into small pieces and rub it into the flour and salt with your hands.
2 Add the egg, mix well and work very briefly with your hand until bound into a soft dough, adding a little milk if necessary.
3 Cover in clingfilm and leave in a cool place to relax for 1 hour.

For the filling:

1 Cut the onions into thick slices.
2 Heat the butter with the oil in a large pan and cook the onions over very low heat and with the lid on for about 30 minutes, until very soft and lightly caramelized, stirring occasionally and adding a little salt.
3 Leave to cool before adding the flour and stirring into the onions.
4 Season lightly with salt and freshly ground white pepper.
5 Beat the cream into the eggs.
6 Line 10 tartlet cases with the pastry leaving a little excess over the side.
7 Line with clingfilm and relax before baking blind with baking beans (10 minutes at 190°C).
8 Leave to cool, remove the baking beans and clingfilm and carefully trim the edges of the paste by cutting away from the edge of the tartlet case.
9 Fill each tartlet with a combination of caramelized onions and grated Stilton.
10 Pour in the cream mixture and bake in an oven preheated to 150°C/300°F/Gas mark 2 for 45 minutes, or until set and golden.
11 Serve hot.

Roast chicken with bread sauce and roast gravy

Method of work

1   Preheat the oven to 450°F/230°C/Gas mark 8.
2   Place the chicken wings over the base of a solid-bottomed roasting tray.
3   Rub the butter all over the chicken, season well and position on top of the wings.
4   Squeeze the lemon all over the chicken, then push the exhausted halves and the thyme inside the chicken cavity.
5   Pour in the sherry and stock.
6   Roast in the oven for about 10–15 minutes, then turn the temperature down to 350°F/180°C/Gas mark 4.
7   Continue roasting for a further 1–1¼ hours.
8   Baste the chicken every 20 minutes.
9   When the skin is crisp and a rich golden colour, skewer the thigh and look for the clear juices that show it's done.
10 Lift out the chicken and tip out its interior juices, thyme and lemon halves into the roasting dish. Put the chicken onto a suitable tray and relax in a warm place (e.g. in an oven that has been switched off).
11 Allow to rest for at least 10 minutes before carving.

INGREDIENTS	4 PORTIONS
Chicken wings, roughly chopped	8 wings
Softened butter	100g
Free-range chicken	2kg (approx.)
Salt and pepper	
Juice of 1 lemon	
Several sprigs of fresh thyme	
Dry sherry	1 small glass
Chicken stock	4tbsp
Bread sauce	
Milk	500ml
Butter	75g
Cloves	8 cloves
Bay leaves	2 large leaves, crumbled
A good pinch of salt	
Onion, peeled and finely chopped	1 small onion
Double cream	3tbsp
Fresh white breadcrumbs	120–130g
Freshly ground white pepper	

Note: 2kg chicken will serve 4 people. Multiple portions can be calculated from this measurement.

Bread sauce

1   Infuse the milk with the cloves, bay leaves, salt and pepper.
2   Heat together the milk (with spices), butter and chopped onion. Bring to the boil and reduce to a simmer.
3   Simmer for 5 minutes and turn off letting the flavours continue to infuse off the heat.
4   Strain through a fine sieve into a clean pan.
5   Add the cream and reheat to just below boiling point.
6   Whisk in the breadcrumbs in gradually until the desired consistency is achieved.
7   Season and pour into a bowl.
8   Keep covered and warm using a bain-marie.

Roast gravy

1   Squash the lemon halves around the roasting dish to extract any remaining flavour, then throw away.
2   Put the roasting tray directly on the heat and stir vigorously with a wooden spoon to displace the roasted sediment (bits).
3   Add more stock, if required, and simmer for 10 minutes, skimming away any fat or impurities that rise to the surface.
4   Strain through a sieve into a small pan.
5   Bring back to the boil and season with salt and freshly ground white pepper.
6   Adjust the consistency using a little diluted arrowroot, if necessary.

Yorkshire pudding

INGREDIENTS	4 PORTIONS	10 PORTIONS
Plain flour	100g	250g
A good pinch of salt to season		
Eggs	3 eggs	8 eggs
Milk	290ml	725ml
Oil	2tbsp	5tbsp

Preheat the oven to 230°C/450°F/Gas mark 8.

Lightly oil the Yorkshire pudding moulds and heat in the oven to get the oil very hot.

Method of work

1 Sift the flour and salt into a bowl and make a well the centre.
2 In a measuring jar, break the eggs into the milk and mix well.
3 Pour half of the liquid into the well of the flour, gradually drawing in more flour to the centre.
4 Beat until the batter is smooth before adding the remainder of the liquid while continuously whisking.
5 Strain and leave to rest for 30 minutes before use.
6 *To cook*: Pour the batter into the pre-heated and oiled Yorkshire pudding moulds. Roast in the preheated oven for 25 to 30 minutes, or until risen and golden brown.

Served as a traditional accompaniment to roast beef.

Salmon and courgette brochette with tomato vinaigrette

INGREDIENTS	4 PORTIONS	10 PORTIONS
Salmon fillet	500g	1250g
Medium courgettes	2 courgettes	5 courgettes
Olive oil for greasing and soaked wooden kebab skewers		
For the vinaigrette		
Tomatoes (skinned, deseeded and diced neatly)	4 tomatoes	10 tomatoes
Fresh basil (chopped)	50g	125g
Olive oil	100ml	250ml
Lemon juice	20ml	50ml
Seasoning (freshly cracked Maldon salt and pepper)		

Method of work

1 Cut the salmon fillet into 1 inch dice.
2 Peel, or use a mandolin, to produce thin ribbons (lengths) from the courgette.
3 Wrap each piece of salmon in a ribbon of courgette and place onto the skewer (5 or 6 in total).
4 Season and brush with olive oil.
5 Cook on the grill for about 5 minutes turning occasionally.
6 Mix all the ingredients for the vinaigrette in a mixing bowl.
7 Serve the brochettes on the skewer with a bowl of the tomato vinaigrette.

10

Prepare and cook food by deep frying and shallow frying

Unit 110 Prepare and cook food by deep frying and shallow frying

LEARNING OBJECTIVES

On completion of this chapter, learners will be able to:

■ Describe the methods of shallow and deep frying

■ Identify foods that can be shallow and deep fried

■ Identify the fats and oils that are used to shallow and deep fry

■ Select suitable techniques to shallow and deep fry

■ List the quality points to look for in food that has been shallow or deep fried

■ List the general safety points to follow when shallow or deep frying food

SHALLOW FRYING

What is shallow frying?

Shallow frying is described as the cooking of food in a small amount of pre-heated fat or oil. This can be achieved by using a variety of different pans or surfaces.

Here are some examples of the methods and equipment used to shallow fry.

Frying pan

Frying pan

A frying pan has shallow sides. This is because the food is cooked by heat being transferred from the base of the pan and into the fat or oil. This is in direct contact with the food and heat is then passed through the food until it is cooked.

During the frying process, we usually have to turn the food over. This is important to ensure that the food is cooked evenly and also to provide an even colour to the food. As the pan is shallow, this is much easier to do than in a pan that has deep sides. To turn food over, we normally use a palette knife or slice. The pictures on the left show an example of this process.

It is important that a frying pan is well looked after and clean before you use it. Many modern frying pans are lined with a coating to prevent foods from sticking. An example of this is Teflon. It is very important that when using and cleaning a frying pan with such a coating that the surface is not scratched or damaged as this will remove the non-stick properties.

Wok (Stir-fry)

A wok

Woks have become a very common piece of equipment in today's kitchens with the increase in Chinese and Far-Eastern foods consumed in the United Kingdom. Stir frying in a wok is a fast method of cookery, where the food is continuously stirred or tossed to ensure that the food is cooked evenly without burning. A wok can also be used to deep fry food but extreme care has to be taken to ensure that the oil or fat does not get too hot and ignite!

Step-by-step: **Shallow frying trout (meuniere)**

STEP 1 A trout which has been washed and gutted

STEP 2 Using a pair of fish scissors, cut the dorsal fins from the back of the fish

STEP 3 Cut the remaining fins from the fish and cut the tail fin square to neaten

STEP 4 Holding the fish by the tail, scope the scales from the fish using a fork or the back of a knife

STEP 5 Lightly coat the fish in seasoned flour

STEP 6 Heat some oil and butter in a frying pan

STEP 7 Place the trout into the oil/butter, service side down (the side you want to present to the customer) and fry

STEP 8 After a few minutes, use a fish slice to carefully turn the fish over to fry the other side

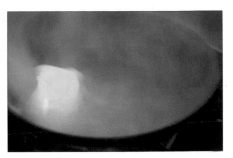

STEP 9 When the fish is cooked, place onto a plate. Heat a frying pan and add cold butter. This will melt very quickly

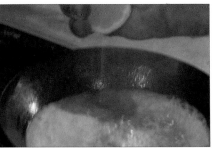

STEP 10 When the butter turns a light, nut-brown colour, squeeze in some freshly squeezed lemon juice

STEP 11 Pour the butter and lemon juice mix (beurre noisette) over the fish and serve

A sauté pan

CHEF'S TIP

Certain vegetables are also suitable to be cooked by sauté, the most common being sauté potatoes. In this case, the potatoes are usually blanched, sliced and cooked in hot oil or fat until cooked through to a light golden brown colour.

Griddle

Sauté pan

The term 'sauté' means to jump or to toss. In this case, the food is cooked quickly in hot fat or oil and usually to a light golden brown colour. When cooking food by sauté, the tossing of the food does not happen as rapidly or as often as it would when stir frying. As this is a quick cookery method, the food must be tender (i.e. without a lot of sinew/muscle). Examples of food that can be sautéed include chicken, which has been cut into portions (thighs, drumsticks, and breast pieces), leaner cuts of meat and offal such as liver and kidneys.

Griddle

A griddle is a heated, solid metal plate which is lightly oiled to produce a frying surface. Griddles are very common pieces of equipment in mobile catering vans that you see at outdoor shows and events. As the surface area is usually quite large, griddles are good for cooking multiple items such as burgers, sausages, eggs, as well as pancakes, scones and potato cakes, etc.

Special pans (omelettes, crêpes/pancakes, blinis, tava)

There are a number of pans that have been designed with a specific purpose. Examples of such pans include an omelette pan, a blinis pan and a tava. Each of these examples has been designed to cook certain types of food. For example, the omelette pan is usually smaller than a standard frying pan as it is cooking a single item. The blinis pan is smaller again as this is designed to cook blinis, which are small buckwheat pancakes usually served with caviar.

Step-by-step: **Stir-fried vegetables**

STEP 1 The ingredients for a vegetable stir-fry – sliced green, red and yellow peppers, shredded leeks, carrots and courgettes and segments of mushroom

STEP 2 Heat some vegetable oil in a wok

STEP 3 Add the mixed peppers and stir-fry

STEP 4 Add the mushrooms and continue to stir-fry

STEP 5 Add the carrots and continue to stir-fry

STEP 6 Add the courgettes and continue to stir-fry

STEP 7 Finally, add the leek and continue to stir-fry

STEP 8 Season with soy sauce, freshly ground white pepper and a little sesame oil (optional) and serve

A tava is a flat pan, which is usually used to cook Indian flat breads such as chapatti and paratha. Tortillas are cooked in a similar way. Oil or fat is not always used to cook on these pans. For example, chapattis are cooked on a dry surface.

THE PREPARATION OF EQUIPMENT FOR SHALLOW FRYING

With the exception of sauté pans and pans that are lined with a non-stick coating such as Teflon, traditional frying pans must go through a process known as 'proving'. This process creates a good frying surface and, if used correctly, the food should not stick to the pan.

CHEF'S TIP

The two ways to prove a frying pan

1 In the first method, the pan is lightly oiled, placed on the stove at a low to medium heat and heated for about ten minutes. After this time, the oil is carefully tipped out into a suitable container and the pan is wiped clean. It is now ready for use.

2 This is often used with crêpe/pancake pans, the pan is filled with salt. This is heated as in example 1. The salt is then tipped out of the pan and the pan is wiped clean. The pan would then be lightly oiled and is ready for use.

THE EFFECTS OF SHALLOW FRYING ON FOOD

It is very important that the fat or oil is heated to the correct degree before adding foods to be shallow fried. If the temperature is too hot, the food will cook too quickly on the outside and even burn. If the temperature is not hot enough, the food will absorb the fat or oil, making the food greasy and increasing the fat content. There is more guidance provided on this subject in the practical examples of foods being prepared and cooked throughout the chapter.

The high temperature of the fat or oil helps to seal foods that are shallow fried. This also helps to retain nutrients and make some foods, such as chicken, more tender and moist. Fried food does, however, naturally absorb some of the fat or oil, increasing the fat content of the finished foods. This is reduced greatly if the process of frying is carried out correctly.

Shallow frying is a quick method of cookery and therefore the foods to be fried need to be suitable. For example, it would be hard to shallow fry large commodities such as a joint of meat, a chicken or a whole vegetable. This

CHEF'S TIP

A Bratt-pan is a versatile piece of equipment that can be used to boil, braise, stew or even poach. As most bratt-pans have a flat base, they can also be used to griddle food.

VIDEO CLIP
Shallow frying salmon

Step-by-step: **Shallow-fried salmon**

STEP 1 Cut diagonally into the tail end of the fillet to expose a little of the skin. Holding the skin firmly, run a sharp knife almost horizontally (with the blade pointing slightly towards the skin) along the inside of the skin of the fish to separate the fillet from the skin

STEP 2 If this procedure is performed well, there will be very little flesh left on the skin

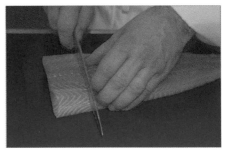

STEP 3 Cut the fillet into evenly sized/weighted supremes

STEP 4 Heat some oil and butter in a frying pan and place the lightly seasoned supreme, service side down, into the pan

STEP 5 When the salmon is ready to be turned, gently press the top of the supreme and place a fish slice underneath.

STEP 6 When cooked, place the supreme onto a plate. In this example the salmon is served with a slice of herb butter and seasonal vegetables

could also be dangerous as the core temperature of the meat would not be high enough to kill bacteria by the time that the outside of the meat is cooked. To make food suitable for shallow frying, it usually has to be cut quite thinly or the texture of the foods has to be such that it allows heat to penetrate through the food quickly without making it tough. Fish provides a good example of such a food, as the flesh of the fish is very delicate and easily digested. This enables the heat to penetrate through the food quickly.

If using meat or poultry, they must be cut appropriately to ensure that shallow frying can be used successfully as a cookery method. Examples include a steak or a chicken escalope. It is also important to note that the structure of the food is suitable for shallow frying. For example, a piece of meat taken from an area that is high in connective tissue will require a long cookery process to tenderize the muscle and sinew. Lean cuts without such a muscular structure can be cooked by much quicker cookery methods and still remain tender. Finally, when shallow frying, it is important that when the outside of the food appears to be cooked, usually to a light golden brown colour, the centre is also cooked through.

Testing the core temperature of a roast leg of lamb

CHEF'S TIP

The core temperature is the temperature in the centre of the item being cooked. To test the core temperature, a temperature testing device called a probe is inserted into the centre. The electronic reading then displays the temperature in the centre of the food, telling you if the item has reached a safe temperature to kill bacteria, making the food safe to eat. The photo above shows this process in action.

ACTIVITY

In the categories below, name two products that would be suitable to shallow fry.

TYPE OF FOOD	EXAMPLE	SUITABLE OIL OR FAT
Vegetables	1.	
	2.	
Dairy products	1.	
	2.	
Fish	1.	
	2.	
Meat and poultry	1.	
	2.	
Fruit	1.	
	2.	
Ready prepared products (convenience products)	1.	
	2.	

THE USE OF FATS AND OILS WHEN FRYING FOODS

Shallow and, particularly, deep frying are not considered to be healthy methods to cook foods due to the high fat content. However, within a sensible and balanced diet, fried foods produce an appetizing and nutritious meal. Fats, such as butter or lard have unique flavours but are high in saturated fat, making them unpopular choices with many people. Lard is also an animal product and would be unsuitable for vegans, vegetarians and those offended by the use of animal products in this way. An un-clarified fat such as butter (butter containing buttermilk) will also burn at a lower temperature than oils. Butter is also an expensive product to use in comparison to vegetable oil.

Therefore, it is much more usual to use oils for frying, particularly when deep frying. As cooking oils come from many sources, their flavours and properties differ. Oils from nuts, such as peanut, hazlenut and walnut oil have strong flavours, making them unsuitable (overpowering) when frying certain foods. They are more commonly used for their flavouring properties.

Vegetable, corn, sunflower and olive oils are the most commonly used oils throughout Europe. Vegetable oils have a very delicate flavour and are the most economical. Olive oil is considered one of the healthiest oils due to its make up of unsaturated fats. However, olive oil is generally more expensive to purchase, particularly virgin (first pressed) olive oil. It also has a stronger flavour than vegetable oil, which will affect the flavour of the food being cooked. Mediterranean and fish dishes are considered to benefit from the flavour passed on through the use of olive oil.

Working safely

It is important to follow safe working practices when shallow frying food. The following points should be considered:

- **Use the right pan for the job!**
  Make sure that the pan is the right size to fit the amount of food to be cooked. This will also make the job of monitoring and turning food much easier.

- **Be very careful when moving a pan when it is hot!**
  This could be during the cooking process when the pan is on the stove or on top of a flame. You also have to be careful after you have finished cooking the food as the pan and the oil or fat will remain hot for quite a long time.

- **Take care when placing food into hot oil or fat!**
  It is important that the oil or fat is heated to the right temperature before placing the item of food to be cooked into the pan. This ensures that the food starts to seal on impact and doesn't absorb excess oil or fat making the food greasy. It is also important that the food is placed carefully and in an action away from the body. Food should be lowered gently into the oil or fat to avoid splashes.

- **Monitor the temperature of the oil or fat!**
  Never walk away from food that is being shallow fried. Oil can catch fire if its gets too hot and this could lead to a serious incident. It is also important to make sure that the item of food is cooking at the right speed

to ensure it is cooked through whilst getting a light golden brown colour on the outside.

■ **Take care when handling hot oil or fat!**

Occasionally, there may be circumstances when you have to handle hot oil and fat. Ideally, oil or fat should be cooled before it is handled or moved. If oil or fat has to be handled when it is hot, extreme care should be applied. You should also ensure that access is clear and that your work colleagues are informed of your actions.

■ **Ensure that appropriate clothing and equipment is worn and used!**

Protective clothing is designed to protect you in the event of hot oil or fat being spilled or coming into contact with the body. Safety shoes will also protect your feet from such spillages and reduce the likelihood of a serious burn. It is also very important that the right equipment is used to handle food when shallow frying. This reduces the need for direct contact and helps to provide a safe distance between the skin and the hot oil or fat.

DEEP FRYING

What is deep frying?

Deep frying is described as the cooking of food in pre-heated deep fat or oil. This can be achieved by using a variety of different pieces of equipment. Here are some examples of the methods and equipment used to deep fry.

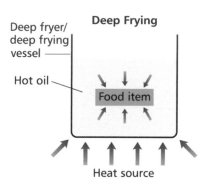

Thermostatically controlled deep fryer

This is the most common type of deep fryer. This is the type of fryer that you would normally see in use in a fish and chip shop. The energy used to heat a deep fryer can be electricity or gas.

In this type of fryer, the oil or fat is held within a deep container. This container heats up the oil or fat to the required temperature. The temperature is monitored and held at the required temperature by a device called a thermostatic control.

Underneath the source of heat is what is referred to as a cool zone. This is designed to catch all the bits of food that may come away from the item of food that is being deep fried. Examples of this include breadcrumbs coming away from a breaded chicken breast or excess batter separating from a piece of battered fish.

Thermostatically controlled deep fryer

Pressure fryer

Pressure fryers seal the air in an airtight container. This retains the heat within the unit, cooking the food more quickly and at a lower oil temperature. Pressure fryers are common in the home due to their safety features and ease of use.

Computerized fryers

Computerized fryers are controlled by circuits of temperature probes, sensors and timers. They can be programmed to control the heat of oil or fat at different stages of the cooking process. They have the capacity to control the food at all stages, lowering the basket of food into the oil for a specific time and raising the food from the oil when it is ready and some even have programmes to clean themselves.

ComputeriZed fryers are commonly used in the fast-food industry. To use pre-programmed equipment minimizes the training required to operate the equipment, while achieving a good quality and consistent finished product.

HEALTH & SAFETY

Never throw or drop items into a deep fryer. The hot oil will splash and could cause a serious burn if it comes into direct contact with the skin

THE EFFECTS OF DEEP FRYING FOOD

When food is being deep fried, it is submerged into a pool of very hot oil or fat. Therefore, it is important that the food being fried can stand up to being exposed to such high temperatures. To protect items of food, they can be coated so that the food is not directly exposed to the very hot oil or fat. The most common coatings are breadcrumbs and batter.

Step-by-step: **Deep frying battered fillets of plaice**

STEP 1 Run the fillet of plaice through some seasoned flour and shake off any excess flour

STEP 2 Holding the fish by the tail end, dip into the beer batter

STEP 3 Lift the fillet from the batter and lightly scrape any excess batter on the side of the bowl

STEP 4 Very carefully, lower the fillet into the deep fryer, releasing the tail-end of the fish away from your body

STEP 5 Half way through the cooking process, use a spider to turn the fillets over

STEP 6 When the fish float towards the surface of the oil and the batter turns a very light golden brown, they are cooked. Remove the fillets from the fryer with the spider and drain onto absorbent paper

In these examples, it is the coating that is in direct contact with the oil or fat, which, if cooked at the correct temperature, will go crisp offering a contrast in texture with the item of food. The coating will also help to prevent the item of food becoming oily as it is not in direct contact with the oil or fat. There are exceptions to this where the item of food can form the crisp outside coating without the addition of a coating.

Chips provide a good example of this process. Normally the potatoes would be cut to an even size of chip. They would then be blanched, this time in the oil, but at a reduced temperature to cook the chip but without colour. The blanched chips can then be stored until required. At this point, the temperature of the oil is raised to finish the cooking of the chips, but also to add the crispy outside coating that you would expect with a good quality chip!

As with shallow frying, it is very important that the fat or oil is heated to the correct degree before adding foods to be deep fried.

Deep frying is a quick method of cookery and therefore the foods to be fried need to be suitable and have to go through a stage of preparation. This can vary quite a lot depending on the type of food. Fish, for example, is very delicate in structure and therefore does not necessarily need to be cut down to speed up the cookery process. An example of this is deep-fried sole. Other fish dishes are more suitable when the fish is filleted or cut into goujons.

Meat and poultry have to be prepared to deep-fry, normally by cutting into slices, strips or dice. This enables the heat to penetrate through the food quickly.

When deep frying, it is important that when the outside of the food is cooked, usually to a light golden brown colour, the centre is also cooked. Therefore, if the meat or chicken is cut appropriately; deep frying can be used successfully as a suitable cookery method. Examples include strips of beef or a chicken escalope. It is also important to note that the structure of the food is suitable for deep frying.

CHEF'S TIP

Potatoes will begin to discolour once they are peeled. A way to prevent this from happening is to place them in a bowl of cold water. However, it is essential that potatoes, or any other foods kept in water prior to cooking, are dried thoroughly before placing into hot oil. This also applies to defrosted frozen food that may have a wet surface.

HEALTH & SAFETY

Water will cause hot fat to spit and will burn if it comes into contact with your skin. The level of oil will also increase causing a possible overspill and a potentially very dangerous situation.

Step-by-step: **Goujons of fish**

STEP 1 Using a sharp filleting knife, cut diagonally into the tail of the fillet to expose a little of the skin. Holding the skin firmly, run the knife almost horizontally (with the blade pointing slightly towards the skin) along the inside of the skin of the fish to separate the fillet from the skin

STEP 2 Cut the fillet diagonally into strips (goujons)

STEP 3 Marinate the goujons in some oil and fresh herbs (optional)

Steps 4–8 over page

STEP 4 Place the goujons into seasoned flour, shake off any excess flour and then place into a tray of beaten egg

STEP 5 Drain off any excess egg and finally place into a tray of fresh breadcrumbs

STEP 6 Place the breaded (panéd) goujons into a frying basket

STEP 7 Lower the basket into the heated oil and deep-fry until lightly golden brown

STEP 8 Lift the basket from the oil and drain the goujons on absorbent paper

Step-by-step: **Apple fritters**

STEP 1 Carefully peel the apples

STEP 2 Cut the apple into quarters and cut out the core from each piece of apple

STEP 3 Cut each piece of apple in half to make eight segments in total

STEP 4 Place the apple segments into water mixed with lemon juice. This will prevent the apple from discolouring

STEP 5 When ready to fry, drain the apple segments on absorbent paper and then coat in flour

STEP 6 Drop the apple segments into the frying batter

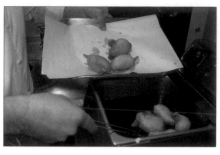

STEP 7 Drain off any excess batter and carefully place each segment into the deep fryer

STEP 8 Once the batter has turned light golden brown, remove the fritters with a spider and drain on absorbent paper

STEP 9 Roll each fritter in sugar and serve as required. Tip – A little ground cinnamon mixed with the sugar produces a great combination with apples

ACTIVITY

In the categories below, name two products that would be suitable to deep fry.

TYPE OF FOOD	EXAMPLE		SUITABLE COATING
Vegetables	1.	2.	
Dairy products	1.	2.	
Fish	1.	2.	
Meat and poultry	1.	2.	
Fruit	1.	2.	
Ready prepared products (convenience products)	1.	2.	

Assessment of knowledge and understanding

1 In your own words, describe the process of deep frying.

2 List three coatings that can be added to foods before deep frying.

3 Why is it important to heat the oil or fat before adding the food to be deep fried?

4 Describe the process of adding foods to be deep fried, explaining the reasons for these actions.

5 List the quality points you would look for in food that has been deep fried.

CHEF'S PROFILE

Name: MARK SALTER

Position: Executive Chef

Establishment: The Inn At Perry Cabin

Training and experience: After leaving Colchester Institute in 1979 I trained at 5 star Properties in France, Germany and Switzerland.

After spending four years in Scotland at Cromlix House I moved to Llangoed Hall in Wales.

In 1993 Sir Bernard Ashley appointed me the executive chef at the Inn at Perry Cabin (Maryland, USA) and in 1999 the Inn At Perry Cabin was bought by Orient-Express Hotels.

My signature dishes include crab spring roll with pink grapefruit, avocado and toasted almonds, my smoked blue fish paté and my honey and tarragon glazed shank of lamb with sun dried tomato sauce.

Over the past 13 years I have tantalized numerous discerning celebrity palates including Margaret Thatcher, John Major, King Hussein of Jordon and Benjamin Netanyahu to name a few.

In 2004 I started my own company Salter's Chesapeake Gourmet, producing Gourmet salad dressings marinades and an Eastern Shore Pub Sauce.

Main responsibilities: Day to day running of the Inn At Perry Cabin Kitchen

Writing menus and meeting with clients.

Best parts of the job: Demonstrations, meeting guests and working with local farms to create signature menus. Travelling and cooking in other Orient-Express properties.

Secrets of a successful chef: Train with great chefs, and always work in restaurants that have great reputations. To begin with don't think about the money, think about the experience you are getting. The money comes later.

Recipe: Crab spring roll with pink grapefruit, avocado and toasted almonds.

Your mentor or main inspiration: My mentors are all the Executive chefs that have trained me and helped me get where I am today.

A brief personal profile: I like to play golf and to watch my children play sports. In the summer I like to pick blackberries from the hedgerows as it reminds me of when I was a teenager back in the UK. Buying fresh produce from the farmers' markets.

CHEF'S RECIPE

Crab spring roll with pink grapefruit, avocado and toasted almonds

CRAB SPRING ROLL

INGREDIENTS	4 PORTIONS
Spring roll casing (use either brick dough or good egg roll wrapper)	4 sheets
Jumbo lump crab meat	4oz
Bok Choy	7oz
Pickled ginger	2 slices
Chopped fresh coriander	1tsp
Juice from ½ lime	
Salt and ground black pepper	
Sliced spring onions	½ bunch
Egg yolks, beaten	4

DRESSING

INGREDIENTS	4 PORTIONS
Pink grapefruit juice	12oz
Juice from 1 lime	
Sugar	½tsp
Grape seed oil	6oz
Salt and pepper	
Clover honey	1tsp

SALAD AND PRESENTATION

INGREDIENTS	4 PORTIONS
Avocado	1
Pink Grapefruit	1
Sliced toasted almonds	2oz
Mesculin greens	2oz

Method of work

1 Shred the bok choy and blanch in boiling salted water or steam. (Approximately 2 to 3 minutes). Slice the spring onions and blanch for 30 seconds.

2 Refresh in ice water, drain and squeeze out most of the water. Add the jumbo crab, chopped coriander, lime juice, salt and pepper.

3 Lay out spring roll casing and place filling on 1/3 of casing. Brush the remaining 2/3 of the casing with beaten egg yolks.

4 Roll up the wrapper 'egg roll' style. Deep fry in vegetable oil at 350°C for 3 to 4 minutes until golden.

5 Melt the sugar in a small stainless steel saucepan over low heat. When melted, add the pink grapefruit juice. Reduce the mixture by 2/3 and then whisk in the honey, lime juice and grape seed oil. Lightly season with salt and pepper.

6 Segment pink grapefruit and peel avocado. Place three pieces of grapefruit and three pieces of avocado around the plate. Sprinkle with toasted almonds. Dress the salad with the pink grapefruit dressing and arrange in the middle of the plate.

7 Cut the spring roll in half on the bias and lay on the salad.

8 Drizzle plate with additional pink grapefruit dressing and serve.

RECIPES

Crêpes *(pancakes)*

INGREDIENTS	10–12 PANCAKES
Plain flour	125g
Salt	2 good pinches
Eggs	2 medium eggs
Melted butter	1tbsp
Milk	300ml

Vegetable oil, to grease the crêpe pan

Method of work

1 Sieve the flour and salt in a bowl and add the eggs, butter and half of the milk and whisk until smooth.
2 Gradually add the remaining milk while continuously whisking.
3 Leave the batter to rest for 20 minutes.

Cooking the crêpes (pancakes)

1 Pour the batter into a jug or bowl and have a small ladle ready for ladling into the crêpe pan.
2 Pour a small amount of vegetable oil into a small measuring jug or cup.
3 Start to heat the empty crêpe pan until you can feel a good heat coming through.
4 Add a few drops of oil, tilt to grease the base of the pan and then tip out any excess.
5 Pour in a small amount of batter from the ladle and immediately swirl the pan so the batter thinly coats the entire base.
6 Put the pan back on the heat and cook until the batter is set and little holes appear in the surface.
7 Slide a palette knife carefully under the crêpe and turn it over.
8 Cook the other side for about 30 seconds.
9 Slide the cooked crêpe out on to a cooling rack lined with a small square of greaseproof paper. Place another square of greaseproof on top and repeat until all the pancakes are cooked.
10 Serve hot or cold.

Deep-fried cod in beer batter with chips

INGREDIENTS	4 PORTIONS	10 PORTIONS
Plain flour (to dust the fish)	200g	500g
Cod fillet (boned, 200–225g pieces)	4 pieces	10 pieces
Squeeze of lemon juice		
Salt and pepper		
Self-raising flour, sieved	400g	1kg
Lager	550ml	1350ml
For the chips		
Large floury potatoes	800g	2kg
Oil for frying		
Sea salt (flaked or milled)	2tbsp	5tbsp

Method of work

Pre-heat the fat-fryer oil to 180°/350°F.

Pre-preparation

1 Leaving the skin on the cod fillets holds the fillet together when it's passed through the batter and placed in the oil.
2 Squeeze a little lemon juice over each fillet and season with salt and pepper and lightly dust with the plain flour.

To make the batter

1 Sieve the flour into a large bowl and whisk in three-quarters of the lager (the consistency of the batter should be very thick). Adjust as necessary using the remainder of the lager.
2 Season with a pinch of salt.
3 Pass the cod fillets, one at a time, through the batter mix, holding the fillet at the thin end, in one corner, between thumb and forefinger.
4 Coat the fish in batter and lift from the bowl. (Some of the batter will begin to fall away slowly.) If the batter falls away too quickly, it means it's too thin, in which case add a teaspoon or two more of flour.

To cook

1 Don't allow too much of the batter to fall off before placing in the deep hot oil.
2 Submerge only an inch at a time and, once three-quarters of the fish is in, the batter will lift the fillet, floating the fish.
3 Submerge the remaining fillet in the same way, being careful not to burn your fingers.
4 Cook for 2–3 minutes before turning the fish over. At this point the fish will not be golden brown but the batter will have sealed and puffed out.
5 Cook until golden brown all around. (A thick slice of cod will take up to 12 minutes to cook, an average fillet 9–10 minutes.)
6 Once cooked, remove from the oil and drain onto kitchen paper. Sprinkle with salt and serve.

For the chips

1 Peel the potatoes and cut them into ½ inch slices.
2 Cut the slices lengthways into ½ inch chips.
3 Rinse in a bowl under a running cold tap until the water is clear to remove excess starch.
4 Drain and pat dry.

To blanch

1 Heat the oil in a deep fryer to 150°C and add the potatoes, not filling the basket more than half-full. If you do you risk the oil overflowing and you will also reduce the temperature of the oil.
2 Fry the chips for 5–6 minutes, stirring occasionally.
3 Check the degree of cooking by removing a chip and inserting a small knife into the centre of the chip. The chips should be soft right through but without colour at this stage. Lift the basket and set aside.

To finish

1 Increase the temperature of the oil to 190°C and replace the chips, frying for 2–3 minutes until golden and crisp.
2 Remove from the fryer, shake dry and then tip onto a tray lined with absorbent paper.
3 Season the chips with the sea salt.
4 Serve immediately.

Thicker cut chips need to be blanched before finishing. This involves cooking the chips at a low temperature to cook the potatoes through before frying at a much higher temperature in order to colour and crisp.

Goujons of plaice

INGREDIENTS	4 PORTIONS	10 PORTIONS
Whole plaice (approximately 300–325g)	2 plaice	5 plaice
Eggs (beaten)	2 eggs	5 eggs
Flour, sieved and seasoned with salt and white pepper		
Fresh breadcrumbs		

Method of work

1 Wash, fillet, skin and trim the plaice.
2 Slice into goujons (approx. 4cm x ½cm strips).
3 Pass through the flour, egg and breadcrumbs.
4 Deep fry in hot fat (170°C) until golden brown.
5 Serve with appropriate sauce (e.g. Tartare sauce).

Escalope of salmon with basil

INGREDIENTS	4 PORTIONS	10 PORTIONS
supremes of salmon (200g)	4 supremes	10 supremes
Salt and freshly ground white pepper		
Lemon juice to taste		
To make the basil sauce		
Shallots, finely chopped	2 shallots	5 shallots
Butter	25g	65g
Basil leaves, cut into julienne	¼ bunch	¾ bunch
Noilly Prat or dry vermouth	50ml	125ml
Fish stock	120ml	300ml
Double cream	60ml	150ml
Butter	20g	50g

Method of work

1 In a saucepan, sweat the shallots in the butter without colour.
2 When they are translucent (see through) add the basil.
3 Deglaze the mixture with the Noilly Prat and cook until almost all the liquid has gone.
4 Add the fish stock and boil to reduce by about half.
5 Add the cream and bring gently back up almost to the boil.
6 Finish the sauce by adding the butter in small pieces and incorporating it by making waves in the sauce.
7 Check the taste, adjust the seasoning and add a few drops of lemon juice as necessary.
8 Keep warm in a bain-marie.

To cook the salmon
1 Season each piece of salmon with salt and pepper.
2 Add a little olive oil and butter to a non-stick frying pan and heat.
3 Fry the salmon over a fairly high heat for 1½ minutes on each side.

To serve
Place the fish on a warmed plate and pour the sauce around it.

Pork escalopes with Calvados sauce and apple compote

INGREDIENTS	4 PORTIONS	10 PORTIONS
Pork escalopes (100g)	4 escalopes	10 escalopes
Shallots – finely chopped	50g	125g
Butter, margarine or oil	50g	125g
Calvados	50ml	125ml
Double cream	125ml	300ml
Apples (e.g. Bramley)	2 apples	5 apples
Granulated sugar	150g	375g
Water (to dissolve)	Splash	Water (to dissolve)
Chopped sage	¼ bunch	¾ bunch
Salt and freshly ground white pepper		

Method of work

For the caramelized apples

1 Peel the apples, cut into quarters and then each quarter into 4 slices.
2 In a saucepan, add the sugar and dissolve with the water. Bring to the boil and cook until a light caramel.
3 Add the apples and stir. The water from the apples will disperse into the caramel.
4 With a perforated spoon, lift out the apples and reduce the liquid back to a caramel.
5 Return the apples until well coated and slightly caramelized.

For the pork escalopes

1 Take a sauté pan and add a little oil and butter. Heat through.
2 Add the seasoned escalopes and fry for 2 minutes on each side.
3 Remove from the pan and keep warm.
4 Using the same pan, add the chopped shallots and sweat them until translucent.
5 Strain off the fat leaving the shallots in the pan and deglaze the pan with the Calvados.
6 Reduce by a half before adding the cream.
7 Season and adjust the consistency of the sauce accordingly.
8 Add the sage to infuse.

To serve

Place a pork escalope onto the centre of a plate. Surround with the sauce and a spoonful of the caramelized apples.

Vegetable stir-fry

INGREDIENTS	4 PORTIONS	10 PORTIONS
Sunflower or vegetable oil	2tbsp	5tbsp
Piece of root ginger, peeled and sliced	25g	65g
Clove of garlic, peeled and cut into slices	1 clove	3 cloves
Onion, finely sliced	1 onion	2 onions
Baby-corn, cut diagonally	75g	175g
Mange tout, topped and tailed	75g	175g
Mushrooms, sliced	75g	175g
Sticks of celery cut into julienne	2 sticks	4 sticks
White of leek, cut into julienne	1 leek	3 leeks
Carrots, peeled and cut into julienne	2 carrots	5 carrots
Red, yellow or green pepper, peeled and deseeded and cut into fine slices	1 pepper	1 of each
Spring onions cut diagonally	3 spring onions	3 spring onions
Soy sauce	2tbsp	2tbsp
Sesame oil	2tsp	2tsp

Method of work

1 Heat the sunflower/vegetable oil in wok.

2 Add the ginger and garlic and fry gently for 1–2 minutes.

3 Quickly blanch the remaining ingredients (apart from the spring onions) in boiling water for 15–20 seconds and transfer into the wok.

4 Stir fry for 2 minutes.

5 Add the spring onions and continue to stir fry for another minute.

6 Season with the soy sauce and sesame oil and serve immediately.

This recipe can be adapted to utilize whatever ingredients you chose. It does not insist on nor is restricted to the use of the ingredients listed above.

11

Regeneration of pre-prepared food

LEARNING OBJECTIVES

On completion of this chapter, learners will be able to:

- Identify the different types of pre-prepared foods suitable for regeneration
- Describe the differences between regenerated, pre-prepared products and other food types
- Describe the purpose of regenerated, pre-prepared foods in the food industry
- State the possible limitations and potential implications of using regenerated pre-prepared foods
- Identify the correct methods for regenerating a range of pre-prepared foods
- List the general quality points and associated products when regenerating pre-prepared foods

TYPES OF PRE-PREPARED FOODS SUITABLE FOR REGENERATION

Dried foods

Drying refers to the removal of liquid from the food. Examples of foods that are dried include stock cubes, powdered sauces and soups as well as batter mixes and scone mixes.

Fresh foods

Many fresh products can be cooked, chilled and then reheated. In the professional kitchen, it is good practice to have food items cooked (blanched) and rapidly chilled. The items can then be quickly reheated and served. Suitable foods include boiled vegetables and certain soups and sauces.

Ready made products

Some ready made products require no further processing to make them edible. Examples of this include cakes, biscuits, cold savoury products (e.g. sausage rolls, quiches, etc.) as well as a whole range of dough products (breads, buns, croissants, etc.).

Other ready products have to be heated before they are safe to eat. Examples include ready made meals, soups, sauces and part-baked roll).

Frozen foods

There are endless products that can be regenerated from frozen. Care has to be taken when regenerating from frozen as some foods have to be fully defrosted before cooking, whereas others may require the products to be strictly reheated from frozen. Manufacturers should produce very clear instructions how to handle their products.

Some frozen foods such as cakes and desserts are ready to eat once defrosted. Such products, particularly the ones which are served cold are ready to eat once thoroughly defrosted.

Freezing is a readily available process for the chef to use to preserve foods for use at a later date. In most cases, foods frozen in this way will require defrosting before use or being reheated. Certain items, such as soups and sauces, may be safely reheated from frozen, although this will depend on the way they have been produced and the ingredients they contain.

Pre-prepared foods

Pre-prepared products can save the chef a great deal of time during the service period. However, quality must also be taken into consideration as certain products are more suited to being pre-prepared and reheated than others.

CHEF'S TIP

The term 'regeneration' or 'regenerated' refers to the fact that a process has to take place to bring pre-prepared food back to a safe and enjoyable condition to eat.

Frozen green beans

CHEF'S TIP

It is essential that defrosting follows the instructions of the manufacturer as such products can take a long time to defrost.

CHEF'S TIP

It is very important that food items are labelled and dated and that good stock control and rotation practices are followed.

Dishes that are sauced and cooked using a long cookery process, such as stewing and braising are generally suited to being pre-prepared, cooled and then reheated. Quality is not adversely affected, although additional liquid may be required to re-hydrate the sauce slightly. Pies can also be pre-prepared and reheated at a later time.

Items that are cooked by the faster cookery methods, such as frying and grilling will lose quality if pre-cooked for use at a later time. They may tend to lose moisture and shrink or, in the case of fish for example, break up.

Canned foods

There is an enormous range of foods available in cans. This includes a whole variety of vegetables, soups and sauces as well as ready to eat dishes such as stews.

DIFFERENCES BETWEEN REGENERATED, PRE-PREPARED PRODUCTS AND OTHER FOOD TYPES

As pre-prepared products have been through a process their nutritional value will be affected as a result. This may be through cooking, freezing or drying, for example. The quality of food will also be affected and usually will not be of as high a quality as fresh food.

The taste of pre-prepared foods normally differs in comparison to a fresh version. For example, a piece of freshly grilled tuna tastes and eats very differently to tuna from a can. Many pre-prepared foods will contain additives and preservatives to increase the shelf-life and flavour of the food concerned. Others such as dried stock cubes contain high levels of salt, making them unsuitable for reducing to intensify flavour when making a sauce.

Pre-prepared products generally require fewer skills than when working with fresh food items. Preparation skills are not required as this part of the process has already taken place. Skills required usually involve the heating and finishing of the food (boiling, baking, etc.) although not all pre-prepared foods require further cooking, frozen gâteaux for example.

Many pre-prepared foods are easy to identify by the trained eye. For example, tinned vegetables have a different appearance to fresh vegetables.

Difference between canned and fresh vegetables

THE PURPOSE OF REGENERATED, PRE-PREPARED FOODS IN THE FOOD INDUSTRY

Pre-prepared foods require fewer skills in preparation and this helps to reduce costs. Foods that are out of season can also be used as the pre-preparation can involve a form of preservation, tinned strawberries for example. This helps to keep the cost of such ingredients down as, once preserved, their shelf-life is extended massively beyond their fresh equivalent. Strawberries are a seasonal fruit and at their prime during the summer months in the UK. Now that rapid exporting of food is much more economical than in previous years, it is possible to purchase fresh strawberries all year round, although imported strawberries can still be expensive and not always high quality in terms of flavour. Another consideration is that fresh fruits and vegetables have a limited storage life, and as such, must be used within a short space of time. Pre-prepared foods, particularly foods that have been canned, frozen or dried will have a much longer 'use-by' period.

Pre-prepared foods also have a few other positive points to consider. The use of pre-prepared foods can also save on the necessity to have the equipment to produce the food from the beginning of the preparation and cookery process. This can range from basic equipment such as a board and knife, through to utensils (saucepans, mixers, etc.) and ovens. Pre-prepared foods also offer a consistent standard as many have been through a standardized mass production line, following very precise procedures.

A microwave meal

It is generally accepted that lifestyles have become a lot faster during recent years and the growth in pre-prepared foods has run alongside this trend. There is a view that many people are too busy to spend time cooking, preparing dishes from fresh ingredients using conventional cookery methods. It is now possible to have a ready made meal within a few minutes by simply popping a dish into a microwave. There are also many sauces and mixes available, reducing the amount of preparation needed to prepare a meal. The idea is to simply cut, mix and cook! However, there have been many criticisms of this trend. This includes the reduction in time that families spend together enjoying a meal, the rise in obesity in the western world, where fast food and ready made meals are most highly consumed, as well as the reducing numbers of people actually spending time preparing and cooking using fresh ingredients.

THE POSSIBLE LIMITATIONS AND POTENTIAL IMPLICATIONS OF USING REGENERATED, PRE-PREPARED FOODS

There is mixed success in the regeneration of pre-prepared foods. Depending on the type of food and the method of processing it has been through, the result can have an impact on quality when regenerated. Soft fruits, for example, are not particularly successful when regenerated from any processed form, particularly if it is intended that the fruit is to be used as if it were fresh. During the process, the composition (structure) of the fruit changes and it is impossible for such fruits to re-form into their original state. A strawberry or raspberry, for example, will never return to its fresh firm state once it has been tinned, frozen or dried. Fish also tends to lose its firmness once it has been frozen and then defrosted, making it very difficult to work with if defrosting back into a raw state. With certain, high risk ingredients, a great deal of care has to be taken to ensure that the product retains quality but also that it remains safe to eat. Eggs provide a very good example of a food item where such measures are necessary.

With nearly all foods that are regenerated, certain changes, whether in appearance, texture or nutritional value, unavoidably take place. This can make them much less appealing than their fresh equivalent. People are now more aware of the consequences of diet and the links this has to health and wellbeing.

The hospitality and catering industry has an important role in providing good quality, healthy options for its consumers. The re-introduction of fresh foods in school meals is starting to happen through various projects and there is a great deal of coverage about eating fresh foods in the media (television, newspapers, magazines, etc.). Eating five portions of fresh fruit and vegetables daily (5 a Day!) is a good example of this type of promotion.

However, everything comes at a cost! It is rarely the cheaper option to use fresh, high quality ingredients in place of pre-prepared foods. Other issues, such as skill requirements in preparation and cooking, the life-span of the food and the spending power of the customer often outweigh the use of fresh ingredients in favour or in place of pre-prepared foods.

CHEF'S TIP

Fast food outlets have undertaken to counteract declining sales of their products. There are now more fresh foods available, such as salads and sandwiches and more emphasis on reduced fat, sugar and salt intake.

CHEF'S TIP

Marketing potential is therefore more increased – catering and hospitality outlets can promote the fact that they are producing meals from fresh ingredients.

THE METHODS USED TO REGENERATE PRE-PREPARED FOODS

The methods used to regenerate pre-prepared foods differs according to the food type (dried, fresh, ready made, frozen, pre-prepared, canned) and the processing the food has undertaken. The methods used include the following regeneration processes.

Step-by-step: **Celery being prepared, refreshed and reheated**

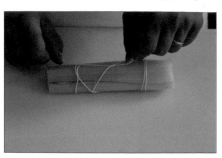

STEP 1 Tying sticks of celery together

STEP 2 Celery is tied into batches for initial cookery

STEP 3 Celery being blanched in boiling water

STEP 4 Refreshing the blanched celery

STEP 5 Braised celery that has been regenerated

STEP 6 Testing the core temperature to ensure that the celery is reheated properly

Reheating

Reheating refers to food that has already been cooked, chilled and frozen. This may be a dish that has been produced from fresh to use at a later date, such as vegetable garnishes and accompaniments, or items made externally by another company, such as ready made meals or sauces.

Re-hydrating

Re-hydrating refers to foods that have had their water content removed to make them dry. Drying foods extends their life-span as the scope for bacterial growth is reduced significantly. As with the majority of life forms, water is essential for survival, growth and reproduction.

To re-hydrate dry foods, the liquid content is placed back into the food. Examples of foods that require re-hydration include dried sauces and soups, dried beans, cereals and grains, such as cous-cous.

Cooking

Other pre-prepared foods will require cooking to ensure they are safe and digestible. Pre-prepared pasta provides an example of a pre-prepared food that can be sold fresh or dried, which requires cooking (boiling, baking) before it is ready to eat. Some ready made meals may also have raw ingredients that require to be cooked through before they are ready and safe to eat.

 CHEF'S TIP

Certain foods will need additional cookery after re-hydration. Examples include pancake mixes, where the mixture will be shallow fried, and scone mixes, where the mixture will be baked.

Dried pasta requires cooking before it is ready to eat

Other products, such as part-baked bread rolls require a degree of cooking before they are ready to eat. In this example, the item is partially cooked and then the cookery process is stopped. At this point, the roll will have a firm structure (shape) but will not be suitable to eat. The roll will normally be packed in a suitable way (vacuum packed) to prevent any bacterial growth or spoilage. When a roll is required, it is cooked again, but this time to complete the cooking process making it safe and enjoyable to eat.

Defrosting

Defrosting can be a complete regeneration process (i.e. no further cooking process is required), and refers to products that simply require defrosting to make them safe and enjoyable to eat. The most obvious examples of this are frozen pastries, cakes and desserts.

THE GENERAL QUALITY POINTS WHEN REGENERATING PRE-PREPARED FOODS

The quality points to look for when selecting, preparing and regenerating pre-prepared foods are very similar to those to look for in any other food items and are described below.

In selection

When buying pre-prepared food items, the following points should be taken into consideration.

QUALITY POINTS

- *Quantity* – is there a sufficient amount of the food item required?

- *Type* – is the food of the type required? Does it meet the specifications for the recipe/dish concerned?

- *Appearance* – does the food look as it should? Is it the right colour, size and shape?

- *Smell* – is there any odour coming from the food? There are very few pre-prepared foods that will have any noticeable smell. The exception to this would be fresh foods that are cooked, chilled and stored to be reheated at a later time. A fresh fish pie, for example, might have a very slight fishy smell, although this should be very subtle and not at all rancid.

- *Temperature* – is the food at the correct temperature depending on its type? – (i.e. fresh, frozen, dried, etc.). This is extremely important as food stored at an incorrect temperature, depending on its type, could be dangerous as it may have developed unsafe levels of bacterial growth.

- *Condition* – is the food in good condition with no blemishes, bruises or breaks?

- *In-date* – is the food within its use by or sell by date? This may have an effect on the food's quality and could also contain potentially unsafe levels of harmful bacteria.

During regeneration

During the regeneration of pre-prepared products, it is essential that correct procedures and instructions are followed to ensure that the product is of the highest possible quality once it has been regenerated.

QUALITY POINTS

- *When re-hydrating* – the correct amount of liquid has been used. The temperature of the liquid is accurate (cold, boiling, etc.).

- *Temperature control* – the food items are placed into, and monitored at, the correct temperatures throughout the cooking process. The temperature is checked to ensure that food items are sufficiently cooked (to a safe level for consumption – core temperature).

- *Time* – the food is cooked for the correct amount of time.

- *Taste* – the food has good flavours and is well seasoned.

- *Consistency* – food items are consistent across all the quality points (size, temperature, appearance, taste, etc.).

- *Texture* – the texture of the food is appropriate to expectations (i.e. crisp, soft, short, etc.).

In finishing

Completing the quality checks in finishing and presenting food items is equally important.

QUALITY POINTS

- *Consistency* – food items should be the same in colour, flavour and temperature. Food items should also be of a consistent portion size and seasoned and sauced in a consistent manner.

- *Presentation* – presentation is a vital element within professional cookery. Service equipment, whether using silver salvers or plates, should be spotlessly clean. Dishes should be garnished consistently and presented in a uniform manner.

The associated products served with regenerated foods

As with all foods, regenerated foods can be enhanced with the addition of further products. This includes the inclusion of appropriate sauces, accompaniments and garnishes.

Assessment of knowledge and understanding

1 Provide one example of a food that can be regenerated from each of the following categories.

DRIED	FRESH	READY MADE	FROZEN	PRE-PREPARED	CANNED

2 List three advantages associated with the use of pre-prepared foods.

i) _____ ii) _____

iii) _____

3 List three possible health considerations associated with the regular consumption of pre-prepared or processed foods.

i) _____ ii) _____

iii) _____

4 Other than health considerations, name three other disadvantages associated with the use of pre-prepared foods.

i) _____ ii) _____

iii) _____

5 How would you ensure that a gâteau was ready to eat if you were regenerating it from frozen?

_____

_____

6 Why do soft fruits change in structure and appearance when processed and regenerated?

_____

_____

7 Provide one example of a food that is regenerated by each of the following methods.

RE-HEATED	RE-HYDRATED	COOKED	DEFROSTED

8 Why do products that have been dried have a longer shelf life (use by date) than their fresh equivalent?

_____

_____

9 After dried foods have been re-hydrated, they may require further cooking. Can you provide two examples of food items and the cookery methods required?

i) _____ ii) _____

10 List four points that you would check to ensure that regenerated dishes were cooked and presented to requirements.

i) _____ ii) _____

iii) _____ iv) _____

CHEF'S PROFILE

Name: GARY RHODES

Position: CHEF & RESTAURATEUR

Establishment: RHODES TWENTY FOUR & RHODES W1 – London
RHODES D7 – Dublin
RHODES RESTAURANT – The Calabash Hotel, Grenada
ARCADIA RHODES & ORIANA RHODES – P&O Superliners

Main responsibilities: Writing and compiling recipes and menus for the restaurants. Cooking and training within the restaurants.

In addition – book writing, TV commitments, cookery demonstrations and presentations.

Best parts of the job: The continual learning that is achieved every day from experimenting and trying out different dishes and menu testing. Also, you can't beat the look of delight on the customer's faces as they enjoy their meal and return an empty plate!

Secrets of a successful chef: Believe in what you are doing and what you are going to achieve. Catering can be a tough career, but the good times far outweigh the bad. To be a part of this exciting industry, you must have the willpower, determination and enthusiasm to want to reach your goals and overcome the challenges that crop up on the way. A good blend of hard work, training and fun will always lead to a successful result.

Recipe: Chicken Fillet steaks

Your mentor or main inspiration: At college, it would have to be Mr Peter Barratt (amongst others), who I am still in close contact with today. A great man with exceptional training skills, knowledge and a passion for cooking.

The Roux Brothers – the godfathers of the industry and a true inspiration throughout my entire career

A brief personal profile: As I'm constantly on the go, I find trying to unwind quite difficult, but with the help of a good workout in my gym, Manchester United on the TV and a relaxing night with my family, I manage to put the day behind me and enjoy the time out from the busy kitchen.

Bread and butter pudding

INGREDIENTS	6–8 PORTIONS
1.5–1.8 pudding dish/basin buttered	1
Medium slices white bread, crusts cut off	12
Unsalted butter, softened	50g
Vanilla pod or few drops of vanilla essence	1
Double cream	400ml
Milk	400ml
Egg yolks	8
Caster sugar, plus extra for the caramelised topping	175g
Sultanas	25g
Raisins	25g

Pre heat the oven to 180°C/350°F/Gas mark 4

Method of work

1 Butter the bread. Split the vanilla pod and place in a saucepan with the cream and milk and bring to the boil. While it is heating, whisk together the egg yolks and caster sugar in a bowl. Allow the cream mix to cool a little, then strain it in to the egg yolks, stirring all the time. You now have the custard.

2 Cut the bread into triangular quarters or halves, and arrange in the dish in three layers, sprinkling the fruit between two layers and leaving the top clear. Now pour over the warm custard, lightly pressing the bread to help it soak in, and leave it to stand for a least 20–30 minutes before cooking to ensure that the bread absorbs all the custard.

3 The pudding can be prepared to this stage several hours in advance and cooked when needed. Place the dish in a roasting tray three-quarters filled with warm water and bake for 20–30 minutes until the pudding begins to set. Don't overcook it or the custard will scramble. Remove the pudding from the water bath, sprinkle it liberally with caster sugar and glaze under the grill on a medium heat or with a gas gun to a crunchy golden finish.

Note

When glazing, the sugar dissolves and caramelises, and you may find that the corners of the bread begin to burn. This helps the flavour, giving a bittersweet taste that mellows when it is eaten with the rich custard, which seeps out of the wonderful bread sponge when you cut into it.

12
Cold food preparation

Unit 112 Cold food preparation

LEARNING OBJECTIVES

On completion of this chapter, learners will be able to:

- State the meal occasions when cold food may be presented
- Identify foods used in cold preparation
- Identify the quality points when preparing cold foods
- Describe a range of hors d'œuvres, salads and sandwiches
- List the techniques used to present cold foods
- List the general safety points to follow when preparing and presenting foods for cold presentation

Some examples of foods suitable for cold preparation

Raw ingredients

Salad items (e.g. lettuces, radish, cucumber, etc.) vegetables (e.g. carrots, onions, peppers, etc.) fruits (e.g. strawberries, melons, oranges, etc.).

Pre-prepared ingredients

Smoked fish (salmon, mackerel, trout, etc.) meat products (e.g. hams, pates or terrines, raised pies, etc.) bread products (e.g. loaves or rolls, speciality breads – ciabatta, naan, pitta; other dough products – croissant, pizza, etc.).

Ingredients that have been cooked and cooled

Roast meats (chicken, beef, pork, etc.) fish/shellfish (poached salmon, prawns, crab, etc.) vegetables (potatoes, fine beans, asparagus, etc.).

It is important to state that food items can come prepared in a variety of formats. This includes frozen, (e.g. prawns) canned (e.g. tuna) or as a convenience product (e.g. ready made pastry cases). This is not limited to any particular type of food.

CHEF'S TIP

Cold food preparation can be described as the putting together of cold food items into a well presented manner. Cold food can be made from raw ingredients, pre-prepared ingredients or items that have been cooked and then cooled.

Step-by-step: **Finely chopping an onion**

STEP 1 Cut off the tip of the root at the top of the onion and trim the base. Peel the onion and cut in half through the root (The root can be identified by a small light brown circle)

STEP 2 With the root pointing away from you, cut thin slices three-quarters of the way up towards the root across the onion. The onion should stay intact as there should be no slices that go right the way through the onion

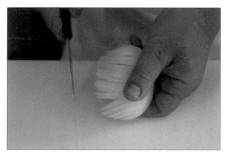

STEP 3 Turn the onion 90°

STEP 4 Holding the knife horizontally, make a cut half way up into the slices of onion. If using a large onion, two cuts can be made across the slices

STEP 5 Cut down the slices to produce finely chopped onion

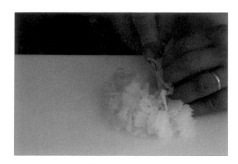

STEP 6 A finely chopped onion

THE MEAL OCCASIONS WHEN COLD FOOD MAY BE PRESENTED

Cold food items can appear at just about any meal occasion. Sometimes cold food items are served exclusively whereas on other occasions they may form part of a meal where hot and cold items will be served. Here are some examples of cold food items being served at a variety of meals.

Breakfast

Throughout most of continental Europe, breakfast usually consists of cold items such as croissant with preserves (jams, marmalade), yoghurt with fresh fruits and selections of cold meats with various styles of bread.

Lunch

Lunch could consist of entirely cold items, a cold buffet for example, with a range of salad items, cold meats, smoked fish, pasta and rice. There are no set rules about the items that can be offered other than that they should be fresh (within use by date), served at the appropriate temperature and safe to eat.

Afternoon tea

It is a traditional meal providing a range of items to enjoy alongside a cup of tea. Examples of items that would commonly be served for afternoon tea include sandwiches, pastries (e.g. Danish, fruit tartlets, etc.) and scones served with fresh cream and sliced strawberries.

Special receptions

A special reception provides the opportunity for chefs to show off their creativity and presentation skills. A special reception may be the launch of a new product for a business or a celebration, or a cocktail party hosted by the captain on a cruise ship.

Dinner

Dinner is usually a more formal occasion and less likely to offer entirely cold items. Portion sizes are generally larger and the quality of food items used are of higher quality. Comparing lunch menus to dinner menus in most restaurants and hotels would confirm this, even by the price difference to customers.

However, similar to lunch, there is scope for cold dishes to be offered as part of a dinner menu and this is acceptable as it provides a range of options for the diner.

CHEF'S TIP

There is also the scope for cold dishes to be offered as part of a menu. In fact, it is good practice to offer a variety of options for the customer to choose from.

CHEF'S TIP

The chef planning has to take the nature of an event into consideration. If guests are standing, for example, they will not be able to use cutlery. Therefore, the food items have to be easily managed by guests and fairly small, maybe even designed to be eaten in one mouthful.

Step-by-step: **Smoked salmon and prawn platter**

STEP 1 The salad ingredients (mixed salad leaves, spring onions, cherry tomatoes, peeled cucumber, fine asparagus tips which have been blanched and refreshed, fresh dill, lemon wedge) and prawns to be prepared for a smoked salmon and prawn platter

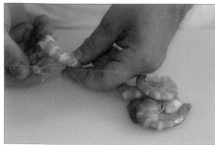

STEP 2 Peel away the shells from the prawns

STEP 3 Place a prawn flat onto a chopping board. Using a small, sharp knife, make an incision into the top of the prawn tail

STEP 4 Using the tip of the knife, remove the intestine from the prawn tail. This is visible as a small black thread

STEP 5 Begin to dress the plate by placing some smoked salmon on a plate. To enhance the presentation, this can be curled and raised to provide the dish with height and dimension

STEP 6 Slice the cucumber and chop the dill

STEP 7 Quarter the cherry tomatoes

STEP 8 Mix the salad leaves with the neatly cut asparagus tips, the quartered cherry tomatoes and sliced spring onions. Put a little vinaigrette into a mixing bowl and toss the salad ingredients to take on the flavour and seasoning from the vinaigrette

STEP 9 Place the salad leaves neatly onto the plate with the smoked salmon. Continue to dress with thin slices of cucumber, the de-veined prawns, brown bread and butter and a wedge of lemon. Spoon over a little more vinaigrette mix with chopped dill

Snacks

One of the most common snacks is the sandwich. A sandwich is the perfect way to satisfy hunger quickly and nutritiously.

There are many examples of snacks and light bites that people often graze on between meals.

FOODS USED IN COLD PREPARATION

Cold food preparation can be described as the joining of food items from raw, pre-prepared or pre-cooked items into the required style of presentation. The range of foods that can be used in cold preparation is huge. There are many classic combinations such as prawn cocktail or Waldorf salad and many other possible combinations.

The following table provides examples of food types that are commonly used in cold food preparation.

TYPE OF FOOD	EXAMPLES
Fruit	Melon, grapefruit, avocado, orange, strawberry, kiwi, grapes, apple, pear, plum, peach, etc.
Vegetables	Onion, garlic, mushrooms, cauliflower, carrot, cabbage, peppers, celery, beetroot, etc.
Meat and meat products	Roast meats and poultry (beef, lamb, pork, chicken, turkey, etc.) hams, pâtés and terrines, pies, etc.
Fish, shellfish and fish products	Smoked fish (salmon, mackerel, trout), tinned fish (sardines, tuna, salmon), pickled fish (herrings), shellfish (prawns, crab, lobster), fresh cooked fish (salmon, sea-bass, cod) etc.
Salad items (also part of the vegetable food group)	Lettuce (lollo rosso, frisée, oakleaf, little gem) cucumber, tomatoes, spring onions, mustard cress, radish, fresh herbs, etc.
Dairy	Cream (sour/acidulated/crème fraiche, fresh cream – single/whipping/double), yoghurt, cheese, milk, etc.
Breads and Pastries	Bread rolls/loaves (wholemeal, white, wholegrain) speciality breads – ciabatta, foccacia, chapatti, naan, pastry products (ragout shells, barquettes, vol-au-vents/bouchées) etc.
Cold sauces, oils, vinegars and dressings	Cold sauces (mustard, Cumberland, horseradish) oils (olive, vegetable, walnut) vinegars (malt, raspberry, white wine) dressings (vinaigrette, mayonnaise) etc.

CHEF'S TIP

If you start work with high quality ingredients, you have more chance of making a high quality finished dish. If your ingredients are of poor quality it is much more difficult to produce a finished dish of high quality.

IDENTIFYING THE QUALITY POINTS WHEN PREPARING COLD FOODS

The quality points to look for in foods will vary between the stages of preparation and cooking. However, it is essential to work with the best quality products available from the offset.

QUALITY POINTS TO LOOK FOR IN RAW INGREDIENTS

- *Freshness* – Ingredients should be as fresh as possible, particularly items such as ripe fruit, vegetables and fish, which are at their peak when only just picked or caught.

- *Appearance* – Appearance plays a big part in the presentation of cold food. Therefore, it is essential that your ingredients have a high-quality appearance in line with the specification for the dish. Appearance covers aspects such as colour, shape and checks for blemishes, breaks or bruising.

- *Smell* – Our sense of smell can inform us if food is off or beginning to turn. Some foods, such as fish have a natural smell, even when fresh, but this is a natural smell from the environment in which they live and should not be too strong. A fish that is off will produce a much stronger and far more unpleasant smell.

- *Temperature* – The temperature at which food is stored is vital to maintain its freshness and appearance, as well as ensuring that it is safe to eat. Checks for temperature should always take place when receiving food items from suppliers.

QUALITY POINTS TO LOOK FOR IN THE PREPARATION OF INGREDIENTS

- *In handling and preparing* – Food items need to be handled and prepared carefully to produce a high quality finished product. Food items should be prepared to the specification required for the dish being produced. This requires knife work to be performed carefully and accurately throughout all the preparation stages.

- *In peeling* – Following the washing of food items such as vegetables and fruits, it may be necessary to peel them. This could be a potato, turnip, an apple or pear. It should be noted that peeling is a technique, and as such, a skill.

- *In cutting and chopping* – Accurate cutting of food into a variety of shapes and sizes can enhance dishes, making them very appealing for the customer. Consideration of the size ingredients are cut and the amount used will also influence the flavour of the dish. For example, if onions were going to be used in a potato salad and they were chopped very finely, their flavour would be delicate and not overpowering. However, if large chunks of onion were used, the flavour would be stronger and the texture much coarser.

- *In carving* – Carving refers to the slicing of cold meats. Carving is quite a difficult skill to master. As meat is an expensive commodity, accurate carving is very important so that waste is minimized. Well carved meat looks very appealing when presented carefully.

- *In slicing* – Slicing is a similar skill but performed on different food items. Smoked fish, such as smoked salmon, is often cut into thin slices. Vegetables, such as tomatoes and cucumber are also often cut into slices when presented as cold food.

- *In shredding* – Many vegetables are shredded when used in cold dishes. For example, to make fresh coleslaw, onion and white cabbage are shredded into very fine strips. Carrots can also be shredded, although many chefs would choose to grate the carrot rather than use a knife. Lettuces, such as iceberg and little gems, are also often shredded in a similar way when being used in cold presentation.

- *In proportion/amount of ingredients* – Many cold dishes consist of more than one ingredient. As such, it is very important to gain an understanding of the quantities (ratios) in which ingredients are mixed together. Flavours should complement (balance) one another and the combinations of foods need to be considered when menu planning.

- *In dressing* – Cold foods, particularly salads, are usually dressed with a cold sauce to provide additional flavours and bind ingredients together. A plain mixed leaf salad without any dressing can be fairly uninspiring to eat. The addition of a well made, flavoursome vinaigrette completely changes the eating quality of such a dish.

> **CHEF'S TIP**
>
> When using vinaigrette, it is good practice to mix the salad with the dressing at the last possible moment before being served. If the salad was mixed and then left to sit, the leaves would soak up the dressing and become limp and soggy. By mixing just before service, the flavours are fresh and the leaves will be in good, crisp condition.

Other dressings regularly used in cold preparations include:

- *Mayonnaise* – e.g. egg mayonnaise, potato salad.
- *Yoghurt* – e.g. raita (yogurt mixed with diced cucumber and mint).
- *Sour/acidulated cream* (cream with lemon juice) – used on a range of salads including Mimosa salad and Japanese salad.
- *Seasoning* – Cold food is greatly enhanced by seasoning. For example, sliced tomato is transformed by the addition of salt and pepper, although salt intake should be monitored for health reasons.
- *Garnishing and presenting* – Garnishes are used to make dishes appealing and can range from simple effective garnishes to elaborate, artistic pieces. Cold food is lifted by its presentation and it is therefore very important that care and thought is put into producing an attractive range of food items.

HORS D'ŒUVRES

Hors d'œuvres is a French term used to describe foods served before or outside (hors) the main dishes of a meal (d'œuvres). The term is often replaced in English with terms such as 'starter' or 'first course'.

Traditionally, hors d'œuvres were served in two styles. These were:

- Hors d'œuvres variés (an assortment of dishes)
- Hors d'œuvres single (a single main food item).

Assorted hors d'œuvres consist of a range of dishes whereby the guest will receive or have the choice of a variety of items. They should utilize a range of food items including meat, fish, vegetable, fruit and dairy based dishes. The customer then has a choice as to which dishes they would like and in the quantities they prefer. A selection of hors d'œuvres can be plated, with a selection of each item being placed neatly onto the plate. Alternatively, the individual dishes could be served separately in ravier dishes, flats, trays or even bowls, giving the customer a choice of preferred items.

Step-by-step: **Vinaigrette**

STEP 1 The ingredients required to make vinaigrette – vinegar (e.g. white wine vinegar, cider vinegar, etc.), oil (e.g. vegetable, olive), mustard (e.g. English, Dijon, whole-grain, etc.), salt and freshly ground black pepper

STEP 2 Place the mustard into a mixing bowl

STEP 3 Mix in the vinegar and season with the salt and freshly ground black pepper

STEP 4 Whisk all the ingredients together

STEP 5 Gradually, pour the oil slowly whilst whisking continuously to form an emulsion (In this example, a mixture of olive and vegetable oils are being used)

STEP 6 Continue to add the oil while whisking until all the oil has been added. A typical vinaigrette is made up of 4 to 6 parts oil to one part vinegar. The liquid should thicken slightly as more oil is added

A single hors d'œuvre focuses on one main food item being the main part of the dish. For example, smoked salmon or pâté could be offered as the principle food item, although it is common practice for the dish would contain other food items to garnish and complement the dish.

SALADS

Salads also fall into two main categories:

■ *Simple salads* – as the title suggests, these are basic salads containing one or a small number of ingredients such as a mixed leaf salad or a tomato salad.

■ *Composite salads* – contain a number of different ingredients and are usually bound together with a suitable dressing (vinaigrette, mayonnaise, etc.). Examples of composite salads include mixed vegetable salad, meat salad and Niçoise salad.

Step-by-step: **Tuna Niçoise salad**

STEP 1 Cut the cooked new potatoes into quarters

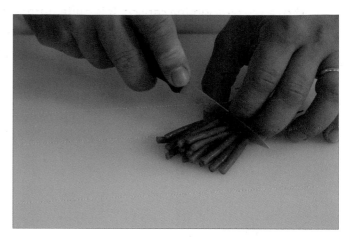

STEP 2 Cut the green beans into neat lengths

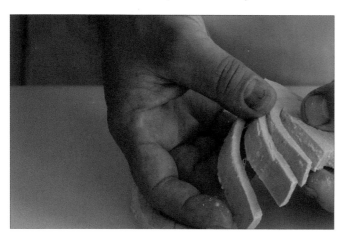

STEP 3 Separate the tuna into its natural flakes

STEP 4 Season, bind with vinaigrette and serve

SANDWICHES

Sandwiches are a very popular and nutritious cold food item enjoyed by millions of people on a daily basis. In professional cookery, there are many ways in which sandwiches are prepared and presented. It should be noted that sandwiches can appear as hot as well as cold items, although in this chapter we will be focusing on cold sandwiches only.

Sandwiches can be made using any form of bread, of which there are many varieties made from a wide range of flours. Breads in styles from around the world are now readily available from suppliers.

A standard sandwich is made up of two slices of bread which is filled with a filling. The range of possible fillings and combinations is endless and is very much dictated by the customer. In many modern sandwich shops, which is now the fastest growing area of the fast food sector in the United Kingdom, sandwiches are made to the customers' exact requirements. This ranges from the type of bread they would like to the type and number of fillings they require. The sandwich is then priced accordingly.

In the hotel environment, sandwiches are often available as room service or as part of an afternoon tea service. It is quite normal practice for the sandwiches to have the crusts removed and be cut into small triangular shapes. From a standard sized loaf, two slices would normally make four small triangular sandwiches.

Sandwich fillings

Sandwich fillings are almost unlimited. However, there are classic fillings and combinations that have become favourites and have stood up to the test of time.

Examples of fillings:

Egg Mayonnaise	Cheese and pickle
Ham and tomato	Tuna and sweet corn
Beef and horseradish	Cream cheese and chive
Smoked salmon	Cucumber

Open sandwiches

Not all sandwiches are made with two slices of bread. The open sandwich is associated with Scandinavia (Denmark, Sweden, Finland and Norway) and its tradition for smorgasbord, a buffet style event. This type of sandwich uses a single piece of bread to which a hot or cold topping is added. Open sandwiches are usually carefully garnished with small cuts of various items to enhance their presentation.

Examples of open sandwiches include:

- Roast beef with tomato
- Scrambled egg with pancetta
- Smoked salmon with dill
- Asparagus, baby plum tomato and Serrano ham.

Once again, the possibilities are endless. However, it is good practice for open sandwiches to be served neatly, with care taken over their presentation. Small garnishes, such as chopped herbs, sliced radishes, brunoise of vegetables, capers and gherkins are often used to enhance the dish.

A platter of mixed sandwiches

Examples of flours and breads include:

FLOURS

White

Wholemeal

Wholegrain

Rye

Granary

BREADS

French sticks

Ciabatta

Cottage loaves

Foccacia

Rolls

Soda

Step-by-step: **A range of sandwiches**

STEP 1 Using an egg slicer, slice a boiled and refreshed egg

STEP 2 Place the egg into a bowl, season with salt and a little freshly ground white pepper and bind with mayonnaise

STEP 3 Place the egg mixture into the centre of a slice of buttered bread

STEP 4 Using a palette knife, spread the mixture evenly across the slice of bread

STEP 5 Sprinkle with some fresh mustard cress

STEP 6 Place another slice of buttered bread on top of the egg and cress to form a sandwich

STEP 7 Using a serrated slicing knife, neatly cut the crusts from the sandwich

STEP 8 Sandwiches can be cut into many shapes and sizes. In this example, cucumber sandwiches are being cut into finger slices

STEP 9 In this example, a round cutter is being used to produced circular smoked salmon sandwiches

STEP 10 Circular shaped smoked salmon sandwiches

STEP 11 In this example, some pate filled sandwiches are being cut into squares

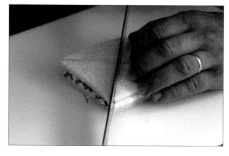

STEP 12 And finally, the egg and cress sandwiches are cut from corner to corner (diagonally) to produce triangular shaped sandwiches

CANAPÉS

Canapés are small, bite-size items usually served at cocktail parties, promotional events or alongside pre-dinner drinks. Canapés can be made from a variety of bases and topped with a variety of toppings. They can be savoury or sweet and served cold or hot.

Canapé bases can be made of fresh bread or bread that has been fried or toasted. Bases can also be made of pastry, such as short, sweet and puff pastry. Occasionally, food items will not require a base. A cherry tomato stuffed with cream cheese, for example, would not require a base as the tomato itself provides a sufficient shell to allow for easy pick up.
As with sandwiches, there are no restrictions on the possibilities of food items used in the production of canapés. It is important, however, that a variety of food items are used in order to satisfy a wide range of tastes.

As canapés are so small, the decorative work involved can be quite fiddly. Therefore, good knife-skills are required to ensure that garnishes are of the same shape and size. Other garnishes may require the chef to pipe a garnish onto the canapé. Once again, this will require a steady hand and precise handling to ensure that the product is neat and well presented. Finally, it is common practice for canapés to be served on flats or trays. In these circumstances, canapés are laid in uniform lines and should look identical. Canapés laid in such lines form a very effective presentation despite being relatively simple. Once again, a variety of food items, such as:

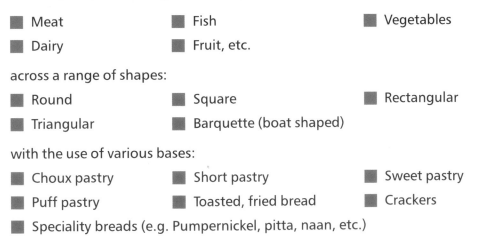

- Meat
- Dairy
- Fish
- Fruit, etc.
- Vegetables

across a range of shapes:

- Round
- Triangular
- Square
- Barquette (boat shaped)
- Rectangular

with the use of various bases:

- Choux pastry
- Puff pastry
- Speciality breads (e.g. Pumpernickel, pitta, naan, etc.)
- Short pastry
- Toasted, fried bread
- Sweet pastry
- Crackers

. . . will provide an effective range of food items, textures, colours and flavours to produce a good quality selection of well presented canapés.

A selection of canapés

SAFETY POINTS TO CONSIDER WHEN PREPARING AND PRESENTING FOODS FOR COLD PRESENTATION

■ Hygiene should be maintained at the highest level. Preparing cold food items involves raw and cooked items, both of which must be handled properly to ensure that the foods do not become contaminated.

■ Cold food items whether served raw or previously cooked will not be cooked again to kill bacteria as with hot items. This is one reason why hygiene standards must be very high when working with cold foods. All equipment and utensils should be clean and well maintained so they do not contaminate the food. Clothing and personal hygiene standards should also be extremely high and food items should be handled as little as possible.

■ All cold food items should be stored in appropriate conditions, which would normally be in a refrigerator between 1°C and 5°C. Food items should always be covered, clearly labelled and dated. When serving cold foods, they should be unwrapped as late of possible and ideally served from refrigerated equipment. The time food is left out for service should be limited to the minimum time possible to avoid any form of contamination. Food items should also be served from clean utensils.

Assessment of knowledge and understanding

1 What is the difference between a simple salad and a composite salad?

2 Why is it important to cut foods into regular shapes and sizes for cold presentation?

3 List four sauces that are regularly used with cold dishes.
   i) _____ iii) _____
   ii) _____ iv) _____

4 What is the difference between an open and closed sandwich?

5 What size should a canapé be served and why?

6 Name four possible bases for a canapé.
   i) _____ iii) _____
   ii) _____ iv) _____

7 What factors would you take into consideration when producing an assortment of hors d'œurves (hors d'œurves variés).

8 Name four items that could be used as single hors d'œurves.
   i) _____ iii) _____
   ii) _____ iv) _____

9 What is the purpose of seasoning and dressing cold food items?

10 Name four types of lettuce.
   i) _____ iii) _____
   ii) _____ iv) _____

11 What is the difference between shredding and chopping?

12 Why should you dress a salad just before it is served?

13 Name three pieces of equipment that could be used to serve an assortment of buffet items.
   i) _____ iii) _____
   ii) _____

14 What quality points would you look for in freshly segmented oranges?

15 Why is it important to have the correct proportions of mixed cold food items when binding them together?

CHEF'S PROFILE

Name: MARK DODSON

Position: Chef/Owner

Establishment: The Masons Arms, Knowstone. Devon

Training and experience:

1975–1978: Colchester Institute – City and Guilds qualifications 705, 706/2, 707/2, 707/3 and the Institute's 'Advanced Cookery Diploma'.

Professional association: The Academy of Culinary Arts (joined 1988).
Academician Mentor 2001.
Invested 2004.

Employment:

1977–1983 Held many positions in UK restaurants and hotels working alongside experienced Head chefs. For instance between 1981 and 1983 worked as Chef De Partie Tournant, Le Talbooth Restaurant, Dedham. After one year promoted to Sous Chef. Also worked part-time at Althorp, the residence of Earl Spencer as the catering was under the supervision of the one Michelin starred Le Talbooth.

September 1983–September 2001 The Waterside Inn, Bray, Berkshire. Joined The Waterside Inn as Commis de Cuisine under the direction of Chef Patron, Michel Roux. In 1988 was made Head Chef (position held for over 13 years). In 1990 The Waterside Inn named Egon Ronay Restaurant of the Year.

June 2005 The Mason's Arms, Knowstone, Devon. Chef-Owner.

October 2005/6 Inclusion in Michelin 2006 and 2007 Eating out in pubs guides 'We liked this one best' symbol.

November 2005 Awarded One Star in 2006 Egon Ronay Guide.

November 2005 Awarded Two AA Rosettes for 2007 guide.

January 2006 Awarded One Michelin star in 2006 guide.

April 2006 Inclusion in Alastair Sawday's Special Places Pubs & Inns 2006.

September 2006 Awarded 6/10 The Good Food Guide 2007.

Main responsibilities: The day to day running of our own business, training of staff and development of dishes and recipes.

Best parts of the job: Satisfaction of knowing that the job has been well done, customer feedback, and the training and development of the team.

Secrets of a successful Chef: Listen and learn, every Chef will have a different technique, a different view on how food should taste and look and a different palate; try to understand what makes your chef special.

Advice for a starter Chef, just beginning their training: Work hard, be alert, absorb as much knowledge as possible and keep a sense of humour.

Recipe: Amaretto parfait with vanilla plums.

Your mentor or main inspiration: Michel Roux

A brief personal profile: I love to eat out and to be entertained, I love to go to the coast on my day off even in the worst Devon weather! I have a love of music and collect records and memorabilia from the 60s, 70s and 80s. I love to unwind with a good blast of The Clash.

Iced Amaretto parfait, vanilla plums and pistachio biscuit

INGREDIENTS	8 PORTIONS
Double cream	350ml
Egg yolks	4 yolks
Sugar	100g
Amaretto	75g
Leaf of gelatine	1 leaf

Plum syrup

INGREDIENTS	8 PORTIONS
Water	300ml
Sugar	300g
Star anise	1 star anise
Cinnamon stick	½ stick
Split vanilla pod	1 pod
Clove	1 clove

Method of work

1 Whisk the double cream until holding but not too firm, reserve.

2 Put the yolks into a mixing bowl and slowly whisk, cook the sugar to 121°C.

3 Pour the sugar onto the yolks and mix, dissolve the pre-soaked gelatine in the warmed Amaretto, pass into the mixture and continue whisking until cold.

4 Gently fold the whipped cream into the egg/sugar mixture until incorporated.

5 Mould and freeze until required.

For the plums

1 Split the plums in half and remove the stone.

2 Make a syrup with the remaining ingredients in table.

3 Add the plums to the boiling syrup, bring back to the boil and then leave to cool.

To Serve

De-mould the parfait and place on the plate, decorate with a little Crème Anglaise and some reduced plum syrup. Garnish with a biscuit (brandy snap or cigarette) sprinkled with finely chopped pistachio nuts.

RECIPES

Chicken Caesar salad

INGREDIENTS	4 PORTIONS	10 PORTIONS
Large cloves of garlic, sliced	2 cloves	5 cloves
Olive oil	150ml	375ml
Lemon juice	1tbsp	2½ tbsp
English mustard	¼ tsp	¾ tsp
Freshly ground black pepper		
Egg, boiled for 2 minutes	1 egg	3 eggs
Anchovy fillets, finely chopped	2 fillets	5 fillets
Slices of bread, crusts removed and cut into 1 inch cubes	2 slices	5 slices
Small cos lettuce	2 lettuces	5 lettuces
Freshly grated Parmesan cheese	4tbsp	10tbsp
Parmesan cheese for shaving		
Chicken Suprêmes (optional)	2 each	5 each

Method of work

1 Remove the best leaves (whole) from the cos lettuce carefully and wash. Drain and carefully place in a tray and chill. Keep the lettuce, if storing, in a moist but cool environment.

2 Mix the garlic with the oil and leave to marinade for 20 minutes.

3 Strain off ¾ of the oil to make the dressing and add it to the lemon juice, mustard, pepper and egg. Whisk well and add the finely chopped anchovies and grated Parmesan cheese. Check and adjust the seasoning as required.

4 Pour the remaining oil into a frying pan, with the garlic, and heat slowly. When the garlic slices begin to sizzle, remove them with a perforated spoon. Add the bread cubes and fry, turning frequently with a slice or perforated spoon until the croutons are crisp and brown.

5 Using a perforated spoon, lift out the croutons and drain on absorbent paper.

6 Toss the lettuce in the dressing. Sprinkle over the croutons and serve in a bowl with fresh Parmesan shavings.

Note: 'Chicken' Caesar Salad has become popular choice throughout the world. This includes the addition of a chicken breast, which has usually been grilled.

Poached salmon with mayonnaise

INGREDIENTS	4 PORTIONS	10 PORTIONS
Pin-boned supremes of salmon (150g)	4 supremes	10 supremes
Court bouillon (poaching liquid)	1 litre	2.5 litres
Small cucumber	1 cucumber	2 cucumbers
Vinaigrette	20ml	50ml
Mayonnaise	250ml	700ml
Water	1 litre	2.5 litres
White wine vinegar	50ml	125ml
Sliced carrots	25g	65g
Sliced onions	50g	125g
A few parsley stalks		
A few sprigs of thyme		
Bay leaf	1 leaf	3 leaves
Peppercorns	8 peppercorns	20 peppercorns

Method of work

1 Bring the court bouillon to a gentle simmer in a wide flat saucepan (e.g. sauteuse).
2 Carefully place the salmon supremes into the liquid and poach gently for 3–4 minutes.
3 Remove from the heat, leaving the salmon in the court bouillon until cold.
4 Once cold, remove from the pan and place on a tray. Carefully cover with cling film and chill.
5 Meanwhile, peel and slice the cucumber very finely and dress with a little vinaigrette.
6 Arrange the dressed cucumber neatly on a plate and place a supreme of salmon alongside.
7 Serve with cold mayonnaise and an assortment of salads.

Mayonnaise

Mayonnaise has a variety of uses, for example, in hors-d'œuvres, in sandwiches or even as a dip.

 VIDEO CLIP Making mayonnaise

INGREDIENTS	4 PORTIONS	10 PORTIONS
Fresh egg yolk	1 yolk	3 yolks
Vinegar or vinaigrette	¾ tsp	2tsp
Salt and ground white pepper (to season)		
Mustard (e.g. English, Dijon, whole-grain)	¼ tsp	½ tsp
Olive or other good quality oil	100ml	250ml
Boiled water (just below boiling point)	1tsp	1tsp

Method of work

1 Place yolks, vinegar and seasoning in a bowl and whisk well.
2 Gradually pour on the oil very slowly, whisking continuously.
3 Add the boiling water whisking well.
4 Correct the seasoning and consistency (i.e. if too thick, a little vinegar or water may be added).

Note: Mayonnaise will curdle/split due to the following:
- The oil is added too quickly.
- The oil is cold.
- The sauce is insufficiently whisked during production.
- The yolks are stale.

The method of rethickening a curdled/split mayonnaise is as follows:
- Take a clean bowl, add a teaspoon of boiling water and gradually whisk in the curdled sauce.
- Take a fresh yolk thinned slightly with ½ teaspoon of cold water. Whisk well before gradually whisking in the curdled sauce.

Coleslaw

INGREDIENTS	4 PORTIONS	10 PORTIONS
Mayonnaise	125ml	300ml
White cabbage, finely shredded (chiffonade)	200g	500g
Carrot, julienne or finely grated	50g	125g
Onion, finely sliced	50g	125g

Method of work

1 To shred the cabbage, first remove the outside leaves.
2 Cut the cabbage into quarters through the stalk.
3 Remove the centre stalk from each quarter at an angle and wash the remaining leaves.
4 Taking a manageable batch of leaves at a time, shred finely using a rocking motion with the knife.
5 Mix with the julienne or grated carrot and finely sliced onion.
6 Bind with mayonnaise and season.
7 Serve chilled in an appropriate bowl.

VIDEO CLIP
Making coleslaw

Pesto sauce

INGREDIENTS	4 PORTIONS	12 PORTIONS
Pine nuts	50g	150g
Olive oil	150ml	450ml
Cloves of garlic	2 cloves	6 cloves
Large bunch of basil	1 bunch	3 bunches
Parmesan cheese	50g	150g
Salt and freshly ground black pepper		

Method of work

1 Colour the nuts lightly under the grill or through the oven, then allow to cool.
2 Take the garlic cloves and basil and grind to a paste.
3 Add the Parmesan cheese, toasted nuts and oil and blend to a purée by placing in a blender or, more authentically (traditionally), using a pestle and mortar.
4 Season with salt and freshly ground white pepper and place in a jar for up to 2–3 days in the fridge.

Classic Niçoise salad

INGREDIENTS	4 PORTIONS	10 PORTIONS
Medium tomatoes	8 tomatoes	20 tomatoes
Hard-boiled eggs	8 eggs	20 eggs
Cooked anchovy fillets or tinned anchovies	8 fillets or 350g (tinned)	20 fillets or 700g (tinned)
Cucumber	1 cucumber	2 cucumbers
Green peppers	2 peppers	5 peppers
Spring onions	4 spring onions	10 spring onions
Small broad beans or haricots verts	200g	500g
Clove garlic, peeled and cut in half	1 clove	3 cloves
Black olives	100g	100g
Olive oil	4tbsp	10tbsp
Basil leaves	4 leaves	10 leaves
Salt, pepper		

Method of work

1 Blanch, peel and quarter the tomatoes.
2 Salt them slightly on the chopping board.
3 Quarter or slice the hard-boiled eggs.
4 Cut each anchovy fillet into 3 or 4 pieces.
5 Peel the cucumber and slice finely.
6 Cut the peppers, onions and broad beans (or haricots verts) into very thin slices.
7 Rub a large salad bowl thoroughly with the two halves of the clove of garlic and put in all the above ingredients except the tomatoes.
8 Drain the tomatoes, salt them again slightly and add to the bowl.
9 Arrange decoratively in a salad bowl and chill.
10 Make a dressing with the olive oil, the finely chopped basil, pepper and salt.
11 Pour on to the salad and serve immediately.

Tartare sauce

INGREDIENTS	4 PORTIONS	10 PORTIONS
Mayonnaise	125ml	300ml
Capers, chopped	12g	30g
Gherkins, chopped; parsley, chopped	25g	60g

Method of work

■ Mix all the above ingredients together to form a blended sauce.

Potato and chive salad

INGREDIENTS	4 PORTIONS	10 PORTIONS
Cooked potatoes or new potatoes (chilled)	200g	500g
Vinaigrette	1tbsp	2½ tbsp
Chives	25g	70g
Mayonnaise	50ml	125ml
Salt and freshly ground pepper		

Method of work

1 Cut the potatoes in to ½ inch dice and lightly coat with the vinaigrette (new potatoes can be left whole or cut in half).
2 Thin the mayonnaise slightly with a tiny drop of water and correct the seasoning, if required.
3 Finely chop the chives and mix into the mayonnaise, reserving some for decoration.
4 Mix the mayonnaise with the potatoes. The mayonnaise should bind the potatoes, rather than provide a sauce!
5 Sprinkle with the remaining chopped chives.
6 Serve in an appropriate bowl or dish.

Vinaigrette

INGREDIENTS	4 PORTIONS
Oil (vegetable, olive – according to required flavour, etc.)	4–5tbsp
Mustard (English, Dijon, wholegrain according to required flavour, etc.)	1tsp
Vinegar (Malt, white wine, raspberry, etc, according to required flavour, etc.)	1tbsp
Salt and freshly ground pepper	

Note: When making vinaigrette, the ratios of ingredients remain the same – e.g. between 4 to 6 parts oil to 1 part vinegar according to taste.

Method of work

1 Place the vinegar in a mixing bowl, add the mustard and seasoning and mix well.
2 Using a whisk, gradually add the oil whisking vigorously until the oil emulsifies with the vinegar.
3 The dressing will thicken slightly as the oil is added.
4 Finally check for taste, particularly sharpness from the vinegar and adjust the seasoning, if necessary.
5 Serve as required.

Tomato, feta and red onion salad

INGREDIENTS	4 PORTIONS	10 PORTIONS
Baby plum tomatoes	200g	500g
Feta cheese, cubed and marinated in olive oil with fresh herbs (e.g. basil, tarragon, thyme, etc.)	200g	500g
Red onion, finely shredded	200g	500g
Fresh pesto		
Freshly torn basil leaves		

Method of work

1 Mix the tomatoes, Feta cheese and sliced red onions in a bowl.
2 Coat with the dressing (pesto) and check for seasoning.
3 Place in a suitable bowl and sprinkle with freshly torn basil leaves.

Vegetable salad/Russian salad

INGREDIENTS	4 PORTIONS	10 PORTIONS
Shelled peas	100g	250g
Green beans	100g	250g
Cauliflower florets	6 florets	15 florets
Potatoes	2 potatoes	5 potatoes
Carrots	2 carrots	5 carrots
Small gherkins, drained and diced	3 gherkins	8 gherkins
Cooked beetroot, diced	1 beetroot	3 beetroots
Egg, hard-boiled, shelled and diced	1 egg	3 eggs
Mayonnaise to bind		

Method of work

1 Cook the peas, beans, cauliflower, potatoes and carrots in separate pans of boiling water until al dente. Drain well and chop into fairly small dice (other than the peas).
2 Put all the vegetables in a salad bowl with the gherkins, beetroot and egg.
3 Stir in enough mayonnaise to provide a coating. Check and adjust the seasoning.
4 Chill in the refrigerator for at least 1 hour.
5 Serve in an appropriate dish or bowl.

APPENDIX 1: AREAS WHERE HAZARDS MIGHT OCCUR

STEP	HAZARD	CONTROL
Purchasing	■ Contaminated high risk foods ■ Damaged goods ■ Growth of pathogens during delivery	■ There must be sufficient storage facilities ■ Purchase only from approved suppliers ■ Deliveries to be delivered under suitable conditions. Chilled food at 8°C or below Frozen food at −18°C or below
Receipt of goods	■ Contaminated high risk foods ■ Damaged or decomposed goods ■ Incorrect specifications ■ Growth of pathogens between the time of receipt and storage	■ All deliveries checked ■ Appropriate labelling ■ Prompt and correct storage
Storage	■ Contamination of high risk foods ■ Contamination through poor handling ■ Contamination by pests ■ Spoilage of food by decomposition	■ Correct usage of refrigeration regimes ■ Foods suitably stored in the correct packaging or receptacles ■ Materials that are in direct contact with food must be of food-grade quality ■ A contract for a pest control service must be in place ■ Correct stock rotation ■ Out of date and unfit foodstuffs removed from the premises
Preparation	■ Contamination of high risk foods ■ Contamination through poor handling ■ Growth of pathogens and toxins	■ Keep raw and cooked foods separate ■ Use pasteurised eggs for raw and lightly cooked egg dishes ■ All food contact surfaces must be fit for purpose ■ Food handlers trained in hygienic food handling techniques ■ Keep the exposure of fresh foods at ambient temperatures to a minimum ■ Label all food that is to be used more than one day in advance of production with its description and use by date
Cooking	■ Survival of pathogens and spores	■ Cook all foods to the minimum recommended temperature
Chilling	■ Growth of pathogens, spores = Toxin production ■ Contamination	■ Cool foods as quickly as possible, to 8°C in 90 minutes ■ Keep food that is chilling loosely covered ■ Use only clean equipment
Hot hold	■ Growth of pathogens and toxin production ■ Contamination by staff and customers especially in self service operations	■ Maintain food at 63°C and discard after two hours ■ Keep containers covered when not in service ■ Use sneeze screens ■ Supervise self service
Cold hold	■ Growth of pathogens and toxin production ■ Contamination by staff and customers especially in self service operations	■ Keep food at 5°C and discard after four hours ■ Keep containers covered when not in service ■ Use sneeze screens ■ Supervise self service
Cold takeaway	■ If the food is kept at ambient temperature there can be increased growth of pathogens and toxin production while in the possession of the customer	■ Keep food refrigerated at 5°C until being sold ■ Meals to be given out no longer than four hours prior to the time of consumption ■ Use insulated containers and freezer pack
Hot serve	■ Growth of pathogens, spores = Toxin production ■ Contamination	■ Serve immediately on removal from holding equipment ■ Keep food covered when service is not in progress

BEEF CUTS CHECKLIST

Timings vary according to the thickness of the meat and the degree of cooking preferred. Timings given are approximate each side.

	Grilling	Frying/ griddling/ dry frying	Stir frying	Roasting	Casserole Stew Pot roast Braising
Beef Steaks					
Sandwich 1–2mm (1/8")	1–2 mins each side	45 secs–1min each side	Not recommended	Not recommended	Not recommended
Thin cut sirloin steaks 1.5cm (5/8")	2–4 mins each side	2–4 mins each side	Cut into strips: 2–4 mins+2 mins with veg	Not recommended	Not recommended
Sirloin, rump, rib eye 2cm (¾")	Rare: 2½ mins Med: 4 mins Well: 6 mins Each side	Rare: 2½ mins Med: 4 mins Well: 6 mins each side	Cut into strips: 2-4 mins+2 mins with veg	Not recommended	Not recommended
Fillet, T-bone, frying, medallions 2–3cm (¾–1¼")	Rare: 3–4 mins Med: 4–5 mins Well: 6–7 mins each side	Rare: 3–4 mins Med: 4–5 mins Well: 6–7 mins each side	Not recommended	Not recommended	Not recommended
Stewing steak (chuck, blade)	Not recommended	Not recommended	Not recommended	Not recommended	Oven temp: gas mark 3, 170°C, 325°F Stew 2–3 hours
Braising steak (shin, leg, neck)	Not recommended	Not recommended	Not recommended	Not recommended	Braise 1½–2½ hours
Beef Joints					
Sirloin, topside, top rump, silverside, rib, brisket	——	——	——	Sirloin, topside, top rump, silverside, rib: Oven temp: gas mark 4–5, 180°C, 350°F **Rare** 20 mins per 450g/½kg(lb) + 20 mins **Medium** 25 mins per 450g/½kg(lb) + 25 mins **Well done** 30 mins per 450g/½kg(lb) + 30 mins	Silverside, rib and brisket: Oven temp: gas mark 4–5, 180°C, 350°F **Pot roast** 30–40 mins per 450g/½kg(lb) + 30–40 mins

Do not use these methods for joints

Glossary

A consistent finished dish A reliable and repeatedly good quality dish.

Abrasions scratches.

Absorb fat or oil soaking up oil in a similar way that a sponge soaks up water.

Accommodation somewhere to stay e.g. a room in a hotel.

Acid ingredient an ingredient that is sharp and acidic such as lemon or lime.

Acknowledging the customer showing the customer that you know they are there.

Additives and preservatives additional ingredients, sometimes chemically based, to enhance (improve) flavours and extend the life-span of the product.

Adversely affected harmed as a result or consequence.

Alloy a mixture of two or more metals (used to make knifes).

Ambient temperature the surrounding air temperature.

Antibacterial gel gel that sterilizes and prevents contamination.

Anti-perspirant prevents sweating.

Appetizing appealing, tasty and attractive.

Aromatic ingredients ingredients that create an aroma or fragrance to the dish – e.g. herbs.

Aspiring chefs those who are aiming to become chefs.

Assessment a measurement or review of skills and/or knowledge.

Benefit from the process become better, helped or improved by using the process being discussed.

Bodily functions the various work the body performs e.g. walking, talking, listening, repairing injuries, etc.

Carcass the skeleton of an animal (after removing the meat).

Career progression changing from one job or role to another, usually as a promotion or to advance a career.

Cell structure the way our cells in our bodies are organized.

Circulation of air the flow of air (evenly).

Circumstances situations, times when a situation occurs

Compensation a payment made for damages (to health, property, reputation, etc).

Comprehensive cleaning thorough, deep cleaning.

Condition to eat state or form in which food is appropriate and safe to eat

Consolidated combined, brought together.

Consumption the intake/eating of certain foods.

Contamination of food affected by bacteria.

Contraction of muscle tightening of the muscle structure.

Contribution the input individuals make towards a goal/target.

Conventional cookery methods traditional cooking using the standard methods of cookery.

Correcting seasoning and consistency adjusting the seasoning and consistency to improve a sauce before eating.

Corrosion something (material) that is subject to decay.

Creativity originality, imagination, vision, inventiveness.

Criticisms people stating their disapproval or disagreement.

Cuisine the style of food produced and offered by a restaurant.

Decorative work the detail that makes food very pleasing to the eye

Delicate flavours subtle, fine flavours (e.g. in a soup or sauce).

Deodorant conceals (covers up) undesired smells.

Dictated by the customer at the choice of the customer/according to their order

Dietician a person qualified to regulate feeding and the kinds of foods eaten.

Digestion food/nutrients being absorbed/processed by the body.

Dimension another level (additional) of flavour.

Directly exposed bare or uncovered/in first line contact with.

Disposable towels towels that are thrown away after use.

Domestic used at home rather than in a commercial (working) environment (situation).

Economical the cheapest or providing the best value.

Economy the relationship between money, industry and employment in a country.

Egg wash beaten egg with a little milk added.

Emergency Services Police, Fire Brigade, Ambulance.

Emphasis on reduced fat, sugar and salt intake stressing the importance that intake of these items has on our diet and health.

Enhance presentation improve the presentation of the dish.

Enhanced improved by the addition (e.g. of herbs).

Excreta waste discharged from the body – faeces, urine.

Exposure being in contact or in the direct environment e.g. exposure to loud noises could cause hearing problems.

Extract flavours bring out flavours.

Fire detection equipment e.g. smoke alarms, equipment that detects smoke and/or heat and raises the alarm.

Flammable substances materials/liquids that will ignite (catch fire).

Food sector a segment or part of the industry as a whole

Hazardous Substances materials/liquids that could cause injury or damage to health.

Health implications consequences/potential impact on our health.

Humidity the amount of moisture in the air.

Immune system the body's natural resistance to disease. This protects the body and promotes recovery.

Impart additional flavours to pass on flavours from one food to another.

Induction a period of induction and initial training in the work place/organisation.

Influence of alcohol the power that alcohol has and the way it changes a person's behaviour.

Infused items immersed/soaked in a liquid to extract their flavours.

Ingestion eating.

Inhalation of smoke breathing in smoke.

Innovation new ideas and styles.

Insulated containers lined, protected.

Intense method severe and powerful.

Intensify flavour make stronger.

Interior of a lower standard.

Interpersonal relationships the way people get along/the relationship (working) between people.

Labour costs the costs of employing staff

Legislation law that has been passed by an official body.

Liaison a combination (association) e.g. of cream and egg yolks.

Licensed sector pubs, e.g. bars and clubs.

Manufacturer the producer of the product (e.g. food).

Marketing potential the opportunity for positive advertising and promotion.

Misinterpretation misunderstanding/misreading a form of communication.

Moist environment wet/humid atmosphere/surroundings.

Monitoring food checking and observing the food throughout the cookery process.

Muscular structure the composition (arrangement) of muscles (i.e. in a piece of meat).

Muslin delicate cotton fabric used in cookery for its infusion and straining properties.

Nausea feeling sick/sickness.

Nutrient imbalance a disproportion – uneven and unsuitable range of nutrients consumed (eaten).

Nutritional deficiency a shortage of certain nutrients in the diet.

Nutritional requirements the nutrients (types of food) the body requires to function properly and efficiently.

Obesity overweight/carrying a higher level of fat than is considered to be healthy.

Obligatory compulsory, absolutely necessary.

Offal the edible innards of an animal, e.g. liver, kidneys, heart, etc.

Organism life form.

Origin of food where the food comes from (its source).

Oven chamber the oven compartment.

Particularly absorbed (e.g. water) is partially soaked up (e.g. when cooking pasta).

Pathogen bacteria that can cause disease.

Penetrate to go through, e.g. for heat to penetrate food.

Portable appliances small pieces of electrical equipment which can be moved from one location to another.

Portion control the number of portions expected from an item of food, e.g. a roast chicken to serve 4 people.

Premises building, property.

Preserve to protect and sustain the life of foods.

Productively the output from staff – how much work is produced in a period of time.

Programmed controlled by an automated system e.g. computerized.

Prohibited forbidden, illegal, not allowed.

Proportion of ingredients the balance of ingredients or ratio.

Remedial action corrective action.

Respiratory the breathing process.

Sanitization very clean and hygienic.

Scalding burn caused by water vapour or hot liquid.

Sector a part/division of the whole (industry), e.g. restaurants are one sector of the hospitality and catering industry.

Septic an injury that has become infected.

Servicing equipment checked/examined by professional people to ensure that it is safe and in good working order.

Smoked foods foods that have been cured or cooked by placing in a smoke-filled environment (e.g. from cindering oak chips) to impart flavour, e.g. smoked salmon, smoked duck breast, smoked garlic, etc.

Specific requirements exactly what is needed.

Specification of a dish the conditions expected or desired in a dish, e.g. quality checks – size, appearance, taste, etc.

Spores a resistant form taken by some bacteria in response to adverse conditions.

Stock rotation ensuring that stock is used in the correct order to minimize waste and/or deterioration.

Submerged placed under/flooded by, e.g. water or oil.

Tainted (by fumes) spoilt by the flavour imparted by the fumes.

Thermostatic control a devise that senses and controls temperature.

To graze to nibble or use as a snack/a light bite.

To lubricate to make fluid and allow movement.

To provide substance to act as a core meal, providing the nutritional intake required at that point in the day, not a snack.

Transfer of heat heat moving from one location to another – i.e. from the heat source into the pan, then from the pan into the oil and finally from the oil into the food (in shallow frying).

Transferable shelf a shelf that can be moved to various areas, e.g. of a grill or oven.

Velouté a french term associated with sauces. It reflects the velvet texture that should be present in the sauce.

Ventilation circulation of clean/fresh air.

Versatility flexible and very useful.

Visually clear apparent by sight, e.g. a surface could be extremely hot but this may not clear by its appearance.

Vulnerable groups people that are at a higher risk than normal.

way in which foods can be processed the methods and procedures that foods have gone through to reach their current state.

Working in isolation working alone – by themselves

Working methodically working in a well organized, systematic and thoughtful way.

Working practices the systems/approaches to work.

Recipe Index

Index